SO-BRS-491

Perspectives in Artificial Intelligence

Volume 9

Editor:

B. Chandrasekaran

Ohio State University
Columbus, Ohio

Editorial Advisory Board:

Rodney A. Brooks

Massachusetts Institute of Technology
Cambridge, Massachusetts

Kenneth Forbus

University of Illinois, Urbana-Champaign
Urbana, Illinois

Mark Fox

Carnegie Mellon University
Pittsburgh, Pennsylvania

Charles Rich

Massachusetts Institute of Technology
Cambridge, Massachusetts

Robert Wilensky

University of California, Berkeley
Berkeley, California

Analogy for
Automated Reasoning

Analogy for Automated Reasoning

Stephen Owen

Hewlett Packard Laboratories
Stoke Gifford, Bristol

ACADEMIC PRESS
Harcourt Brace Jovanovich, Publishers
Boston San Diego New York
London Sydney Tokyo Toronto

006.3
0 97

ACADEMIC PRESS LIMITED
24–28 Oval Road, London NW1 7DX

This book is printed on acid-free paper.

Copyright © 1990 by Academic Press, Inc.
All Rights reserved
No part of this publication may be reproduced or
transmitted in any form or by any means, electronic
or mechanical, including photocopy, recording, or
any information storage and retrieval system, without
permission in writing from the publisher.

United States Edition Published by
ACADEMIC PRESS, INC.
1250 Sixth Avenue, San Diego, CA 92101

ISBN 0-12-531715-8

Library of Congress Cataloging-in-Publication Data is available

Printed in Great Britain by
St Edmundsbury Press Limited, Bury St Edmunds, Suffolk

90 91 92 93 9 8 7 6 5 4 3 2

For Lucy

Editor's Note

By now it is a truism in artificial intelligence (AI) and cognitive science that metaphor and its parent, analogy, are ubiquitous in human cognitive behavior. A central problem in analogy is how to match a given situation with situations stored in memory so that the most analogous one can be brought to the fore. A deep logical problem exists here, as suggested by Watanabe's Theorem of the Ugly Duckling (Watanabe, 1969), to wit: "Any pair of two objects are as similar to each other as are any other pair of two objects, insofar as the degree of similarity is measured by the number of shared predicates." Is the degree of analogy between two situations inherent in a given pair of situations, a function of the context and the goal of the agent, or some combination of the two? The first alternative, which would lead to matching routines that are functions of only the descriptive vocabulary for situations, is ruled out if one supports Watanabe's theorem. Belief in the second alternative means that, given any two situations, one can find goal descriptions of the agent for which the two situations are the most analogous. Of course, the third alternative appears suitably moderate, being a *via media* position, but figuring out how to combine the two alternatives is actually quite difficult.

Steve Owen's work on analogy is a good step forward in attempts to understand how analogies work. By concentrating on a well-defined set of goals (proving theorems) and a well-defined domain (several areas of mathematics), he has built a powerful experimental system that can be used to investigate various matching heuristics. One of the uses of analogies in problem solving is that once an analogy is found, the solution of the old problem is somewhat transferable to the solution of the new problem. Owen also investigates the range of options available for controling this solution transfer process.

Another aspect of Owen's book that workers in analogy will find useful is his analysis of previous work in this field. His framework enables him to cast the matching and solution-transfer strategies of earlier researchers in a more uniform language so that they may be compared experimentally.

It seems to me that complex problems such as analogy can be investigated only by experiments in different domains, experiments of appropriate size and scope that do not trivialize the problem of finding and using analogies. Owen's work is an excellent example of such much-needed research. I am happy to present it to the AI and cognitive science community as part of the Perspectives in Artificial Intelligence series.

—B. Chandrasekaran

References

Watanabe M. S., *Knowing and Guessing*, John Wiley & Sons, New York, 1969.

Contents

List of Figures

Foreword: Alan Bundy

Human thought and reasoning is replete with analogies: from the use of metaphor in everyday speech to the association of ideas that inspires a new theory. It has long been a dream of researchers in artificial intelligence to build a computer program that uses analogy, so that we may better understand how human analogical reasoning is possible, and so we can apply it to solve technological problems. In recent years this interest has grown significantly with the work of Gentner, Carbonell, Holyoak, Winston and many others.

There have been many attempts to build an analogical reasoning program, but they have all been rather unsatisfactory. It is almost impossible not to 'cheat' by building into the program the very analogy you wish it to discover. Firstly, you think of an analogy between two situations, for instance, the particles in an atom *vs* the planets in the solar system, or radiation attacking a cancerous growth *vs* armies attacking a city. Secondly, you represent these situations symbolically in your program. Thirdly, your program 'discovers' this analogy by some kind of matching process between the two representations. Lastly, it demonstrates its analogical reasoning by applying a solution known in one situation to an 'unsolved' problem in the other.

One is never sure what understanding has been gained in such demonstrations. There is always the suspicion that the symbolic representations of the two situations were consciously or unconsciously chosen to simplify the task of the analogical matcher. It is unclear how the program would fare give some huge database of situations provided by some third party and asked to find an analogy suitable for solving some previously unsolved problem. Would the best analogies prove elusively beyond the abilities of the matcher? Would the matcher become bogged down in the computational complexity of finding all possible connections between all pairs of situations? We do not know because we do not have access to a suitably encoded huge database. Nor is one likely to become available in the foreseeable future.

There is one exception to this. The world of mathematics provides a potentially huge database of situations in the form of different mathematical theories, theorems and proofs. It is also especially rich in the potential for analogies within and between these theories. Moreover, an independent encoding of these situations is readily available from the work of mathematical logicians, and it is a relatively simple matter to encode large numbers of them in a machine readable form. This mathematical world provides a domain in which analogical reasoning mechanism can be thoroughly tested and compared.

Despite these methodological advantages the domain of mathematics has been only a minor player in the history of automated analogical reasoning. The exceptions are researchers like Kling, Munyer and Bledsoe. Their goal has been the use of analogies between formulae to guide the search for the unknown proof of a new conjecture using the known proof of an old theorem. To find and apply such analogies they have built fuzzy matchers which look for near isomorphisms between the new conjecture and the old theorem. These matchers all have rather an *ad hoc* flavour. They relax the normal constraints of isomorphism in whatever ways occurred to the human designer and were needed to find the analogies they knew were present.

Steve Owen has built on all this work and has made a significant step forward. He has surveyed and analysed these previous matchers and discovered the underlying principles on which they are based. This has enabled him to build a general purpose, modular matcher, which calls on a set of heuristics. These heuristics can be readily modified, enabling the experimental investigation of different combinations of heuristics. Owen has conducted thorough experiments with this machinery to find which combinations of heuristics perform best in the long run.

Once a match has been found between the old theorem and the new conjecture it can be used to map the old proof into a new proof. Unfortunately, life is not quite this simple; a step of the old proof may not be a legal proof step when mapped across. For instance, mapping an axiom to a new formula may not produce another axiom. The mapped old proof must be considered as a rough plan, which requires filling out to become a proof of the new conjecture. Owen has also applied his analytical and experimental methodology to this problem. He has surveyed previous work on plan application and investigated the choices available for implementing plan appliers. Using this analysis he has built a modular system which allows different options to be rapidly chosen and compared. He has then conducted his usual thorough testing of the different options in order to assess their relative merits.

At last we have a basis for the empirical study of analogical reasoning. Owen has shown us how to test the properties of analogy finding matchers and plan appliers on a body of independent data. His modular matcher

and plan applier enable us to formulate and test different hypotheses about
the mechanisms of analogical reasoning. I believe this book will represent a
major milestone in the computational investigation of analogical reasoning
and become required reading for the new generation of researchers that it
will inspire.

Alan Bundy
University of Edinburgh

Chapter 1

Introduction

1.1 The goal

The goal of the research described in this book is to enhance automatic problem solving systems with **analogical ability**: that is, a capacity to use a known solution to a problem to aid in the solution of a similar problem.

The goal is primarily a technical one. However, much of the inspiration for the endeavour comes from the accepted human ability to reason by analogy — this apparently natural ability, when set alongside the inability of even a powerful theorem prover to make use of its experience, motivates the study of analogical reasoning in artificial intelligence (AI).

The previous paragraph gives an informal definition of analogical problem solving: the solution of a problem using knowledge of the solution to a similar problem as a guide. As we shall see, we will need to refine this definition, for example to exclude reasoning by inductive generalisations, which certainly fits the definition given. However, the definition given forms the focus of this book.

Motivation for the research comes from a desire to build more powerful and adaptable problem solving systems. An automatic problem solver with analogical ability would be an **extensible reasoning system**: that is, a system able to increase its problem solving power over the course of experience in solving specific problems. As more problems were solved, the system would extend its knowledge base and power through being able to use analogies with a larger set of past problems. We would thus hope to see increased problem solving power as one direct result of the analogical ability. However, it may be that analogical ability proves most useful in other ways: knowledge of useful analogies in a domain can indicate directions for generalisation. Such generalisations can represent major breakthroughs in the understanding of a domain. In this way analogical ability can be of more

1

significance than simply in improving a system's ability to answer questions: it can help to ask new questions.

Such a system remains a long term aim. Many problems will have to be overcome before one is built; some of these problems are addressed in this book, some are not. Section 1.6 discusses the scope and limitations of the book.

The work described in this book is not intended primarily to represent a model of human analogical reasoning, despite being motivated by the corresponding human ability. The goal is to build computer systems which can use analogy. However, the work is influenced by the models of analogical reasoning which have been proposed by cognitive psychologists (we discuss these in the next chapter); and it may well be that the research will prove useful to psychologists by feeding back experience of the technical aspects of analogical reasoning.

1.2   The Basic APS framework

Figure 1.1 illustrates schematically the operation of an analogical reasoning component. The problem solver is set problem P_1 to solve (the **target problem**). It finds, or is directed towards, another problem P_2 (the **base problem**) whose solution S_2 it knows. A **match** is found between the two problem statements; the match represents the similarities, and perhaps differences, between the problems. Given such an analogy match, the system constructs out of S_2 a **plan**, X, for the solution of the target problem; as noted above, an analogy is used to *guide* the problem solver; the guidance is encapsulated in the analogical plan. The system then attempts to **apply** the plan, which means following the guidance encoded in the plan, as far as possible, in the hope of constructing a solution to the target problem. In the language of search, the problem solver uses the analogical plan to choose which steps to take in attempting to solve P_1. If the analogy is a good one, the steps suggested will, on the whole, be the right ones, and the search required to solve P_1 will have been greatly reduced. We will call this approach to analogical problem solving (APS) **Basic APS**.

As indicated above, the Basic APS framework is not intended as a model of human analogical reasoning (although it bears resemblances to many such models); but it describes how APS researchers have attempted to introduce analogy into automatic problem solvers.

The Basic APS framework leaves open the issue of where the base problem comes from and how it is found. In almost all analogy research done so far, the base problem is provided by the user of the analogy system. A realistic analogical reasoning system will have to find promising base problems

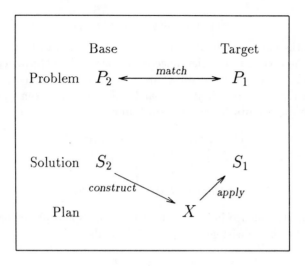

Figure 1.1: Basic APS

for itself from among a large knowledge base of known and solved problems — we refer to this problem as the **base filtering problem.** Many analogy researchers have included base filtering as part of their model of analogical problem solving, particularly those concerned with providing a model of human analogical reasoning. It augments the Basic APS model as a prior stage.

1.3 Examples

We discuss here some examples of problem solving analogies. These are the kinds of analogy which we might wish an analogy system to handle. They give a feel for the potential utility of an analogy in guiding the search of an automatic problem solver, and also for the task that we face in building an analogy system.

Elementary number theory

Consider the following simple results of elementary number theory:

$$even(x) \wedge even(y) \rightarrow even(x \cdot y) \qquad (1.1)$$

$$odd(x) \wedge odd(y) \rightarrow odd(x \cdot y) \tag{1.2}$$

In a mathematics textbook, it is common for a result like the first to be derived in the text just after the concepts of *even* and *odd* have been defined, and then for the second to be set as an exercise for the student.

We can represent the similarities and differences between the problems by the following **symbolic correspondence**:

$$even(x) \wedge even(y) \rightarrow even(x \cdot y)$$

$$odd(x) \wedge odd(y) \rightarrow odd(x \cdot y)$$

This correspondence indicates the structural isomorphism between the problems, and the consistent mapping of symbols

$$
\begin{array}{ccc}
x & \longleftrightarrow & x \\
y & \longleftrightarrow & y \\
even & \longleftrightarrow & odd \\
\cdot & \longleftrightarrow & \cdot
\end{array}
$$

between the two. The mapping indicates differences as well as similarities between the problems. In embarking on a target proof by analogy to the base proof, the hope is that the differences do not seriously affect the *form* of the base proof. The use of the word 'hope' in the previous sentence is significant: we are not usually sure that the analogy will work before trying it out; often, the similarity between the problem statements is misleading, and the attempt to use the base proof as a guide for the proof of the target fails. In the next chapter, we argue that this uncertainty is an important aspect of analogical reasoning. In this case, the analogy turns out to be a good one, as we now describe.

The derivation of 1.1 might go as follows:[1]

Expand the assumptions *even(x)* and *even(y)* by the (re-cently introduced) definition of *even*:[2]

$$x = 2 \cdot a \quad \text{(for some } a\text{)}$$

---

[1]We use a somewhat informal style to present this example – just enough detail to illustrate the analogy. When we return to the example, later in the book, we use a refutation style for the example.

[2]We use the following definition of *even*:

$$\forall x \,.\, even(x) \leftrightarrow \exists y \,.\, x = 2 \cdot y$$

$$y = 2 \cdot b \quad \text{(for some } b)$$

Then multiply these equations:

$$x \cdot y = (2 \cdot a) \cdot (2 \cdot b) \tag{1.3}$$

Then rearrange 1.3 to get:

$$x \cdot y = 2 \cdot (a \cdot (2 \cdot b))$$

and lastly reapply the definition of *even*, this time contracting it:

$$even(x \cdot y)$$

Formula 1.2 can be proved in a similar way (i.e. 1.1 and 1.2 are analogous):

Expand the assumptions $odd(x)$ and $odd(y)$:

$$x = 2 \cdot a + 1 \quad \text{(for some } a)$$

$$y = 2 \cdot b + 1 \quad \text{(for some } b)$$

Then multiply as before:

$$x \cdot y = (2 \cdot a + 1) \cdot (2 \cdot b + 1)$$

Then rearrange (but this part is harder than before):

$$x \cdot y = 2 \cdot (a \cdot (2 \cdot b + 1) + b) + 1$$

Lastly reapply the definition of *odd* as before, obtaining:

$$odd(x \cdot y)$$

In overall shape, and many details, these two proofs are very similar. Just as the first proof helps the student to find the second, we would hope that an analogy system would be able to use the first as guidance in its search for a proof of the second. Intuitively, the guidance is encapsulated in expressions such as 'multiply as before': at each intermediate stage, a problem solver (human or machine) would find that were many possible steps that *could* be made. The base proof can be used to suggest which one of these *should* be made. Notice that the analogy does not amount simply to applying the same sequence of operators that worked in the base (although this does sometimes work). For example, expansion and contraction of the definition of *even* is replaced by those for *odd* — here the proofs are *correspondingly different*. More seriously, the rearrangement stages of the two proofs are quite different:

for the target this stage involves six basic steps, whereas there was just one for the base. For this stage, the base proof is not much help, and the student (or machine) must do more work. So the proofs are not *precisely* analogous, but enough so for the analogy to be useful. The analogist[3] must be able to follow the base proof where it is useful, while being prepared to fill in gaps where it is not. It is a challenge for the designers of analogy systems to achieve this behaviour. We describe how this has been attempted in a later chapter.

Before we move on to the next example, notice one more thing: we described the base proof in a way that also validly describes the target proof (once it is found): there are corresponding stages, and the description of the 'rearrange' stage is chosen so that it applies to the corresponding target stage. Sometimes humans are given similar descriptions to work with, which may be helpful; sometimes there are no such descriptions, or the descriptions given turn out to be misleading. Indeed, sometimes a person is able to form a common description as a result of applying the analogy; these descriptions can be an important part of the learning gained from the analogical problem solving.

Boolean algebra

In Boolean algebra, there is a well known *duality* between meet ($\cup$) and join ($\cap$).[4] Consider, for example, the following two theorems:

$$\text{BASE} \quad x \cup x = x$$
$$\text{TARGET} \quad x \cap x = x$$

The base states that $\cup$ is **idempotent**; the target that $\cap$ is also. The structural correspondence shown indicates the analogy. Figure 1.2 shows refutation proofs of both theorems side by side.[5] All the steps of the proofs

---

[3]We use the term analogist to refer to the person or machine who is reasoning by analogy.

[4]The meet and join functions of Boolean algebra are written $\cap$ and $\cup$ respectively to distinguish them from the logical connectives $\wedge$ and $\vee$.

[5]For those not familiar with refutation proofs, here is a brief explanation. If the goal is to prove a universally quantified statement such as $x \cup x = x$, we first assume that it is false; that is, that there exists an a such that $\neg a \cup a = a$ (first line of base proof). We then draw consequences from this assumption until a contradiction is reached (*nil*, last line). This means that our assumption of the existence of such an a was false; or, that the theorem is true. Note that the constant a introduced is *arbitrary*; that is, we are not allowed to assume anything about it during the proof.

are shown. It is easy to see that the proofs are structurally isomorphic, with a mapping that includes and extends that of the problem statements:

$$
\begin{aligned}
= &\longleftrightarrow\ = \\
\cup &\longleftrightarrow\ \cap \\
\cap &\longleftrightarrow\ \cup \\
0 &\longleftrightarrow\ 1 \\
1 &\longleftrightarrow\ 0 \\
- &\longleftrightarrow\ -
\end{aligned}
$$

We can regard the application of the analogy as being the extension of the initial match between the problem statements to the complete proofs, including the corresponding axioms that were applied. The analogy is perfect, unlike that of the first example given. If the problem solver was aware of the formal duality within Boolean algebra, it could infer that the analogy was bound to succeed without going through the application stage. If the solver was not aware of the formal duality, it would need to go through the application. In fact the success of the analogy could be used as a clue to the existence of the duality (this is similar to, though more formal than, the suggestion of the proof descriptions by the analogy in the first example).

Lattice theory

We give a brief example to illustrate that even in perfect analogies we must be prepared to permute the arguments to predicates or functions in a match. Suppose that we are defining lattice operations in a partially ordered set with finite least upper and greatest lower bounds. We might define $\cup$ and $\cap$ as follows:

$$x \cup y = lub(x, y)$$

$$x \cap y = glb(x, y)$$

where lub and glb are the least upper bound and greatest lower bound functions respectively. Consider the analogy between the following properties of the newly defined $\cup$ and $\cap$:

$$x \leq x \cup y$$

$$x \cap y \leq x$$

As above, this is a perfect analogy, and is part of the same duality as the previous example (we do not show the isomorphic proofs here). But notice that to describe the problems as isomorphic we need a concept of isomorphism which allows arguments of functions and predicates to be permuted.

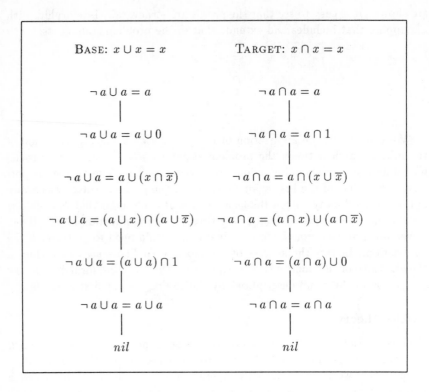

Figure 1.2: Isomorphic proofs in Boolean algebra

We will see that a number of analogy researchers have defined the concept of analogy match to exclude argument permutation. In such accounts, therefore, even perfect analogies like the current one are excluded.

Notation for matches   The current example indicates the need for a more detailed representation of symbolic correspondences than the notation

$$\leq \longleftrightarrow \leq$$

which we have used so far. In this example, the arguments to $\leq$ are permuted and we may wish to encode this important information in the correspondence. We therefore sometimes use the more detailed but less evocative notation

$$(\leq, \leq, [(1,2),(2,1)])$$

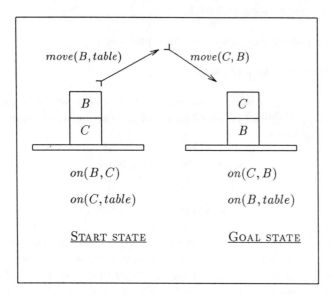

Figure 1.3: Reversing a stack of two

to indicate the argument pairings in an association. The third component of the triple above gives the argument pairings — in this case the first argument of the left symbol with the second of the right, and vice versa. The above association has different implications for an analogy system from

$$(\leq, \leq, [(1,1),(2,2)])$$

in which argument order is preserved. This is why the more elaborate notation is sometimes necessary. We will switch fairly freely between the two notations in this book. It is important that the reader understands the equivalence.

The blocks world

For our next example, we visit the blocks world. Suppose that we know how to reverse the positions of two blocks, one on top of the other. The start and goal states and the operations necessary for this are displayed in Figure 1.3.

Suppose now that we are set the task illustrated in Figure 1.4. We are given a stack of three and asked to construct a configuration in which the stack is reversed. We can describe this problem as 'reverse a stack of three blocks'

just as we could have described the base problem as

'reverse a stack of two blocks'

This strongly suggests an analogy as follows (here we use a correspondence between English sentences to stand for one between corresponding formal descriptions):

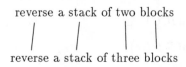

reverse a stack of two blocks

reverse a stack of three blocks

In a way, using these descriptions for the problems directly is cheating or, at least, assuming sophistication in the problem solver: these descriptions implicitly make a generalisation which encompasses the analogy. As with the previous examples, we would like an analogy system to be able to cope without being provided with the generalised description, rather the straightforward ones given in Figures 1.3 and 1.4.

It is clear that there is no isomorphism between the descriptions of Figures 1.3 and 1.4 since they have different sizes and numbers of variables. This makes the construction of the analogy harder than the earlier examples. We might attempt to associate the whole of the base with parts of the target (i.e. pick two blocks in the target to correspond to those in the base); but this approach fails to express the full analogy between the problems. In Chapter 4, we describe mechanisms by which the problems can be re-expressed into formal versions of the English forms given above as part of an attempt to construct an analogy match between them.

If such re-expression can be performed on the problems, it is important also to re-express the known base solution in terms similar to the new version of the base problem. Specifically, we would like to describe the base solution in terms of operations on a stack of blocks (in this case, two) rather than in terms of applications of basic operations to specific blocks, as it is initially presented to us. This will enable us to construct a corresponding plan for the solution of the target. It turns out that these feats of re-expression can be performed on this example and the target problem solved by application of the plan.

This example is an instance of an important feature of analogical reasoning: the perception of an analogy between two problems (or situations) often involves re-expressing their descriptions. To put it another way: the

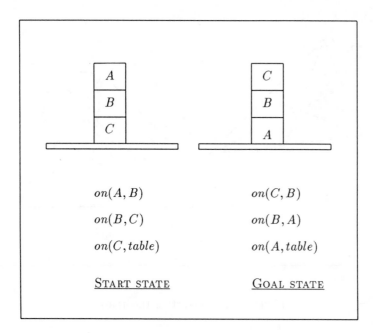

Figure 1.4: Reversing a stack of three

given representations of problems often obscures a potential analogy between them. The next example also exemplifies this phenomenon. A powerful analogy system must be able to cope with this.

Geometry

We now discuss an example from geometry which is similar to the previous one from the blocks world. Again, we first describe the two problems in English which suggest the analogy, and consider how to find the analogy given more straightforward formal descriptions which obscure it somewhat. The problems are:

1. The three lines joining the vertices of a triangle to the midpoints of the opposite sides meet at a point (the orthocentre).

2. The four lines joining the vertices of a tetrahedron to the orthocentres of the opposite faces meet at a point.

Figure 1.5 illustrates these two theorems geometrically.

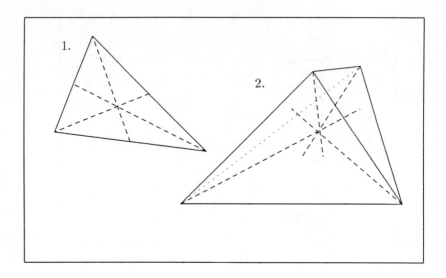

Figure 1.5: Intersection theorems

As before, if the analogy system starts off with (formal versions of) these descriptions, the apprehension and exploitation of the analogy is much easier than if the problems are represented as in Figure 1.6. Again we argue that a powerful analogy system must be able to cope with just the Figure 1.6 descriptions.

In a later chapter we will argue that the essence of perceiving the analogy is noticing that the problems as stated in Figure 1.6 can be rewritten in terms of *sets* of points in the following way:

$$\bigwedge_{s \in S} pt(s) \longrightarrow pt(o(S)) \wedge \bigwedge_{s \in S} lies\_on(o(S), line(s, midpt(S \backslash \{s\})))$$

$$\bigwedge_{s \in S'} pt(s) \longrightarrow pt(o(S')) \wedge \bigwedge_{s \in S'} lies\_on(o(S'), line(s, orth(S' \backslash \{s\})))$$

where $S = \{x, y, z\}$ and $S' = \{x, y, z, w\}$. This allows a close syntactic correspondence to be constructed, as shown. As in the previous example, we can re-express the base proof in terms of sets, then construct and apply a plan from the new proof.

We briefly describe two more examples which we will discuss further in later chapters. We introduce them here in order to illustrate aspects of

HYPOTHESES
point(x) ∧
point(y) ∧
point(z)

CONCLUSIONS
point(o(x, y, z)) ∧

lies_on(o(x, y, z),
    line(z, midpt(x, y))) ∧

lies_on(o(x, y, z),
    line(x, midpt(y, z))) ∧

lies_on(o(x, y, z),
    line(y, midpt(z, x)))

HYPOTHESES
point(x) ∧
point(y) ∧
point(z) ∧
point(w)

CONCLUSIONS
point(p(x, y, z, w)) ∧

lies_on(p(x, y, x, w),
    line(w, orth(x, y, z))) ∧

lies_on(p(x, y, z, w),
    line(x, orth(y, z, w))) ∧

lies_on(p(x, y, z, w),
    line(y, orth(w, z, x))) ∧

lies_on(p(x, y, z, w),
    line(z, orth(w, x, y)))

Figure 1.6: Geometry theorems

analogy matches which must be taken into account in the design of analogy matchers.

Real number theory

Consider the following two propositions of elementary real number theory:

1. The sum of a rational number and an irrational number is irrational.

2. The product of a non-zero rational number and an irrational number is irrational.

A potential analogy is immediately suggested by reading these two propositions together. The following match between formal representations of the propositions makes the correspondence explicit:

$$\wedge \, (\, rational\,(x),\, \neg\, rational\,(y)\,) \longrightarrow \neg\, rational\,(x + y)$$

$$\wedge \, (\, rational\,(x),\, \neg\, x = 0,\, \neg\, rational\,(y)\,) \longrightarrow \neg\, rational\,(x \cdot y)$$

The first proposition can be thought of as one about addition, and the second as a corresponding one about multiplication. It turns out that these propositions can in fact be proved in corresponding ways (again, we do not give the proofs here, but leave them until Chapter 6). However, the correspondence is not an isomorphism — some of the symbols of one of the propositions are left unmatched, those that make up the non-zero condition. This is because there is nothing in the other proposition which corresponds to the non-zero condition — it is part of the difference between the propositions. There is a corresponding mismatch between the proofs: at least one extra step needs to be put into the proof of the second proposition to handle the non-zero condition (see Chapter 6). However, the mismatches between the propositions and between the proofs do not seriously disrupt our intuition that there is an analogy here (apart from the extra step, the proofs correspond closely). Many intuitively close analogies turn out to involve unmatched symbols: sometimes, as here, unmatched atoms, sometimes unmatched arguments to predicates or functions. Thus we take the view that an analogy system will have to allow matches of this form if it is to be useful.

Irrationality of roots theorems

To illustrate another property of analogy matches, we consider an example involving one of the most famous theorems in mathematics:

1. The square root of 2 is irrational.

2. The cube root of 2 is irrational.

Again, we can immediately recognize a potential analogy, which, given formal representations, we can make explicit as follows:

$$\neg\, rational\,(\,root\,(2,2))$$

$$\neg\, rational\,(\,root\,(3,2))$$

Our suspicion is again borne out by the fact that the two propositions can be proved in very similar ways (we describe the application of this analogy in Chapter 6). However, notice that the match between the propositions is, in a sense, inconsistent; that is, a symbol on one side, 2, is associated with two *different* symbols on the other side, 2 and 3. Just as with unmatched symbols, there is nothing about this situation which prevents a person from recognising the analogy. Inconsistencies frequently occur in analogies. We therefore take the view that we cannot rule out inconsistent matches, such as this one, from our analogy system without seriously restricting its generality.

Flexible notion analogy match

The examples given above indicate that a competent analogy system, in the context of automated reasoning, will need to have a flexible notion of analogy match. Some of the examples given above led to isomorphic matches, possibly after necessary re-representation. However, some did not, and it turns out that the majority of 'naturally occurring' analogies are not perfect isomorphisms. The examples already given indicate the following features of matches:

- Predicate, function and constant symbols may be matched with *different* predicate, function and constant symbols.

- The arguments to predicates or functions which are matched may be permuted by the match; i.e. we may have matched subterms of the following form:

$$
\begin{array}{c}
f(a,b) \\
| \hspace{0.1em} \times \\
g(c,d)
\end{array}
$$

  Since the argument order of functions and predicates is often arbitrary, it is clearly unreasonable to insist that matches preserve argument order.

- Matches may contain **inconsistencies** where a symbol on one side is matched with two distinct symbols on the other. While this is not a desirable property for a match to have, we cannot exclude the possibility without missing intuitively clear matches.

- Symbols and subterms may be left unmatched in an analogy. Again, this is not a desirable property, but we must allow it.

It is interesting that almost all of the accounts of analogy outside the context of automated reasoning adopt a definition of analogy match which excludes some or all of the features just described. It seems that it is the pull of intuitively close analogies, such as those described above, which forces a flexible notion of analogy match. These analogies are well known outside of the realm of analogy research, and hence have to be tackled directly, without convenient intervening simplification.

Other issues in analogy

The examples given above have touched on many of the issues which will
be discussed in detail in later chapters. There are other important issues
in analogy which they do not suggest. Firstly, the examples are given in
neat analogous pairs of problems. While this is often true in textbooks, it
is rarely so in practical problem solving. The problem of finding a suitable
base problem is a very important one. The issue of how analogical reasoning
is embedded in, and contributes to, wider problem solving activity is also
important and not addressed by the examples. Most of the research done
in automated analogical reasoning has concentrated on the isolated version
of the phenomenon expressed in the examples. The content of this book
reflects this.

1.4   Other uses of analogy

Analogy is useful for more than just guiding the solution of given target
problems. In this section, we discuss some other activities to which analogy
can contribute. We argue, however, that the Basic APS framework is a
crucial component of most other uses of analogy.

   It is well accepted that people are able to use analogies in diverse ways,
not all fitting into Basic APS. We briefly consider some other uses; each
possibility has its counterpart among potential applications of analogy within
automated reasoning.

Definitions

Definitions are frequently made by analogy: given an analogy between an unfamiliar domain which is being explored and a better understood domain, we
might make a definition of a new concept in the former domain by analogy to
one which has proved useful in the latter. We hope that the analogy remains
fruitful, and the new concept leads to interesting results. Mathematics has
numerous examples of definitions by analogy: many of the concepts of abstract mathematics were defined by analogy to those in well known concrete
areas — the operations on vector spaces by analogy to those on Euclidean
spaces; in ring theory, the concept of a prime ideal is defined by analogy
to that of prime number in number theory; in geometry, concepts from Euclidean geometry are imported as far as possible into projective geometry.
When mathematicians are exploring a new abstract system, it is common
for them to ask 'can we define a notion of X?' where X is a concept from
some well known area which they believe or wish to be analogous to the new
system.

In analysis, concepts such as limit occur in slightly different forms in many settings; for example, suppose the theory of real-valued series is mature and we are exploring the area of real-valued functions; we might define the property of a function tending to a value at a point by analogy to the familiar property of a series tending to a limit as $n \to \infty$.

Definition by analogy often precedes generalisation (when it is successful). For example, the motivation for category theory was to generalise the concept of 'freeness' which had been defined analogously in numerous branches of abstract mathematics ([31]). The concept of an abstract algebra grew out of the observation that a closely analogous set of concepts could be defined in many different areas of algebra (group theory, ring theory, field theory, etc.). As indicated in Section 1.4, such influential generalisations are perhaps the most significant product of analogical reasoning. The instances of analogy which give rise to a generalisation are superseded by it and can therefore be hard to identify (they tend not to be mentioned in textbooks).

In less formal areas, such as natural science, the distinction between definition by analogy and metaphor can be fuzzy. For example, the concept of the *orbit* of an electron around the nucleus in an atom could be regarded as defined by analogy to the orbiting of a planet around the sun, according to Rutherford's famous solar system model of the atom (see [17] for a discussion of this analogy); but we could also regard the use of the term 'orbit' when applied to an atom as just an evocative figure of speech (that is, a metaphor). Which interpretation we choose depends on whether we regard the concept of orbit as an intrinsic part of the mathematical model of the atom or just a descriptive term.

Conjectures

Analogies are frequently used in making conjectures: given an analogy between two domains and a known property of one of them, we might suspect there to be an analogous property in the other; we could conjecture an analogous property to hold in the latter domain, and then attempt to verify the conjecture by analogy to the demonstration of the known property. This can give a useful focus to the exploration of an unfamiliar domain. To pursue the analysis example introduced in the previous section, once the concept of convergence to limits at points has been defined for real valued functions, known properties of limits of series might be conjectured to hold of the new concept for functions: for example that the sum (or product) of two functions, which tend to limits at a point, also tends to a limit at the point which is the sum (or product) of the separate limits. We shall discuss analogies in this area in more detail in Chapter 6.

In physics, the fluid model of electricity may be used to make predictions about the behaviour of electricity: for example the formula for the combined resistance of two resistors in series (or parallel) may be predicted by the analogy which maps resistors to constrictions in a pipe. The Rutherford model of the atom was used to make predictions about the allowable energy levels of atoms.

While conjecture and definition are undoubtedly important aspects of human analogical reasoning, it is a challenge to describe an automated reasoning (AR) system sophisticated enough to have need of them and make use of them. Such a system would need to have discovery as one of its principal goals — most current AR systems solve problems in a fixed and delimited domain. Perhaps the nearest example to date is Lenat's system AM ([30]). AM is a discovery system which has mechanisms for making definitions and conjectures, and can use a simple notion of analogy as one way of doing these things. More ambitiously, a discovery and reasoning system such as that proposed in [5] might well be able to make use of a definition/conjecture making and verifying ability.

Teaching and explanation

Another area where analogies are frequently used by humans is in teaching and explanation: we often explain an unfamiliar situation by analogy to another situation more familiar to the recipient of the explanation. For example, we might explain electricity using the flow of fluids as an analogy. Explanation by analogy has been proposed as a potentially useful part of the explanation facilities of expert systems and tutoring systems, though practical benefits have yet to be demonstrated. Gentner and colleagues ([21]) have been concerned with this aspect of analogy, among others. Burstein ([7]) has produced a computer model which learns about the behaviour of assignment in procedural languages using an analogy with putting objects in boxes.

Generalisation

In most of the examples that we have already discussed, the analogy has suggested that some kind of generalisation can be made. We have argued that this product of analogy is perhaps its most useful one, and have given examples from abstract algebra and category theory.

The use of the analogy is to suggest feasible and useful directions for generalisation: roughly, we generalise away the differences between the problems and solutions, and maintain the common parts. In the next chapter, we compare reasoning by analogy to direct generalisation techniques such as **explanation-based generalisation**.

1.5 History of analogy in AI

Now that we have introduced the problem to be addressed in this book, we give a brief overview of the work done in artificial intelligence on the subject.

Much of the work done on analogy in AI has not been concerned with the *use* of analogies in problem solving, and hence turns out to be of little interest to our concerns here. In later chapters, we shall look mainly at problem solving accounts of analogy. For the purpose of this brief history, however, we shall be more discursive.

Now that our investigation has been motivated with some examples, we can see, in some cases, how the accounts of analogy are too restrictive for our purposes.

Evans

One of the earliest computational accounts of analogy is due to Evans [14].

Evans wrote a program which attempted to solve geometric analogy problems of the kind which occur in intelligence tests. These problems test the ability to perceive relations and analogies, or rather the ability to perceive the same analogy as the person who set the problem. The analogies are not used for any external purpose.

Evans' concept of an analogy match is as follows: a bijective relation between geometric objects such that identical geometric relations hold between corresponding objects. An example of such a match is the following:

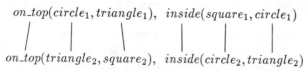

$$on\_top(circle_1, triangle_1), \quad inside(square_1, circle_1)$$
$$on\_top(triangle_2, square_2), \quad inside(circle_2, triangle_2)$$

which represents the correspondence between geometrical figures shown in Figure 1.7.

The examples given in the previous section indicate how Evans' notion of analogy match is too restrictive for the purposes of this book. Nevertheless, Evans' early work on analogy is an important part of the development of analogy within AI – as far as the present author is aware, Evans was the first person to articulate analogies as symbolic correspondences between formal representations. This notion of what an analogy is exists implicitly in the work of both Hesse ([24]) and Polya ([38]), but is not developed to the stage of being made explicit.

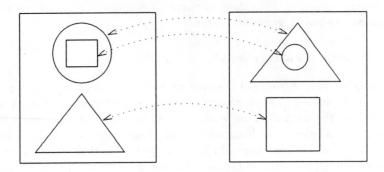

Figure 1.7: Geometrical correspondence

Kling

Kling [29] reports an analogical reasoning system for use with an existing
resolution theorem proving system. It is, as far as the present author is
aware, the earliest attempt to automate the *use* of analogies to solve problems. Kling was the first to introduce the paradigm for reasoning by analogy
which we have called Basic APS into AI. Kling was mainly concerned with
the analogies that exist between different branches of abstract algebra, particularly group theory and ring theory. An example of such an analogy
between problem statements is:

> The intersection of two subgroups of a group is also a subgroup.

> The intersection of two subrings of a ring is also a subring.

Kling represents the problems and the analogy as shown in Figure 1.8.

The fact that these analogies from abstract algebra are not perfect isomorphisms has forced Kling to adopt a more flexible notion of analogy match
than many subsequent authors have done. We defer detailed discussion of
this notion and of Kling's matching algorithm until Chapter 3.

It is perhaps misleading to describe the later stages of Kling's system as
the construction and application of analogical *plans*: Kling uses an analogy
to find analogues for the axioms which were used in the base proof; the
axiom base of the theorem prover is then restricted to these analogues, and
the theorem prover attempts to prove the target by its normal uniform search
procedure. Thus the order of application of the axioms and any intermediate
steps generated in the base proof are discarded. In AI, the term plan is
usually taken to mean a structured entity which represents an intention

```
HYPOTHESES                          HYPOTHESES
group(g, *)                         ring(r, *, +)
subgroup(h₁, g, *)                  subring(s₁, r, *, +)
subgroup(h₂, g, *)                  subring(s₂, r, *, +)
intersection(h₁, h₂, h₃)            intersection(s₁, s₂, s₃)

CONCLUSION                          CONCLUSION
subgroup(h3, g, *)                  subring(s3, r, *, +)

                  h3      ⟷    s3
                 [*]      ⟷    [*, +]
         intersection     ⟷    intersection
                  h1      ⟷    s1
                  h2      ⟷    s2
             subgroup     ⟷    subring
                group     ⟷    ring
                    g     ⟷    r
```

Figure 1.8: Abstract algebra example

to proceed in a particular way, including some notion of order. We need to generalise this definition to include Kling's candidate analogue axiom sets as plans: they represent an intention to proceed in a particular way, namely to attempt a proof of the target using only the analogous axioms, but without any specification of order. We will consider Kling's application routines in greater detail in Chapter 6.

Winston

Winston [47] has considered analogies between simple representations of the plots of stories. He restricts his analogies to being 1-1 correspondences between objects from the plots, which are considered analogous by virtue of bearing some of the same relations to each other in both stories. For example, the following match between a pair of propositions would contribute to one of Winston's analogies:

$$loves(Romeo, Juliet)$$
$$|\quad\quad|\quad\quad|$$
$$loves(Tristan, Isolde)$$

Both of these requirements on analogies are too restrictive for the types of analogy with which we are concerned in this book: the examples given earlier in this chapter indicate that analogical correspondences need not be bijective, and that the relations and functions which give an analogy strength need not be the same on one side as the other.

Winston defines a notion of the *strength* of a match. This depends on the number of matching objects and relations, as well as a notion of *importance* for some relations: the relation **cause** is always deemed to be important; other relations are important if the teacher says so. Matches between important relations are scored more highly than others. The motivation for treating causal relations as more significant than others seems to be that the central thread of the plots with which Winston is concerned is composed of a series of causal connections, for example:

Lady-Macbeth *cause* {Macbeth *murder* Duncan}

For two story plots to be regarded as analogous, the causal threads should correspond well.

Winston's algorithm for finding the best match between a pair of plot descriptions is to generate all syntactically possible matches, to score each and to pick the best. Winston acknowledges that this approach is infeasible for large problems. In Chapter 4 we discuss in detail work done by other researchers on more sophisticated matching algorithms.

A limitation of Winston's work and several other accounts is that the analogies are not *used* in any wider task for which there is an objective success criterion. It is usual for such accounts to use an over-simplified notion of analogy match.

Munyer

Munyer [33] describes a system for reasoning by analogy. Like Kling's, Munyer's system fits into the Basic APS structure. Also like Kling, Munyer is concerned with analogies between problems in mathematics. This has led him also to adopt a flexible view of an analogy match, and to face a correspondingly difficult analogy matching problem. An example of the sort of match Munyer is concerned with is:[6]

$$\sum(i,0,n,R^i)$$
$$\big/ \big/ \big/ \big/ \; \big\backslash\big\backslash$$
$$\sum(i,0,n,i \cdot R^i)$$

---

[6] We have re-expressed the usual notation $\sum_{i=0}^{n} f(i)$ as $\sum(i,0,n,f(i))$ in order that we can exhibit the analogy match clearly.

Notice that this match is not an isomorphism. Again, we postpone detailed discussion of Munyer's matcher until the next chapter.

Munyer describes two analogy application systems, the **implicit planning method** and the **explicit planning method** (the latter was not implemented). In both of these, the base solution is used to construct a plan for the solution of the target. These plans are constructed out of the intermediate steps which were generated in the base solution; the order in which they occur in the base solution is also used in the plans; the axioms (or operators, in Munyer's terminology) which were applied in the base solution are ignored. It is interesting that Munyer's and Kling's analogical plans make use of disjoint sets of information from the base solutions.

Carbonnell

Carbonnell has discussed how a problem solving system can be augmented with an analogy component. In [9], he proposes a model essentially the same as the Basic APS model of Figure 1.1 except that the plan construction phase is omitted – the base solution is taken as the plan for the target.

Carbonnell gives no definition of, nor algorithm for finding, analogies. His main concern seems to be with the plan application stage. He proposes various operators which may be applied to a faulty plan in the hope of transforming it into a valid target solution. Examples of these are:

'insert an operator application at a particular point in the plan'

and

'swap a consecutive pair of operator applications in the plan'

Carbonnell gives no details as to how these solution transformation operators are to be controlled, nor examples of their application to actual problems. The control of these transformation operators (we will use the term *patching operators* for corresponding objects in Chapter 6) is an important issue, and no account of how to apply an analogy can be considered complete without some solution to it. The reason for this is easy to see: the branching rate at the solution transformation level is much greater than that at the original state space level, and the solution at the plan level may at the same time lie at greater depth than at the object level; thus, without some account of the control regime at the transformation level, the use of the analogy is likely to make the target problem harder to solve.

Carbonnell's paper ([9]) is widely quoted as being the first formulation of analogical reasoning as being a planning activity at the level of solutions. This does not do justice to Munyer ([33]) who introduced such a model, along with detailed procedures for implementing it, well before Carbonnell.

Derivational analogy In [8], Carbonnell proposes a new model for reasoning by analogy within an automated problem solver, for which he coins the phrase **derivational analogy**. This is different from the Basic APS model and his previous model in the following respect: instead of looking for analogies between the problem representations alone, analogies are sought between initial segments of problem solving activity between the target and the base; that is, the target problem is attacked by the problem solver (presumably with some general-purpose search technique); the entire trace of the problem solver's search at any stage is retained, including all failed branches and intermediate states; matching takes place between this structure and corresponding initial traces for candidate base problems; once an adequate match is found, the later stages of the process proceed in a way similar to Carbonnell's earlier model.

The motivation behind this model seems to be that an initial segment of problem solving activity contains more information about the form of a potential solution than the problem does alone. This is certainly an attractive idea. But, once again, Carbonnell gives no examples or technical details with which his model can be tested.

Carbonnell makes the following criticism of his earlier model, in justification of his new model: the earlier system bases its decision of which base problem to pursue entirely on the comparison between problem representations, without regard to the progress of solutions. His criticism certainly carries some weight. However, while Carbonnell's earlier system may well have had this property, Basic APS systems in general need not: the development of an analogical plan can be frequently re-assessed during plan application; if the plan is doing well it can be developed further; if not, or if there is a higher-rated alternative plan, the current plan can be suspended in favour of the other. Thus the process of choosing the right base problem can extend into the application phase and thus be sensitive to more than just the original problems. In Chapter 6, we consider the design of such systems in more detail.

Indurkhya

Indurkhya [27] describes a knowledge representation scheme, very similar to first-order logic, and defines a notion of analogy within it. While Indurkhya does consider the problem of reasoning with an analogy, both his problems and his concept of analogy are idealised: he requires an analogy to be an isomorphism between formulae; i.e. predicates and objects may be associated with different predicates and objects (unlike in the accounts mentioned above), but only in a strictly consistent manner. There can be no permutation of arguments between associated terms and formulae, and there can be no unmatched arguments. Thus most of the examples given in Section 1.3 cannot be captured in Indurkhya's system.

Gentner et al

Gentner and colleagues have done considerable work on analogy from both a psychological and computational standpoint ([18, 19, 15]). They have developed a model for analogical reasoning called **structure mapping theory**, which is very similar to Basic APS. In the **mapping** stage a symbolic match is formed between the base and target descriptions. Such a mapping is then used to make predictions about the target domain from known properties of the base domain.

Gentner's work has been concerned with modelling famous scientific analogies such as Rutherford's solar system model of the atom and the fluid flow model of electricity, and also analogies used in cognitive experiments, such as Duncker's well known tumour/fortress problem ([13]) .

Gentner uses what, for our purposes, is a too restrictive notion of analogy match: matches must be isomorphisms between parts of the base and target descriptions, with relations being matched only with identical relations. This again seems related to the fact that Gentner does not use the analogies in a genuine problem solving context. However, the matching system developed by Gentner and her colleagues ([15]) is capable of somewhat more flexible use than its specific instantiation in [15], and will be discussed in Chapter 4.

Gentner has also considered the problem of **base filtering** ([22]): that is the determination of a small set of plausible base problems/descriptions from a potentially vast base of descriptions.

Bledsoe et al

Some of the best work on the use of analogies in genuine problem solving has been done by Bledsoe and his students at the University of Texas ([1, 2]). Their model for analogy fits into the Basic APS framework. They have been concerned mainly with analogies from analysis such as:

$$\lim_{x \to a} f(x) = l \wedge \lim_{x \to a} g(x) = k \longrightarrow \lim_{x \to a} [f(x) + g(x)] = l + k$$
$$\lim_{x \to a} f(x) = l \wedge \lim_{x \to a} g(x) = k \longrightarrow \lim_{x \to a} [f(x) \cdot g(x)] = l \cdot k$$

Most of their effort has been put into the application stage — the initial matching is not done automatically. The analogy example given above, and others like it (see [1]) are not trivial to apply (i.e. the base and target proofs are not isomorphic); this has led Bledsoe and his colleagues to develop some interesting mechanisms for analogical plan application, which we will describe in more detail in Chapter 6.

Holyoak and Thagard

Some very interesting recent work on analogy has been done by Holyoak, Thagard and others ([26, 25, 44]). This work is principally motivated by cognitive psychology — the main goal is to produce a model of human analogical reasoning. However, this work has also contributed from a computational point of view, particularly in the matching stage.

The model of analogy is component of a wider model of human problem solving, called **PI**. Problems (or parts of problems) may be attempted by analogy or by normal search. A distinguishing feature of this work is the neural net approach to both filtering and matching.

We describe the overall PI model further in Chapter 2, when we are discussing psychological models of analogy, and the matching algorithm in Chapter 4.

Owen

The current author has concentrated on the use of analogy to guide the search in theorem proving systems ([34], [35]). The goal has been to develop mechanisms for constructing and exploiting simple analogies between mathematics problems such as:

$$\wedge\,(\,rational\,(x),\,\neg\,rational\,(y)\,) \longrightarrow \neg\,rational\,(x+y)$$

$$\wedge\,(\,rational\,(x),\,\neg\,x = 0,\,\neg\,rational\,(y)\,) \longrightarrow \neg\,rational\,(x\cdot y)$$

As with other work on genuine problem solving analogies, a flexible notion of an analogy match is necessary. Much of the effort has been towards a more flexible, powerful and understandable matching algorithm than those of Munyer and Kling. We describe this algorithm (called **FHM** — flexible heuristic matcher) in detail in Chapter 4. Procedures for the construction and application of analogical plans are developed in [35], and demonstrated on a number of simple analogies. This work is also described in later chapters.

Further, work has been done on how an APS system can improve its analogical ability over time through the construction of global analogies (or **dualities**).

1.6   Overview of the rest of the book

The rest of the book is structured around the component processes of the Basic APS model. Successive chapters deal with analogy matching (Chapters 3 and 4), plan construction (Chapter 5) and plan validation (Chapter 6). In each case, we describe in detail the best and most relevant work done on the topic in question and indicate directions for future research.

Before we describe the component processes, in Chapter 2, we analyse the concept of analogy. All computational accounts of analogy must be based on a some theory of what analogy is — for example, analogy matchers prefer certain kinds of match to others because these are believed to be more promising analogies. We therefore discuss work done in philosophy and psychology on both normative and cognitive theories of analogy. One particular topic of concern is the tradeoff between analogical reasoning as we have described it (where a base problem is used as a model for a target problem) and inductive reasoning (where the base problem is pre-generalised in such a way that the generalisation applies to the target problem. This tradeoff has been a concern of philosophers and has practical ramifications: inductive reasoning indicates generalisation techniques from machine learning, whereas analogical reasoning indicates the Basic APS framework. In Chapter 2 we also compare the features of Basic APS systems with a sample of generalisation techniques from machine learning.

We do not discuss in detail work done on the retrieval of potential analogues for the target problem from a large base of known problem/solution pairs — the base filtering problem. A certain amount of interesting work has been done on this issue (see [44], [22]), which we will discuss briefly in the next chapter. The work done has not been directed towards analogies in automated reasoning. Furthermore, the analogy researchers in automated reasoning have not worked with problem bases which are large enough to require a separate retrieval stage. Hence, while work on analogue retrieval is important and interesting in its own right, it does not yet connect closely to work done on the rest of the Basic APS model, which is the theme of this book. Hence, we refer the reader to the references given for more detailed discussion of this issue.

Chapter 2

What is analogy?

Before we invest effort in analysing and developing programs to perform analogical reasoning, it is wise to look more closely at the phenomenon of analogy, for the following reasons:

- Research in philosophy and psychology has shed light on the nature of analogy; we should allow this work to inform our program design and understand the likely significance of an analogical ability.

- In particular, it is important to understand how analogical reasoning fits into a wider reasoning context: how it compares and what are the tradeoffs with other machine learning techniques which transfer experience from the solution of one problem to that of another. Research which has been done on the same tradeoffs for human reasoning is applicable here. It is important to ensure that we are not merely reinventing other machine learning techniques in a different guise.

In this chapter we review and analyse both **normative** and **cognitive** accounts of analogical reasoning. By normative accounts, we mean those which attempt to provide an analytical *justification* for reasoning by analogy (why *should* the target solution be similar to the base solution?). By cognitive accounts, we mean those which attempt to model human analogical reasoning and hence gain insight into how people are able to benefit from analogy. Both sorts of account are relevant to our endeavour of building automated analogical reasoning systems. This chapter will provide us with a view of analogy which will motivate the rest of the book.

2.1 Analogy in human reasoning

2.1.1 Normative accounts

Philosophers since Aristotle have tried to understand analogy by considering what reason we have for believing an analogy to be useful; that is, why should its predictions about the target situation be true frequently enough to justify its use. The purpose of this section is not to review comprehensively the literature in this area but to describe briefly the results of this research. We therefore concentrate on Hesse's theory of analogy in scientific reasoning ([24]) which is, in the current author's opinion, the best description of the justification of analogy and of its applicability relative to reasoning from general laws.

Hesse's theory

Hesse's theory of analogy [24] is concerned with the use of analogical models to make predictions in science. When scientists are investigating some new and unfamiliar system (the target system), with only a few properties of the system known to them, they may use an analogy with a more familiar system (the base system) in order to predict new properties of the unfamiliar system; these predictions can then be tested by experiment.

Famous examples of scientific models, quoted by Hesse, are Newton's particle theory of light and Rutherford's solar system model of the atom.

Typically, the base domain is well enough understood that its basic mechanisms are known; that is, there is a successful theory which predicts the observed properties. The model is used to assert properties of the target because corresponding properties are known to be true of the base.

Hesse analyses the situation in the following way: the model is initially proposed on the basis of *recognisable similarities* between *observable properties* of the base and target systems; say the base has properties

$$\{B_1, \ldots, B_r\}$$

which are recognisably similar to known properties of the target

$$\{B'_1, \ldots, B'_r\}$$

This part is known as the **positive analogy**. There are also properties of each domain known not to hold in the other; say

$$\{A_1, \ldots, A_n\}$$

in the base, and

$$\{C'_1, \ldots, C'_m\}$$

in the target. This part is known as the **negative analogy**. There are, moreover, properties of the base of which it is not known whether corresponding properties hold in the target (remember that the target is sparsely understood). This part is known as the **neutral analogy**. The terms positive, negative and neutral analogy are Hesse's.

Say that property R is in the neutral analogy. The use of the analogy is to predict that R' holds in the target. This prediction can then be tested by experiment; if the analogy is good, the prediction will turn out to be true, or at least close enough to be useful. But there will be many properties which are currently in the neutral analogy but which will be false in the target. How is it that the properties to predict and investigate are chosen from the neutral analogy? The fact that the base domain is well understood means that there will be **causal relations** known between the properties of the base. The properties from the neutral analogy which are chosen to form hypotheses for the target are those which are causally connected with properties from the positive analogy.

Perhaps a direct causal connection between the positive analogy and R is known. This would amount to the knowledge of (or belief in) a general law

$$B_1 \wedge \ldots \wedge B_r \longrightarrow R$$

Such a law could (and should) be used to *infer R'* in the target by direct inference, without using the analogy at all. But (Hesse claims) such general laws are not often known; what is known is that

$$B_1 \wedge \ldots \wedge B_r \wedge A_1 \wedge \ldots \wedge A_n \longrightarrow R$$

but precisely which factors are responsible for R in the base cannot be determined. For example, the motion of elastic balls may be taken as a model for the propagation of sound in air; the fact that balls rebound off hard surfaces may be correlated with (i.e. is causally connected to) their basic properties, using, say, Newtonian mechanics; but

> we cannot empirically separate the characteristics which are in common between the throwing of a ball and the uttering of a sound, and those which are different, in order to infer a general causal relation applicable also to sound: 'throwing is correlated with rebound,' in such a way that it is independent of the occurrence of the other characters of the ball. [24]

Thus the echoing of sound could be predicted (or explained) *by analogy* to the bouncing of balls, but not using a general theory, given the existing state of understanding.

So Hesse's argument is that, while arguing by general law is preferable to arguing by analogy when it applies, the latter is applicable in many more situations than the former. According to Hesse, analogies tend to be 'pre-theoretic', with respect to the target domain anyway; a successful analogy will lead to a deeper understanding of the target domain and hence, perhaps, to a causal theory of the target which will replace the analogy. Thus analogical models can be seen as complementary to general theories.

Hesse is rather vague about what constitutes the 'recognisable similarity' on which her theory is based. Notice that her theory requires not only that we should be able to *recognise* the similarity between analogous properties A and A', but also that, given a property R in the neutral analogy, we can predict the analogous property R' in the target: i.e. we need to be able to *construct* the analogue of a property.

A recent account published in the AI literature has attempted to provide a more precise normative theory of analogy than Hesse's ([12]). This account tightens Hesse's vague notion of causality in the base domain being transferred to the target with the notion of a **determination**. A determination holds between attributes A and B of a system if the value of A strictly determines that of B — for example, a person's age determines his or her eligibility to drive a motor car. The use of an analogy, in this account, is to infer the value of attribute B of the target system from the knowledge that the base and target have the same value for attribute A, and the knowledge of the value of attribute A in the base. According to this account, therefore, an analogical inference is guaranteed to be correct.

Hesse's theory would categorize reasoning by determination under reasoning from general laws, not analogy, since a knowledge of the base and the determination allows the following general law to be inferred which applies to the target:

$$A = A_0 \longrightarrow B = B_0$$

where A_0 and B_0 are the known values of A and B in the base. While there may be pragmatic reasons why such a generalisation would tend not to be made in advance of the target situation (such as the need to store all such generalisations), the point is that Davies and Russell's theory excludes most interesting instances of analogical reasoning, where knowledge as strong as determinations is not available.

Hesse's theory of analogy is weaker (in the sense that her notion of analogy does not guarantee correct inference) but correctly captures the heuristic and experimental nature of analogical reasoning. This is the view of analogy which motivates the work described in this book.

2.1.2 Cognitive accounts

In this section, we briefly review the attempts of cognitive psychologists to model human analogical reasoning. Early models tended to concentrate on isolated analogies, such as those used in IQ tests, and did not consider the purpose or use of analogy. More recent models construe analogy as a part of wider human reasoning; not surprisingly, these turn out to be more relevant to our interests in this book.

2.1.3 Cognitive models for simple analogies

Simple analogies are problems of the form

$$A : B :: C : X$$

(which reads 'A is to B as C is to X'), where A, B and C are given and X is to be determined, usually chosen from a small set of options. This form of problem is common in intelligence tests. Psychologists became interested in providing models for the solution of such problems apparently because they believed this would help them understand the nature of intelligence. With simple analogies, the problem is recognising the analogy — we are not *using* the analogy to solve another problem.

Rumelhart and Abrahamson [40] give a model for the solution of simple analogies. In this model, the terms are represented as points in a multi-dimensional space, the dimensions being properties relevant to the terms in question, such as size, ferocity, etc. for animals:

$$A : B :: C : X \quad \text{if} \quad \underline{B}\text{-}\underline{A} = \underline{X}\text{-}\underline{C}$$

That is, the analogy relation holds if the differences in the predefined dimensions are the same on each side. Thus, the analogy is defined purely in terms of intrinsic properties of the entities in question rather than external relationships between them. So a simple analogy such as

$$DOG : CAT :: CAT : MOUSE$$

where the common relationship is a tendency for one term to chase the other, could not be adequately represented in this model. Similarly, scientific analogies, such as those studied by Hesse, typically involve systems of external relationships between entities. So the representational system chosen by Rumelhart and Abrahamson is inadequate for most interesting analogies. Perhaps the fact that the simple analogies are not used for anything, and thus that there is no objective criterion for their success, led Rumelhart and

Abrahamson to propose such a restricted model. Also, spatial models were
fashionable in cognitive psychology at that time.

Sternberg ([43]) gives another model for the solution of simple analogies.
In this model, terms are represented by some (unspecified) semantic memory,
a semantic network for instance. An analogy is represented by the same
relation occurring between different objects. Once again, analogies are used
to get the 'right' answer on IQ test simple analogies This definition for
analogy is too restrictive for the analogies which we are seeking in problem
solving, in which relations on one side may match with different relations
on the other. However, Sternberg's representation language can at least
express a wider range of relationships between objects than Rumelhart and
Abrahamson's. Again, not surprisingly, a model of simple analogies does not
shed much light on the *use* of analogy in problem solving.

2.1.4   Cognitive models of analogical problem solving

More recently, cognitive psychologists have moved on from simple analogies
to consider the role of analogy in problem solving.

Gentner et al

Gentner's structure/mapping theory, introduced in the previous chapter,
is illustrated schematically in Figure 2.1. The analogy retriever looks for
potential analogues for the current state of working memory (which might
include, for example, the current problem to solve) and past experience
stored in long term memory (LTM). Potential analogues are then passed to
the analogy engine, which is the heart of the analogy system. The engine
does full matching on the potential analogues, and then may make candidate
inferences about the target situation (i.e. what came from working memory),
and structural evaluations of the strength of the analogy. These suggestions
are then merged with the agent's other plans and goals.

A significant feature of this model is that the analogy component exists separately from the rest of the problem solving and reasoning apparatus
(represented in the diagram by the 'plans and goals' ellipse. Gentner's model
construes analogy matching and analogical inference as being isolated syntactic operations; i.e. it does not allow semantic or pragmatic factors (such
as the current goal of the problem solver, or semantic information about
the symbols in the base and target descriptions) to influence directly the
analogical process. Gentner ([20]) argues that these factors influence analogy by determining the state of working memory when the analogy engine
is invoked. This issue is clearly relevant to computational analogy — what
information/knowledge should the analogy system have access to and how

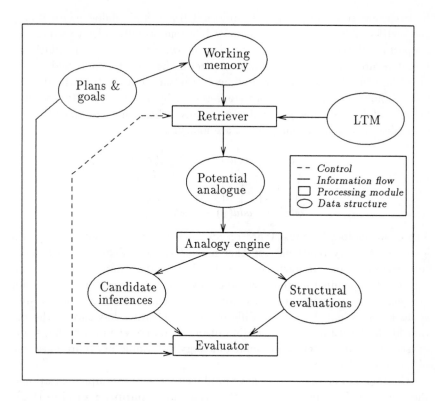

Figure 2.1: Gentner's model of analogy

should it use it. The PI model of Holyoak and Thagard takes a different
view on this issue.

Gentner's model of analogy can be seen as a fleshing out of Hesse's,
being based on the same idea of what analogy is, but defining the notion of
similarity, about which Hesse is vague, so that a computer implementation
is possible (and effected).

The notion of similarity which Gentner uses is similar to that used by
Sternberg and mentioned above, except that it is more fully and clearly
defined. Gentner uses a kind of semantic network to represent physical
systems. An analogy between two such networks is defined to be a mapping
between the objects of the networks so that the same relations hold between
corresponding objects.

This definition is too restrictive for the purposes of problem solving by
analogy, as pointed out above. Gentner also considers unary relations to

be irrelevant to analogies, and so does not try to find analogues for them;[1]
she justifies this by saying that unary relations usually refer to superficial
properties of the objects (such as the yellowness of the sun), which are
therefore not part of the causal structure of the base domain, and so will
never be helpful in making predictions in the target. In automatic problem
solving, however, unary relations (represented by unary predicates) seem to
be as useful in looking for analogies as any other kind. In the following
example, the *only* relations present are unary:[2]

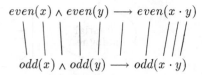

$$even(x) \wedge even(y) \longrightarrow even(x \cdot y)$$

$$odd(x) \wedge odd(y) \longrightarrow odd(x \cdot y)$$

These two factors (the insistence on identical non-unary relations, and the
ignoring of unary relations) together make Gentner's definition of analogy
too restrictive for our purposes. Gentner's structure mappings are clearly
very much dependent on the particular way in which the systems in question
are represented; a complicated, real-world system such as the solar system
could be represented in many different ways; Gentner has chosen the one
that fits best with her representation of the atom, i.e. she has, perhaps sub-
consciously, anticipated the intended analogy in forming her representations
of the physical systems.

Gentner and her colleagues have produced a computer implementation of
the structure/mapping theory — the **structure/mapping engine** ([15]).
While the concept of analogy match used in the theory is over-restrictive,
the mechanisms used in the SME for constructing matches can potentially
be used with a less restrictive notion of analogy. We discuss the matching
procedures further in Chapter 4.

Holyoak, Thagard et al

Some of the best work in cognitive modeling of analogical reasoning has
been done by a group comprising Holyoak, Thagard and others, and has
been developed over a number of years ([23, 26, 25, 44]).

The work of Gick and Holyoak in [23] addresses the issue of the level
of representation of the base and target systems. They show how people
represent the systems in such a way as to maximise the similarity between
them (their notion of similarity at that time, given representations, is very

---

[1]Brown ([3]) takes exactly the opposite view, namely that unary relations should form
the cornerstones of analogical matches.

[2]We discuss the application of this analogy in Chapter 6.

similar to Gentner's structure mapping). They liken this ability to change representation to a theory of text comprehension, in which a story can be described in many different ways, each being a summary of the story at some level of generality. While explaining the problem clearly, they do not suggest any computational mechanisms either for constructing the representations or for matching them once constructed. The issue of changing representation in order to construct analogies is an important one for analogy in problem solving: several of the examples given in Chapter 1 required some such ability. Furthermore, if analogy is to be useful in genuine dynamic problem solving, we cannot expect the examples to be presented neatly and optimally for the analogy which is being sought. This indicates that analogy matching will have to do more 'cleaning up' itself.

In more recent papers ([26]), a model of problem solving, called **PI** has been proposed. This model is illustrated schematically in Figure 2.2.

PI takes a heuristic, experimental view of analogy, like Hesse and SMT: analogies are used to propose actions to a problem solver for which there is an independent success criterion (i.e. whether the problem is solved or not); analogies do not guarantee success.

PI is a spreading activation model in which currently active concepts (for example, those involved in current goals) spread activation to other concepts with which they are associated. As Figure 2.2 shows, analogy is tightly coupled with normal problem solving. The loop in the figure represents the principal cycle of rule retrieval and application in PI. If the current problem (encoded in working memory) has not been solved yet (the diamond-shaped question box), production rules are retrieved which are relevant to the problem. These are then fired to update the working memory. At each cycle of rule activation analogous problems may be retrieved and matched. The use of the analogy is to suggest plausible rules to fire for the current state. Holyoak and Thagard [26] argue that this is a distinguishing feature of PI from SMT, and an advantage.

The PI model has a number of contributions to computational analogy. Firstly, there is an implemented mechanism for the filtering stage; then there is an interesting approach to analogy matching; and the PI researchers, unlike others in the field, have considered how the analogy can be both used to benefit problem solving activity and integrated with 'normal' problem solving. The algorithms for both filtering and matching are implemented on neural nets. The motivation for this is that, in analogy, there are a number of weak criteria that we would like a match to have, but we cannot enforce such criteria; neural nets appear to be good at performing tasks with these properties. We discuss the neural net matching algorithm in more detail in Chapter 4.

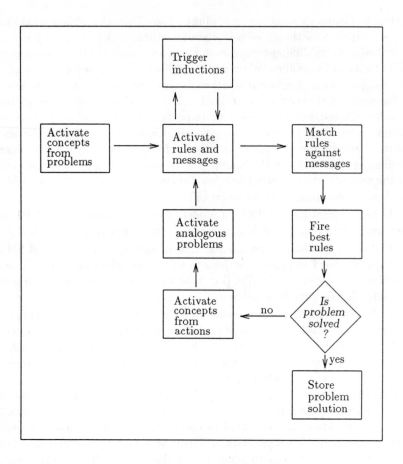

Figure 2.2: Problem solving in PI

2.2   Analogy as machine learning

As explained in the previous chapter, the goal of APS is to enable a problem
solving system to improve its performance by exploiting its past experience
in solving similar problems. Thus APS is a form of machine learning. There
are other machine learning techniques which have the same overall goal,
although their means of achieving it is different from APS. In assessing
the power and applicability of APS, therefore, we should compare it with
other machine learning systems. In this section, we compare APS with
three existing machine learning systems which have been used to transfer

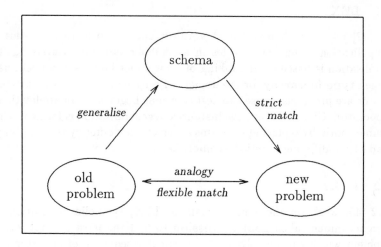

Figure 2.3: Analogy and generalisation

problem-solving experience: LEX [32], LEX2 [45] and LP [41]. The three systems are chosen as representative of different kinds of machine learning — LEX embodies an inductive form of learning, LEX2 uses an analytical, explanation-based technique, and LP is an example of learning by meta-level analysis. Together, the three systems exemplify the most widely-used symbolic machine learning techniques.

All three are spontaneous generalisation systems; that is, given an example or examples of problem solving behaviour, they form a generalisation of both the problem and (aspects of) the solution. Faced with a new problem, they look for a generalisation which subsumes it (strict subsumption); when one is found, they attempt to instantiate the generalised solution to solve the given problem. In contrast, APS makes no spontaneous generalisation, but attempts to match old problems with new ones by *flexible* matching. These different approaches to exploiting past experience are illustrated schematically in Figure 2.3. In each case, there is a notion of the potential generality of the process: that is, across what sort of variation in problems can old experience be exploited. As well as the potential generality across problems, there is the issue of the potential variation in the form of the solutions. These two issues are crucial to the assessment of the generality (in terms of applicability) of the techniques. We compare the existing systems to the hypothetical Basic APS system with particular regard to these issues. Firstly, we give a brief description of the existing systems.

2.2.1   LEX

LEX [32] used a technique called **version spaces** to learn heuristics for
the application of particular rules in a symbolic integration system. The
generalisation is based on the taking of least upper bounds in a fixed, user-
supplied **type hierarchy** for the domain. Positive instances for a particular
operator are problems whose shortest solutions begin with an application of
the operator. Given two positive instances, a generalisation is formed, which
subsumes both, by replacing subterms at which they differ by the least upper
bound of the differing function symbols in the hierarchy.

2.2.2   LEX2

LEX2 [45] works in the same domain as LEX, symbolic integration. It
uses a technique called **goal regression** to find the most general form of
a problem which can be solved by a particular sequence of operators. Its
generalisations stay within the **object language** — that is the language in
which the examples and operators are expressed.

2.2.3   LP

LP [41] learns schemata for the solution of equations from single examples presented by the user. It first characterises the original equation, and
the user's solution in terms of a sophisticated description language, quite
separate from the object language — this language is termed the **meta-
language**, since it describes object level terms. The idea of the meta-level
description is to abstract away from the details of the solution and to express
just the 'strategic shape'. The meta-level operators used are mainly those
from the preceding PRESS system ([42]): a particular operator application
in the solution might be described as a 'collection' step, in which the number
of occurrences of the unknown is decreased, or a 'homogenisation' step, in
which the equation is rearranged so that the unknown occurs only within
instances of one compound term. Meta-level operators (called **methods**)
have pre- and post-conditions.

  LP then uses a technique called **pre-condition analysis** to construct a
schema by performing a simple kind of goal regression in the meta-language:
the schema expresses the conditions under which the entire sequence of methods which describe the given base solution can be expected to apply. LP's
schemata are expressed in the meta-language. The schemata are used on new
problems by checking their pre-conditions against the problems; if a match
is found, an attempt is made to apply the sequence of methods making up
the schema to the problem in order to solve it.

The intuition for this form of learning is as follows: if the description of the solution in terms of methods does capture its important aspects, we might expect another problem which has a similar description according to the methods (though it might look different) to be solvable with the same (or a similar) sequence of methods.

2.2.4 LEX vs APS

A LEX generalisation has the same top-level structure as the problems which gave rise to it; it differs from the problems in that instances of particular functions have been replaced by typed function variables. The part of the original problems which has not been generalised (the greater part in most cases) must match the new problem exactly. More complicated types of match, such as

$$
\begin{array}{c}
(x + y) - x = y \\
\diagdown\diagdown\diagdown\,\bigm|\bigm|\bigm| \\
x = 0 \vee (x * y)/x = y
\end{array}
$$

where there is an extra condition on one side, are not allowed. Matches in an APS system may also permute arguments and omit function symbols. Thus the range of problem generality in an APS system is potentially much greater than that in LEX.

With respect to the solution generality, LEX only makes generalisations relating to the application of *single* operators; thus it cannot capture variations in the solution which may correspond to variations in the problem. For example, LEX could handle the following problem variation (within Boolean algebra):

$$
\begin{array}{c}
x \cap x = x \\
\bigm|\bigm|\bigm|\bigm|\bigm| \\
x \cup x = x
\end{array}
$$

(assuming it knew the appropriate types) but could not represent the fact that *correspondingly different* operators need to be applied in the solution of the problems.

Thus, in both respects, APS offers greater generality than LEX, and would thus be applicable in many more situations. Referring to Hesse's theory described above, we can think of LEX as forming general laws inductively from instances which it has observed. That is, it abstracts out certain of the properties of the instances (in Hesse's terminology) and forms general laws (or rather beliefs) involving those that remain. However, its single method of generalising through a type hierarchy means that it can abstract out only certain sorts of property (the identity of certain functions). If a potential generalisation involves abstracting out other sorts of property, such as the order of arguments, LEX will not be able to capture it.

Furthermore, even within its range of variation, the reliability of LEX generalisations is questionable. As Hesse points out, arguing by general laws (or beliefs) involves claiming a causal link between the form of problem (expressed by the type hierarchy) and the form of solution (in this case, which operator was applied first). In the case of LEX, this link is not based on any theory of the problem solving process, as it is in, say, LP (see below), but is represented by a domain-level belief that the type hierarchy gives good dimensions for generalisation. While this may be true for some sets of problems, it is unlikely to be true throughout a non-trivial domain, and in any case depends on the user supplying a *good* hierarchy. Thus, the causal links will not be strong enough to support reliable generalisations. As a result, LEX would make serious over-generalisations after extended experience.

In summary, APS offers greater scope for variation in both problem and solution, and thus will be more widely applicable than LEX's inductive generalisation technique, as predicted by Hesse's theory. Furthermore, it is questionable whether LEX's inductive technique is powerful enough to support valid generalisation.

2.2.5   LEX2 vs APS

LEX2 uses a form of **explanation-based generalisation**. That is, its generalisation from a solution to a problem is obtained by answering (at some level) the question 'why did this solution work?' LEX2 is very cautious – its answer is simply that it worked because the sequence of operators applied was seen to solve the problem (an answer which would be considered bloody-minded of a human). Its generalisation technique (goal regression) looks for the most general problem which can be solved by the same sequence of operators. Thus, its generalisations are very strong (theorems, in fact), but the range of problem and solution variation is limited: new problems must match perfectly with old ones, except for subterms which have been generalised to variables, and new solutions must be identical to old ones. Thus APS is more widely applicable than LEX2. This is not to say that LEX2 is not a useful system; as Hesse shows, arguing by generalisation, where applicable, is preferable to arguing by analogy. In a given non-trivial domain, there will be a tradeoff between the strength and the generality of the generalisations: LEX2's are cautious, i.e. not very general, but very strong.

2.2.6 APS vs LP

LP's generalisation technique, like LEX2's, is a form of explanation-based generalisation. The difference is that LP's answer to the question 'why did this solution work?' is much less cautious and is based on sophisticated domain knowledge; it gives its answer not in terms of the particular operators which were applied but of the effect which they had on the terms to which they were applied, expressed in a meta-level description language. Thus the generalisations of which LP is capable are much greater than those of LEX2; on the other hand, the generalisations are not as reliable, and schema application may fail.

The potential variation in problem obtainable by LP's meta-level technique goes beyond simple syntactic similarity; this is because LP's schemata are expressed in terms of the description language, and will be applied to new problems which satisfy a particular description. But the descriptors in question (which may say, for example, that the equation must contain a pair of identical subterms) do not characterise the *syntactic* form of equations to which they apply. That is, we cannot write down the most general equation which satisfies a particular meta-level description. So the range of variation is much greater on the problems. Similarly, the solutions can vary considerably as well: the operators applied in the new situation do not have to be the same as the old ones, but can be any from a class of operators capable of producing similar meta-level effects. LP can also insert extra operators in the application of its schemata.

While the problem variation in APS is wider than that in LEX and LEX2, it is still syntactically based, and thus cannot express the leaps of generalisation available to LP. Similar remarks are true of the solution variation. Note that it is still possible, in theory, for APS to exploit variation which LP cannot: if the syntactic match between problems does not preserve the meta-level descriptors, LP would not regard the new problem as an instance of the schema derived from the old. Furthermore, an LP schema is only applicable within the domain (equation solving) in which it was formed; APS can potentially work across domains – indeed this is perhaps the most interesting application for analogy.

The success of LP's schemata is clearly dependent on the accuracy of the meta-language – that is, on the extent to which the (meta-level) form of a problem determines the (meta-level) form of the solution. In LP's domain of equation solving, the meta-language seems extremely appropriate: it represents a theory of *how* to solve equations, which enables large generalisations to be made.

In the terms of Hesse's theory, there is a theory which underlies and explains the observed (meta-level) properties independently of the other characteristics of the equations. This makes LP's generalisation, when it applies, preferable to APS. As Hesse shows, models or analogies are useful when general theories are not available. Thus, in domains which are not as well understood as equation solving, APS will become more attractive since LP's techniques will not work.

2.2.7   Summary of analysis

The above analysis shows that APS has a role to play in an advanced learning and reasoning system. The only generalisation system we have discussed which can produce greater variation in both problem and solution, LP, relies on sophisticated domain knowledge. Where such knowledge is lacking, such as when a new domain is being explored, APS could provide a means of exploiting past experience. The following spectrum illustrates our conclusions:

analogy	generalisation
knowledge-free ————————————————	knowledge-based
empirical	analytical

On the left-hand side, in the absence of sufficient domain-specific knowledge, analogy will be the preferred technique for learning from past experience; on the right-hand side, in the presence of sophisticated domain knowledge, generalisation techniques such as LP's pre-condition analysis will be preferred.

Hybrid systems

The question naturally arises of whether we could have a learning system in the middle of the spectrum; that is to say, one which combines a certain amount of spontaneous generalisation with a certain amount of flexible, analogical matching. If the meta-language for the domain was not fully developed, analogical techniques could supplement analytical techniques in the following ways:

- If the meta-language was not as general as it could be, i.e. if there was more scope for generalisation in the domain than it knew, flexible matching could be used between schemata and new problems; this would have the effect of 'stretching' the schemata a bit further. The question would then arise of whether the results of the attempted applications could be used to increase the power of the meta-language so that it could express the greater generalisation. If this could be

done, we would have a powerful system, capable of directing its generalisation language by experience; analogical reasoning would be a step
towards reasoning by generalising, just as reasoning from models is a
step towards the construction of theories in science.

- If the meta-language was over-general, and was producing schemata
  which failed much of the time, analogical matching between the object-
  level problem statements could be used to select the most promising
  of a number of schemata which matched at the meta-level. The results
  of this could perhaps be used to refine the meta-language.

Any analogy system which uses information other than the bare syntactic form of problems and operators is a sort of hybrid system. For example,
Winston's analogy matcher ([47]) is told that causal relations are more 'important' than non-causal ones; this amounts to a (weak) claim about the
domain: that the outcome of stories is correlated with the causal pattern of
the plot. In the PI model ([26]) certain associations are given prior plausibility as a result of **semantic similarity**: this also is a weak form of domain
insight — while we cannot say just how or why, we expect that semantically similar objects will behave in similar ways, and hence make plausible
analogues.

2.3 Summary of chapter

We summarise the conclusions of our analysis of the concept of analogy:

- Analogy is applicable to transferring experience when reasoning by
  generalisation is inapplicable through lack of knowledge of the domain.

- Analogy involves going beyond what the system already knows; since
  analogy will be used when existing generalisations do not apply, the
  use of analogy is based around the belief that there is more generality
  within the domain (or across domains) than has yet been expressed in
  laws.

- While analogy tends not to be necessary in cases of strong domain
  knowledge, any (weak) information that is available about the domain
  is potentially useful for analogy, and should not be neglected.

Chapter 3

Heuristics for analogy matching

We have already introduced the notion of an analogy match (in Chapter 1); we now define it more precisely. An analogy match is a set of **positional associations** between symbols in the logical terms; i.e. consists of elements of the form

$$((symbol_1, position_1), (symbol_2, position_2))$$

where $symbol_1$ has $position_1$ (a position is represented as a sequence of successive argument positions) in $term_1$ and likewise for $symbol_2$, $position_2$ and $term_2$. The two symbols in their respective positions are regarded as being *analogues* in the analogy represented by the match. For example, given the terms

$$f(a, g(b)) \quad and \quad f(g(c), a)$$

an analogy matcher might produce the match

$$\{ \, ((\, f, [] \,), \, (\, f, [] \,)), \, ((\, a, [1] \,), \, (\, a, [2] \,)),$$
$$((\, g, [2] \,), \, (\, g, [1] \,)), \, ((\, b, [2,1] \,), \, (\, c, [1,1] \,)) \, \}$$

which can be graphically represented as

$$f(\; a, \; g(\; b \;))$$
$$f(\; g(\; c \;), \; a)$$

We often talk about the mapping or correspondence associated with a particular match. In this we abstract away the positional information in the full match, to leave the set of pairs of symbols which are associated, possibly

together with argument pairing information. For the example above, the
two presentations of the mapping would be:

$$
\begin{array}{ll}
f \longleftrightarrow f & (f, f, [(1,2),(2,1)]) \\
a \longleftrightarrow a & (a, a, []) \\
g \longleftrightarrow g & (g, g, [(1,1)]) \\
b \longleftrightarrow c & (b, c, [])
\end{array}
$$

All of the computational accounts of analogy involve a notion of an analogy match as a symbolic association. However, as we saw in the previous
chapter, researchers have differed considerably over the details in the following respects:

- Whether a match must be bijective, or whether unmatched symbols
  are allowed — for example, unpaired arguments to paired functions.

- Whether the arguments to functions which are paired can be permuted
  in a match.

- Whether a match must be **consistent** (a symbol is always matched
  with the same symbol on the other side).

- Whether predicates/functions/objects can be matched with *different*
  predicates/functions/objects.

In the previous chapter we discussed a number of examples of problem
solving analogies which indicated that, for our purposes anyway, we must
make the permissive choices on all of the issues above.

The function of an **analogy matcher** is to construct analogy matches
between terms which are presented to it. As described in Chapter 1, matching is the first stage of the Basic APS framework. However, it turns out that
matching can be an important part of the later stages as well; in fact, we
can think of the function of the later stages as being the extension of the
initial match between the problems to the solutions.

The first analogy matcher, as far as the current author is aware, was
written by Evans ([14]) to construct correspondences between descriptions
of simple geometric configurations. Evans's notion of a match was restricted
(see the previous chapter), and his matching algorithm relies on the restrictions, so we do not describe it here.

The first matcher to use a reasonably flexible concept of analogy was
that of Kling ([29]). He used it to construct analogies between theorems in
abstract algebra. We discuss Kling's matcher in detail below; we also discuss
Munyer's matcher ([33]) which embodies a considerably more flexible notion
of analogy match than Kling's.

Winston ([47]) used exhaustive enumeration and scoring as his method of matching. We argue below that this method is inadequate for all but small terms, as the combinatorics quickly become overwhelming.

More recently, various matchers have been published based around the idea of flexible application of heuristic criteria — the PMH matcher ([35]), the ACME matcher ([25]) and the SME matcher ([15]). In the following sections and the next chapter we discuss the more interesting approaches to analogy matching in detail.

3.1 There is no formal rule for analogy

There seems to be no general, formal rule which tells us what constitutes a reliable analogy match. It is in the nature of analogy that it is partly empirical — we only know for sure whether a particular match is good or not after the application procedure has used it in trying to solve the target problem. Hesse's theory of analogy, discussed in the last chapter, helps us to understand this: analogy (as opposed to generalisation) is useful when the causality in a domain is not well understood: that is, when we cannot say, in general terms, why the solution to the base worked. According to Hesse, therefore, we turn to analogy precisely when we are not *sure* whether we can apply our old experience to a new situation.

We could attempt to restrict the notion of analogy to one where we had a specification of a match which guaranteed successful application (the theory put forward in [12] does essentially this). But this would prevent us from attempting to exploit looser analogies (looser, that is, relative to the state of knowledge of the system at the time, not necessarily so objectively). The motivating examples of the last section, and the great majority of analogies people seem able to exploit are of this form.

Almost all analogy researchers have adopted the heuristic view, though some more explicitly than others. Therefore analogy matching algorithms use **heuristic criteria** to guide them in searching for good analogies. The heuristics that a particular matcher uses determine its (or rather its designer's) idea of what constitutes a promising analogy.

While heuristics are first apparent in the matching stage, it will become clear in later chapters that the other stages of Basic APS include similar criteria (implicitly or explicitly) as part of their design. The notion of analogy heuristics is a very useful tool in analysing and building analogy systems.

Since analogy is heuristic, it is likely that different criteria will be successful in different situations. It is therefore desirable for analogy matchers to be flexible with respect to the criteria that they use: that is, the specific criteria used should not be engrained in the architecture of the matcher.

The descriptions given in the literature of early matchers (particularly [29] and [33]) do not make it clear generally what heuristics their matchers are using, where they are using them, or why they are using them. In Section 3.3 we analyse both these matchers to determine the heuristics that they are using and to assess their power and limitations in terms of the heuristics.

More recent matchers ([25], [15], [35]) have been more explicit with their criteria. But there has been little discussion (except in [35]) of *why* the criteria are used: that is, why should we expect matches which score highly according to the criteria to lead to success. In Section 3.4 we discuss the justification for the use of the most common general heuristics.

3.2   What should a matcher know about?

Recently, a subject of debate has been the issue of what knowledge about its context a matcher should have. By context, we mean relatively static domain knowledge (operators/axiomatisations, semantic type hierarchies) as well as 'current state' (current goals, purposes, etc.).

As discussed in the previous chapter, Gentner's SMT does not allow any context other than the syntactic structures which are being matched. Gentner argues that relevant considerations can be adequately reflected in these structures alone. On the other hand, the PI model allows similarity judgements and 'pragmatic centrality' judgements to influence the matching process (these latter seem to assess to what extent a rule or concept is relevant to the task at hand). In a similar vein, Kedar-Cabelli ([28]) has argued that the current purpose of the analogy system is important to matching; and Carbonnell ([8]) argues that the current trace of the problem solver working on the target problem should be used in matching (as well as corresponding structures for the base).

This issue is related to that of what heuristic criteria should be used, as certain criteria require some parts of the context but not others. For example, preferring matches between entities of the same or similar semantic type (we will later call this the **semantic type heuristic**) requires the presence of some sort of type hierarchy or other means of making similarity judgements.

We can understand the motivation for introducing context into the matcher using Hesse's theory of analogy discussed in the previous chapter. We are going to use the analogy to make predictions about the target system; these predictions are based on transferring known (or believed) correlations from the base to the target: the correlations which are transferred relate parts of the positive analogy (which have analogues) and parts of the neutral analogy (which do not have yet). We can see two reasons for introducing context: firstly, it is plausible to search for matches with base systems/problems whose positive and neutral analogies are connected by known base correlations; such matches are likely to be strongly *predictive*; this motivates giving the matcher access to these correlations. Secondly, we may wish to maximise the likelihood that the analogy will make predictions *relevant to our current goals*; this indicates checking the relevance of the correlated parts of the neutral analogy (in the base) with our current (target) intentions.

For the purposes of this book, we will take a pragmatic, application-oriented, view of this issue. We will introduce context into our discussion of matching only as our target examples require it. If context is vital, we will find that without it our APS system will break down on some intuitively straightforward example; we will then know that we must introduce some context, and the example concerned will motivate and guide its introduction. For this approach to be successful it is important that the analogy matcher is easily extendible. Behind this approach to the issue of context is the claim that while extra context may well prove useful (and we will see examples of this in later chapters), a competent analogy system should be able to operate without it, though perhaps not so well.

For an automated problem solver, the current goal of the system tends to be encoded in the structures being matched (i.e. the problem representations): in a theorem prover the goal is 'prove this theorem'; in a STRIPS-like planner ([16]), the current goal is encoded in terms of start and goal states. One lesson is that we should not match on the start states alone, but this is rather obvious.

Perhaps, as theorem provers get more sophisticated, we will find that a prover can have more specific goals than simply to prove a particular theorem. Consider, for example, a proof planning system such as that proposed in [6]; such a proof planner views the enterprise of trying to prove a theorem at a strategic (meta-)level, as well as at the usual object level of assumptions, axioms and inference rules. A subgoal in such a system might therefore have a strategic, meta-level description (such as 'reduce the number of occurrences of the unknown in the equation'), rather than being a normal object level goal (such as 'prove this equality') — the examples are motivated by the PRESS ([42]) and LP ([41]) systems discussed in the previous chapter. It seems clear that an analogy matcher should match at this meta-level as well as at the object level.

We discuss various sorts of context that might benefit the matcher in a Basic APS system in Section 4.5 and elsewhere: semantic types, known analogies, domain axiomatisations, meta-level matching.

3.3   Analysis of existing matchers

In this section we develop the concept of analogy heuristics by analysing the analogy matchers of Kling and Munyer. These two matchers were developed for problem solving use in mathematical domains and hence are of interest to this book. Furthermore, in the publications on these matchers ([29], [33]) there is no discussion of what heuristics are used by the matchers — the heuristics are embedded in the algorithms. It will help us to understand the concept of heuristics to tease them out.

3.3.1   Munyer

Munyer's algorithm takes two terms (representing the base and target problems) together with a small amount of information about the symbols (see below). It constructs a single analogy match between the terms.

Munyer calls the terms which his matcher accepts as input **logical terms**. They are well formed in the sense of being representable as trees in the usual way (so that each symbol has a unique position in a term and heads a unique subterm) but are not necessarily first-order since variables can have arguments (i.e. there can be variable functions and predicates).

Munyer's matcher makes no distinction between predicates and functions. If logical *formulae* are to be matched, the logical connectives in them are treated as predicate/function symbols just like any normal predicates or functions in the formulae. So the matcher operates with an unrestricted and rather uniform syntax. The only contextual information about the symbols that the matcher uses is the commutativity or otherwise of functions and predicates.

The algorithm

Munyer's matcher works in three stages, constructing intermediate matches from the first two. They are: **grounding, deleting** and **adding**. The matching strategy may be briefly described as follows: in the first stage, an initial match of *a priori* plausible associations is constructed; in the second stage, this match is whittled down to a subset of associations which fit together well; in the third stage, holes are filled in the whittled down match. More recent matchers (in particular the SME of [15]) have been based along similar lines, although Munyer's contribution to the field is rarely acknowledged.

Grounding   In this stage, an initial map is created in which

- Any pair of identical symbols, one from each term, are associated.

- Any variable in either term is associated with all symbols in the other term.

Deleting This stage takes as input the output of the previous stage, i.e. two terms and an initial map between them, and deletes some (or all or none) of the associations in the initial match. The choice of which maps to delete is made on the basis of how well each map **supports** the maps which **directly dominate** it in the existing match. To explain what 'directly dominate' means, note that the associations in a match can be partially ordered in the following way: for symbols a and b in a term, define $a > b$ if b occurs in the (unique) subterm headed by a; for associations (a_1, a_2) and (b_1, b_2), (a_1, a_2) **dominates** (b_1, b_2) if $a_1 > b_1$ and $a_2 > b_2$; the relation of domination puts a partial order on the associations in a match. Now we can define the relation of direct domination as follows: (a_1, a_2) **directly dominates** (b_1, b_2) (in a match M) if (a_1, a_2) dominates (b_1, b_2) and there is no (c_1, c_2) in M, dominated by (a_1, a_2), which dominates (b_1, b_2).

The procedure is first to mark certain associations as being exempt from deletion, and then to delete those which have not been exempted and which share a node[1] with another association.

To be exempt from deletion, a match must give **support** to an association which directly dominates it. The notion of support is defined so that one association supports another if together they tend to preserve the structure of the terms being matched. For example, in the match

$$f(\ a,\ g(\ x,\ d\ ))$$

$$f(\ g(\ c,\ d\ ),\ a)$$

the (x, c) and (d, d) maps are directly dominated by the (g, g) map and both give it support. The (x, d) map, however, which is also directly dominated by (g, g), does not give it support.

Support is a relative concept; that is, map$_1$ supports map$_2$ if there is no map$_3$ **competing with** map$_1$ which supports map$_2$ better. The definition of 'competes' is important: in the above example (x, c) competes with (x, d) at x; (x, d) competes with (d, d) at d, whereas (x, c) and (d, d) do not compete at all (all this with respect to the directly dominating map (g, g)).

---

[1]Munyer uses the term 'node' to refer to an occurrence of a symbol at a position in a term.

The formal definition is that two maps compete on the left (w.r.t a map which directly dominates them both) if their left nodes occur in the same argument position of the left node of the dominating map. (Similarly for competition on the right.)

A map supports a directly dominating map on the left if it has minimal **left penalty** among all the maps with which it competes on the left. Munyer defines the left penalty of a map (l_2, r_2) w.r.t a directly dominating map (l_1, r_1) as the sum

$$C.P. + P.P.$$

where $C.P.$, the containment penalty, is the number of unmapped symbols above l_2 and below l_1 in the tree structure of the left term, and $P.P.$, the permutation penalty, is 1 if (l_2, r_2) permutes arguments of (l_1, r_1) and neither l_1 or r_1 is commutative, and 0 otherwise. If the minimum is not unique, all maps achieving it are deemed to give support.

In the above example, (x, c) and (x, d) compete on the left w.r.t. (g, g); both have $C.P. = 0$, (x, c) has $P.P. = 0$ and (x, d) has $P.P. = 1$, so (x, c) supports (g, g) on the left and (x, d) does not.

The notion of supporting on the right is defined analogously using the notion of competing on the right.

Lastly, Munyer defines a map to be exempt from deletion if it gives another map *either* left support *or* right support.

After the marking stage has been completed, those maps which have not been marked and which share a node with another association are removed from the match. This removal stage (but not the marking stage) is iterated, as an association which was removed may have been the only one which another association supported and so the latter should be removed also.

The motivation behind this complicated procedure seems to be that we should retain a set of associations which preserve the structure of the terms (this is behind the notion of direct dominance), and remove any other sets (this is behind the notion of competition).

Adding   This stage takes as input the result of the deleting stage and adds an association between any pair of nodes in the two terms which are both unmapped in the existing match but whose parent nodes are mapped to each other.

Also, if the head symbols of the two terms are both unmapped an association between them is added.

This step is not iterated.

Heuristics

What are the analogy heuristics which are being used in this algorithm? That is to say, what did Munyer believe about analogies that led him to design the algorithm in the way which he did?

In the grounding stage, all possible identical associations are put in the initial match: thus Munyer must have believed that identical associations make good analogues, and matches containing high proportions of identical associations make good analogies. Let us call this belief the **identical symbols heuristic**.

In the deleting stage, the initial match is whittled down to a subset of the original; this is done so that the associations in the subset tend to support each other well, in the sense of respecting the structure of the terms which are being matched. Thus, Munyer must, in addition, have believed that matches which respect the structure of the terms make promising analogies. Let us call this belief the **partial homomorphism heuristic** (a homomorphism, in algebra, is a mapping which respects, in a formal sense, the structure of the entities which it relates).

In the adding phase, associations are added to the match which fit in well, again in a structural sense, with those left after deletion. So this stage also makes use of the partial homomorphism heuristic.

Reconstruction

In [34], Munyer's algorithm is reconstructed (in Prolog), tested and analysed. It is found that the matcher, as described by Munyer, is not able to construct many of the analogies that Munyer claims it can in [33]. In [34], certain alterations to the algorithm are suggested which enable it to find Munyer's target analogies. These are:

- In the computation of the **containment penalty** (which penalises structural deformations in a match), only *unmapped* intermediate nodes are counted. It turns out to work better if *all* intermediate nodes are counted.

- The condition for exemption from deletion is changed so that a map is exempt if it supports another map *both* on the left *and* on the right, as opposed to the previous condition which only required *either* one *or* the other.

- In the deleting stage, all maps which are maximal in the match with respect to **partial dominance** (a refinement of dominance) are exempted from deletion.

We do not discuss the changes in detail here, since Munyer's matching examples were not drawn from real problems and his target matches are not intuitively clear analogies.

The latter two changes were principally motivated by the desire to make the algorithm *complete for first-order unifiable terms*: that is, if the terms are first-order and unifiable, the matcher will construct the match which represents their most general unifier (see [39] for an explanation of these terms). Munyer claims that his matcher is complete in this way; in fact, the algorithm, as stated, is not even complete for *identical* first-order terms.

Perhaps Munyer had in fact incorporated the three improvements into his algorithm, but forgot to update his written description of it. Otherwise, it seems odd that he should quote examples that his matcher could not carry out.

Assessment of the algorithm

The first thing which is notable about Munyer's algorithm, or at least the reconstruction of it, is its enormous computational cost. For example, in constructing the match

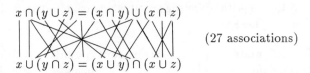

$$even(x) \;\wedge\; even(x) \longrightarrow even(x \cdot y)$$
$$odd(x) \;\wedge\; odd(y) \longrightarrow odd(x \cdot y)$$

the program took 40 seconds of c.p.u. time (interpreted Quintus Prolog on a Sun3 workstation); and on the match

$$x \cap (y \cup z) = (x \cap y) \cup (x \cap z)$$
$$x \cup (y \cap z) = (x \cup y) \cap (x \cup z)$$

(27 associations)

took 185 seconds.

While the reconstruction of the algorithm has not been particularly concerned with efficiency, the high cost seems to be an inherent feature of the structure of the algorithm, in particular the treatment of variables. In the grounding stage, associations are placed between a variable and all symbols in the other term, on the basis that no *a priori* restriction can be placed on the possible bindings for a variable. In the above examples, there were 67 and 146 associations respectively after the grounding stage. In general, the number of maps at this stage would be of the order of the square of the length of the terms.

The deleting stage then has to perform fairly complex computations on this set of associations, and this is where most of the c.p.u. time is used. The complexity of the deleting stage is of the order of the square of the size of the match produced by the grounding stage. The adding stage is linear in the size of the intermediate match. Therefore, the whole algorithm is n^4 in the size of the original terms. Unlike many 'worst case' analyses, this is also a typical case analysis, as the algorithm does not exploit features of particular terms to cut down its computation. Munyer's justification for his bottom-up approach to matching (as opposed to the top-down approach of unification algorithms) is that, since an analogy match may disrupt the structure of the terms, no top-down restrictions should be placed on associations. This philosophy contrasts with that of Kling [29], who uses the notion of semantic type to constrain the possible mappings between variables (see below). Kling's approach is to enforce type correspondence if possible, but to allow a small amount of deviation in order to find interesting analogies; in any case, in Kling's matches, variables are mapped only to other variables. Munyer has no type restrictions, and furthermore allows the binding of variables in his matches. This, in theory, enables him to find a much wider range of analogies, but he pays for this generality in c.p.u. time. The matcher in PI, which we discuss below, also has a bottom-up structure; however, it uses the spreading activation control of a neural net to enable the computation to be efficiently parallelised.

Having observed the inherent complexity of Munyer's approach, there are ways in which the algorithm could be guided which would not violate the approach:

- **Consistency.** No attention is paid during matching to the consistency of the match, particularly the variable bindings which it entails. Matches with inconsistent variable bindings are rejected at a later stage of the analogy process ([33]). But the complexity would be reduced if only consistent sets of variable bindings were considered in the first place. This would involve the development of several possible matches between a pair of terms which Munyer, for some reason, seems to want to avoid. The (relative) consistency of the predicate and variable mappings could be used to prune unpromising matches.

- **Syntactic types.** Munyer's matcher blurs some syntactic distinctions which analogies tend to respect, for example the special status of the propositional connectives, and the distinction between predicates and functions. In all the analogies considered in this book, propositional connectives are mapped only to other logical connectives, predicates are mapped only to other predicates, and functions to other functions.

One way of exploiting these syntactic type distinctions would be to construct only those associations which respect the syntactic types during grounding, and to put in those which do not (if at all) during adding. These proposals introduce more typing into the representation, but only at a very general, domain-independent level.

The issue was raised above of the construction of more than one match between a pair of terms, which Munyer's algorithm cannot do. The following intermediate match after the grounding stage illustrates the usefulness of such a facility:

$$a(\ a(\ a(\ b\ )))$$

$$a(\ a(\ x))$$

There are two main competing 'chains' of supporting associations, one drawn as dotted lines and one as continuous lines. Munyer's original algorithm would delete both chains iteratively from the left, finishing the deleting stage with a null match. The version with third change would retain the continuous chain, because it connects the head function symbols, delete the dotted one, and thus come up with the first-order unification. But there seems to be a disjunction here — either of the chains represents a plausible match which could be investigated further. The present criterion for deciding between them is unsatisfactory as it does not relate to the structure of the various possibilities. It seems sensible at this stage to split the match into the disjuncts and investigate them separately.

Analysis in terms of heuristics

In the previous section we saw how Munyer's matcher could be improved in certain ways without departing from the overall, bottom-up approach which Munyer takes. However, there is a serious problem with Munyer's algorithm which will not be solved by any of the remedies which have been suggested. The problem can be understood in terms of the way in which the matcher uses its analogy heuristics: the **identical symbols** and the **partial homomorphism** heuristics. The matcher relies entirely on the identical symbols heuristic to propose initial associations (apart from variable bindings). Non-identical associations, which are not variable bindings, can only be introduced by the adding stage. The effect of this is that the matcher is unable to construct useful matches which involve a significant number of non-identical associations. The two examples given above to illustrate the computational cost of the algorithm also illustrate this defect. There are strong matches between the problem pairs, which Munyer's algorithm misses — this is because they involve significant non-identical associations. In the second example, the identical symbols heuristic is positively misleading, since the terms do contain common function symbols, but these are not associated in the strong match.

Generally, the identical symbols heuristic can only be considered as a fairly weak heuristic (see Section 3.4 for further discussion of this, and of other heuristics). The partial homomorphism heuristic is stronger, however (see Section 3.4). Nevertheless, no amount of clever computation at the deleting stage, which is based on the latter heuristic, can rectify the errors in the initial match constructed by the grounding stage, which is based on the former. Most interesting analogies will contain a significant number of non-identical associations; thus the heavy reliance of Munyer's matcher on the identical symbols heuristic will restrict the generality of the matcher, preventing it from finding many interesting and easy analogies.

Summary

Munyer's algorithm, even with the improvements which have been made to it, does not provide an adequate analogy matcher, even for simple analogies. The broad diagnosis of the problem with the algorithm is that it relies too heavily on a weak heuristic – the identical symbols heuristic. Quite apart from this, the algorithm is extremely expensive computationally, which makes the prospects for it scaling up to larger examples remote.

3.3.2 Kling

Kling's algorithm for matching up pairs of problem descriptions is called INITIAL_MAP, and is part of his analogy system ZORBA. INITIAL_MAP accepts as input two theorem descriptions, each of one of the forms

$$H_1 \wedge H_2 \wedge \ldots \wedge H_n \ \rightarrow \ C_1 \wedge C_2 \wedge \ldots \wedge C_m \quad \text{or} \quad C_1 \wedge C_2 \wedge \ldots \wedge C_m$$

where each of the Hs and Cs is of the form

$$P(x_1, \ldots, x_r)$$

P being a predicate and the xs variables. The variables are implicitly universally quantified. Thus there are no functions or constants. Note that this is a more restricted syntax than that accepted by Munyer's matcher. Kling claims that this subset of predicate calculus is suitable for mathematics. This seems an odd thing to say, as normal mathematics has as many constants and functions in it as anything else. It is true that a much wider class of sentences can be transformed into semantically equivalent sentences of the above form (skolemise the existential variables; if P is a (unary) predicate, f a function symbol and $t_1, \ldots, t_n$ terms, replace $P(f(t_1, \ldots, t_n))$ by $f'(t_1, \ldots, t_n, x) \rightarrow P(x)$, where x is a new variable and f' is the functional relation associated with f (similarly for n-ary functions); iterate the last step until there are no functions or constants (0-ary functions) left). What comes out of this procedure is a very unnatural looking sentence, and, importantly for analogy matching, the functionality of the new predicates is not represented in the syntax. Note also that, unless the functionality of the predicates is stated explicitly in the form of axioms, the theory which results from this transformation is weaker than the original — in particular it is decidable.

However, the theorems of abstract algebra on which Kling bases his matcher do fit naturally into this form.

INITIAL_MAP also has access to **semantic templates** for each of the predicates in the sentences to be matched. For example, the predicate *group* has semantic template

$$structure(set, operation)$$

The intended meaning of this (although Kling does not explain it) seems to be that a group is a *structure* consisting of a *set* and an *operation*.

INITIAL_MAP outputs an **analogy match** between the sentences, which consists principally of an association between the predicates in the sentences, and, as a by-product, an association between the variables. In Kling's system ZORBA, this match is then passed to the EXTENDER module, which applies the match to the axioms used in the proof of one of the theorems in order to find analogous axioms, extending the match in the process. The latter stages will be analysed further in Chapter 5.

The algorithm

The matching strategy of INITIAL_MAP (I-M) is as follows: assume the hypotheses of one theorem match those of the other, and similarly for the conclusions (so the match breaks up into two submatches); do one of these first, and then the other, using the intermediate match obtained from the first to help the second; use the semantic templates to constrain the association of atoms between the theorems, and use the existing predicate and variable associations to choose where there is ambiguity in the semantic templates.

Kling does not say in what order the two submatches are attempted. In the reconstruction described in [34], whichever of the conclusions and the hypotheses contains fewest atoms is attempted first, on the basis that it is usually easier to match smaller structures.

So, if the theorems to be matched are

$$A_1 \wedge A_2 \wedge \cdots \wedge A_n \to B_1 \wedge B_2 \wedge \cdots \wedge B_m$$

$$\text{and } C_1 \wedge C_2 \wedge \cdots \wedge C_r \to D_1 \wedge D_2 \wedge \cdots \wedge D_s$$

and $m + s < n + r$, the module SETMATCH is called first on the conclusions, then the hypotheses.

SETMATCH breaks up into two submodules, SINGLEMATCH and MULTIMATCH, where SINGLEMATCH is first called to pair up the atoms in the sets which have unique semantic templates, and then MULTIMATCH is called to pair up the rest using the partial match generated by SINGLEMATCH to guide it.

When either SINGLEMATCH or MULTIMATCH decides to associate a pair of atoms, a procedure called ATOMMATCH is called to extract predicate and variable correspondences from the atoms, which are added to the evolving match. If the atoms have identical semantic templates, the associations are just those which preserve argument order. But Kling also wants to be able to find analogies in which, for example, groups are associated with rings — that is, $group(Set, Op)$ is associated with $ring(Set_1, Op_1, Op_2)$ — and these predicates do not have the same semantic templates. Their semantic templates are $structure(set, operation)$ and $structure(set, operation, operation)$ respectively. Kling's solution to this problem is as follows. He allows a variable in one of the atoms to be associated with a consecutive sequence of variables in the other as long as: (a) all the types involved are the same, and (b) the correspondences preserve argument order. In this case, he would get

$$group \leftrightarrow ring, \quad Set \leftrightarrow Set1 \quad and \quad [Op] \leftrightarrow [Op_1, Op_2]$$

If conditions (a) and (b) cannot be satisfied, ATOMMATCH fails.

The job of SINGLEMATCH and MULTIMATCH, then, is to decide on pairs of atoms to pass to ATOMMATCH. SINGLEMATCH uses the following criteria in its decision:

1. If there is only one unpaired atom left on each side, associate them by default.

2. Associate pairs of atoms having the same semantic template.

3. Associate pairs of atoms whose predicate symbols are associated in the existing match.

4. Associate pairs of atoms whose predicate symbols have the same type, where this gives a unique association.

Condition 1 is checked after any association is made. Otherwise 2, 3 and 4 are checked in that order.

If SINGLEMATCH cannot pair up all the atoms with unique semantic templates on each side, it fails. If it can, the partial match produced is passed on to MULTIMATCH, which considers the atoms on each side which have the same semantic templates as others. Firstly, the atoms are grouped into their semantic blocks; then blocks are paired up using the following criteria in the same way that SINGLEMATCH used its criteria:

1. If there is only one unpaired block on each side, associate them by default.

2. Associate pairs of blocks which contain atoms whose predicate symbols are associated by the existing match.

3. Associate pairs of blocks whose atoms have predicates with the same semantic type.

When a pair of blocks is associated by the above criteria, the submodule MULTIMATCH1 is called to pair up the atoms within the blocks. MULTI-MATCH1 has a single criterion for doing this, based on the existing variable associations: if there is a pair of variables associated by the existing match, each of which occurs in only one atom in the appropriate block, then pair up the two atoms.

This completes the description of INITIAL_MAP.

Heuristics

What are the analogy heuristics which are used in Kling's algorithm? The most obvious guidance is given to the matcher by the semantic templates; associations are made which preserve the semantic type of predicates whenever possible. Thus Kling must believe that matches which tend to preserve semantic type make promising analogies. Let us call this the **semantic type heuristic**.

As well as the semantic types of predicates (for example, *structure* and *relstructure*[2]), the templates give types for the argument positions to the predicates (for example, set and operation). These argument types are used in the procedure ATOMMATCH, which insists that variable associations preserve the argument types. We call this the **argument type heuristic**.

---

[2]*relstructure* seems intended to denote a substructure.

These types seem to be of a different kind from the semantic types of the predicates (although Kling does not discuss the meaning of either); the argument types could well be unary predicates from the object language, or the types within a typed logic, whereas the semantic types denote heuristic sets of predicates from the object language. This is why the two heuristics are distinguished here.

Thirdly, the **partial homomorphism heuristic**, used by Munyer, is also used by Kling; the overall top-down structure of the algorithm ensures that the symbol associations made in a match preserve the syntactic structure of the terms being matched. Furthermore, the default rules in SINGLEMATCH and MULTIMATCH are also based on the belief that analogy matches ought to be structure-preserving — the association between atoms made by default fills a structural hole in the associations which have already been made. The default rules in INITIAL_MAP are similar in spirit to Munyer's adding stage.

SINGLEMATCH, MULTIMATCH and MULTIMATCH1 all contain criteria for pairing up atoms, or blocks of atoms, on the basis of existing associations in the intermediate match; pairings are made so that the associations are likely to be repeated — that is, an attempt is made to keep the match as **consistent** as possible. Thus, Kling must believe that consistent matches make promising analogies. Let us call this the **consistent translation heuristic**.

Lastly, note that INITIAL_MAP never considers associating symbols unless they have the same **syntactic type**; i.e. propositional connectives are only ever associated with propositional connectives, and similarly for predicates and variables (unlike Munyer's algorithm, INITIAL_MAP makes no attempt to bind variables in matching). This is not done by explicit criteria, but is built into the structure of the algorithm; let us call this the **syntactic type heuristic**. Given the restricted syntax which the matcher accepts, we can think of this heuristic as being implied by the partial homomorphism heuristic (or vice versa); however, in more general situations, the two would be separate, which is why they are listed separately here.

Reconstruction

A detailed reconstruction of Kling's matcher and its testing on examples is given in [34]. It is instructive to work through the performance of the algorithm on one of Kling's abstract algebra examples. Figure 3.1 shows one of Kling's theorem pairs and the resulting match obtained by the program.

SETMATCH is first called on the conclusions, and SINGLEMATCH immediately defaults to ATOMMATCH, since there is only one atom in each. The

HYPOTHESES   HYPOTHESES
$group(g,*)$ $ring(r,*,+)$
$propernormal(m,g,*)$ $properideal(n,r,*,+)$
$factorstructure(x,g,m)$ $factorstructure(y,r,n)$
$simplegroup(x,*)$ $simplering(y,*,+)$

CONCLUSION   CONCLUSION
$maximalgroup(m,g,*)$ $maximalring(n,r,*,+)$

$$
\begin{array}{rcl}
maximalgroup & \longleftrightarrow & maximalring \\
m & \longleftrightarrow & n \\
g & \longleftrightarrow & r \\
[*] & \longleftrightarrow & [*,+] \\
factorstructure & \longleftrightarrow & factorstructure \\
x & \longleftrightarrow & y \\
propernormal & \longleftrightarrow & properideal \\
group & \longleftrightarrow & ring \\
simplegroup & \longleftrightarrow & simplering
\end{array}
$$

Figure 3.1: Abstract algebra example

semantic templates of the conclusions are not identical, but they do match
in the weak sense outlined above, giving the first four elements of the match.
SETMATCH is then called on the hypotheses, with the partial match being
passed along. The atoms in the hypotheses which have unique semantic
templates:

$$\{propernormal(m,g,*),\ factorstructure(x,g,m)\}$$

from the left-hand theorem above, and

$$\{properideal(n,r,*,+),\ factorstructure(y,r,n)\}$$

from the right-hand theorem, are passed to SINGLEMATCH.

Condition 2 from SINGLEMATCH pairs up the *factorstructure* atoms
and passes them to ATOMMATCH which adds two more associations to the
analogy. Then the default condition in SINGLEMATCH pairs up the remaining
two atoms and passes them to ATOMMATCH which adds one more association
to the match.

Next, MULTIMATCH is called on the two atom partitions which have
identical semantic templates:

$$\{group(g,*),\ simplegroup(x,*)\}$$

$$\{ring(r,*,+),\ simplering(y,*,+)\}$$

These are paired up by the default condition, and are passed to MULTI-MATCH1 to pair up the atoms within the partitions. The existing $g \leftrightarrow r$ variable association is used to pair up one atom from each partition, and the $x \leftrightarrow y$ association to pair up the remaining atoms, giving the final match.

While the program performed as desired on Kling's algebra examples, the heavy use of the semantic templates was worrying. All of Kling's theorem pairs come from essentially the same global analogy between group theory and ring theory. It seemed that it was Kling's knowledge of this global analogy which led him to choose the particular semantic templates that he did for the examples. Thus it is no surprise and no great achievement that the algorithm finds the correct matches in these cases. This issue is discussed further below.

When the reconstruction was tested on different examples, shortcomings emerged. Some of these were dealt with by minor modifications to the algorithm:

- MULTIMATCH is given the extra semantic template condition that SIN-GLEMATCH has (condition 2); this enables the matcher to construct the following match:

$$-(x + y) = -x + -y$$
$$|\ \ |\ |\ |\ \ |\ \ \backslash\backslash\ |\ |\ \backslash$$
$$1/(x \cdot y) = 1/x \cdot 1/y$$

- In the published version, SINGLEMATCH fails unless it can pair up all the atoms on each side; allowing SINGLEMATCH to succeed if there remains just one unpaired atom on one side enables the construction of the following match:[3]

$$rational(p) \ \wedge \ irrational(q) \rightarrow irrational(p + q)$$

$$rational(p) \ \wedge \ irrational(q) \ \wedge \ unequal(p, 0) \rightarrow irrational(p \cdot q)$$

- The control structure of the matcher should be more flexible to allow co-routining between applications of MULTIMATCH1 to the various pairs of partitions. This change was not implemented in the reconstruction, but provided motivation for the design of a new matcher, which is described in the next chapter.

---

[3]The predicate *irrational* had to be introduced in place of ¬*rational* as the matcher cannot handle negation.

Assessment of the algorithm

While Kling's algorithm performs competently on his algebra examples with
the given semantic templates, its limitations were made apparent by the
reconstruction:

- As explained above, ATOMMATCH makes only variable associations
  which preserve argument order. While this is understandable if the
  predicates of the atoms are the same, it is not otherwise — the relative order of arguments between two different predicates is the result of
  arbitrary decisions made when the domain was formally represented,
  and should therefore have no influence over analogy matching. Furthermore, if the predicates are commutative in some of their arguments,
  the particular presentations chosen for the atoms determine the possible variable correspondences that ATOMMATCH can make; that is, no
  account is taken of the commutativity which might allow ATOMMATCH
  to permute the order of the variables in the atoms.

- MULTIMATCH1 makes use of existing variable associations only, and in
  a fairly simple way — this is all that was necessary for Kling's target
  algebra examples. There seems to be no reason why it should not use
  existing predicate associations as well, as SINGLEMATCH and MULTI-
  MATCH do. This would make it more powerful. The way in which
  MULTIMATCH1 uses the variable associations could also be strength-
  ened so that it can make use of multiple associations, like $* \leftrightarrow [*, +]$,
  as well as single associations.

- Conversely to the previous point, there seems to be no reason why SIN-
  GLEMATCH and MULTIMATCH should not use existing variable associations, as well as predicate associations, to pair up atoms and blocks
  of atoms.

- A more serious problem with the matcher is shown up by the following
  example:

Equation	In Kling's syntax
$\sqrt{x} + a = b$	$root(x,z) \wedge plus(z,a,y)$ $\rightarrow equal(y,b)$
$\sqrt{x+1} + a = b$	$plus(x,1,y) \wedge root(y,z) \wedge plus(z,a,w)$ $\rightarrow equal(w,b)$

In the first sentence, all the atoms have unique semantic templates,
whereas in the second the two plus atoms are in a semantic block together. Thus, SINGLEMATCH pairs up the two root atoms and the two

equal atoms, and leaves the plus atom in the top sentence unmatched. Then MULTIMATCH is called between a single block on one side and nothing on the other, and so fails.

It is the basic SINGLEMATCH/MULTIMATCH distinction which is at fault here: where there is an atom which ought to be unmatched, its semantic template may coincide with that of another which ought to be matched by SINGLEMATCH, which will prevent the latter from ever being considered by SINGLEMATCH. It seems likely that this situation will occur often in non-trivial analogies, and thus that the matching strategy of INITIAL_MAP will have to be changed to cope.

- The expectation that matches will preserve type is built into the overall structure of the matcher, in particular the distinction between SINGLEMATCH and MULTIMATCH. As explained above, this rigid structure restricts the generality of the matcher, causing it to fail on fairly easy examples, even when the intended match would preserve types. In order to avoid this problem, the main procedures of the algorithm would have to be rewritten.

- It is a consequence of the design of the algorithm that almost all of the predicate associations which are made will preserve semantic type; it is possible for non-type-preserving associations to be added by the default rules, but not significantly many. But we can think of the types as (partially) encoding potential analogies; for example, the type structures shown in Figure 3.2 suggest an analogy which includes the associations *group* ↔ *ring* and *subgroup* ↔ *subring*. So INITIAL_MAP is unable to extend significantly the analogies which are encoded in its type structure. Thus it is doubtful whether the matcher can be said to discover analogies at all — its use of types seems to involve a circular argument. As explained above, on the algebra examples, the matcher repeatedly reconstructs parts of the same global analogy between group theory and ring theory, which is the analogy suggested by the semantic templates. The problems with the use of the semantic types in matching are discussed further in Section 3.4.

Analysis in terms of heuristics

From the point of view of the discovery of new analogies, the shortcomings of Kling's matcher can, like Munyer's, be understood in terms of the way in which it uses its analogy heuristics. The matcher relies on the **semantic type heuristic** to propose initial associations between atoms, and uses the

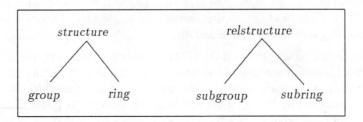

Figure 3.2: Algebraic type structures

other heuristics only to add new associations on the basis of the existing ones. Thus, just as Munyer's matcher is unable to break free of its reliance on the identical symbols heuristic, Kling's is unable to break free of the semantic type heuristic.

But some analogies will preserve a given set of types, some will respect them (in the sense of inducing a consistent mapping between types in the base and target[4]), and others will do neither. We would like a matcher to be able to use the type information in a flexible way, along with other criteria for analogy, so that matches which respect types may be preferred, but those which do not will not be ruled out.

Summary

Kling's matcher turns out to be inadequate for many of the simple analogies which we would hope that a matcher could find. Perhaps this is not surprising since the matcher was designed around just a few algebra examples, for which it was provided with much of the information about the intended analogies.

We have seen that there are various straightforward alterations which can be made to the algorithm to improve its performance while not affecting its overall strategy. However, it has also become clear that, in order to improve the algorithm much further, its reliance on the semantic type heuristic, including the SINGLEMATCH/MULTIMATCH distinction, which is the basis of the algorithm, would have to be dropped. This would entail a complete redesign of the matcher. The distinction, and hence the matching strategy, is based on the rigid use of types and 1-1 associations between atoms; where these cannot be guaranteed, the matcher will be inadequate.

---

[4]Brown [3] describes analogies of this kind.

Heuristics	Munyer	Kling
Partial homomorphism *(strong)*	✓	✓
Consistent translation *(strong)*	✗	✓
Semantic type *(weak/circular)*	✗	✓
Identical symbols *(weak)*	✓	✗
Syntactic type *(strong)*	✗	✓
Argument type *(variable)*	✗	✓

Figure 3.3: Heuristics used

3.4 Justification for the heuristics

Figure 3.3 lists the heuristics which have been found to underlie the matchers of Kling and Munyer, and which matchers use each of them. The heuristics used are all reasonable; it is the inflexible use which the matchers make of the heuristics which is the cause of their deficiencies. In fact, the heuristics listed in Figure 3.3 are the principal ones used in all of the matchers which have been published. We now consider the justification for the use of the heuristics in analogy matching.

Partial homomorphism (PHH)

Firstly, we note that almost all computational or quasi-computational accounts of analogy are based around a notion of structural matching, which is what the PHH recommends. For example, in her **structure-mapping theory**, considered in Chapter 2, Gentner introduces the notion of the **systematicity** of a structure-mapping; this is the extent to which matched objects are mutually constrained by identical relations. Apart from the strange restriction to identical relations, Gentner does not consider the looser forms of structural correspondence which arise in mathematics, and which both Munyer and Kling are concerned with. Both these restrictions of the structure-mapping theory seem related to the fact that Gentner designed the representations of the physical domains herself, and thus was able, by anticipating the analogy, to smooth away many of the matching problems. Interestingly, the partial homomorphism heuristic is the only one shared by both Kling's and Munyer's matchers.

But why is it a good idea to look for matches which respect the structure of the terms being matched? Although most authors have considered structural matching crucial to analogy, there has been very little discussion of its justification. However, within automated problem solving, we can understand why structural matching is important. The goal of analogy is to use the base proof to guide the search for a target proof. The base proof consists of a sequence (or tree structure) of applications of axioms or lemmas to intermediate clauses, starting with the problem and ending with a recognised goal state (the empty clause, for instance). The applicability of an axiom to a step is determined by unification, a strict structural matching procedure. The hope in analogy is that we will be able to make corresponding steps in the target. In the target too, we will need structural matches between axioms and intermediate steps. If we can find a structurally similar problem to the target problem, we can reasonably hope that, if we can also find structurally similar axioms to those used in the base, there will be a good chance of being able to make corresponding steps in the target — that is, that the corresponding clauses will unify and produce corresponding inferences. If this is so throughout the proof, the application procedure (see Chapter 6) will have no difficulty in solving the target problem by analogy to the base problem. Of course, many things can go wrong: we may not be able to find similar axioms to apply in the target, or, even if we can, the corresponding steps may not go through because of the loose structural matches (see Chapter 6 for a discussion of how the application procedure can get into difficulties). But a structural match between problems is still an important factor. To put it another way, if we do *not* have a structural match between problems, it is almost certain that the application of the analogy will be difficult.

Therefore, we consider the PHH to be strong. It is important that our notion of structural similarity be flexible, in order to encompass the sorts of structural match between even closely analogous problems which occur in mathematics.

Consistent translation heuristic (CTH)

Again, the notion of consistency of the translation implied by an analogy match is taken to be important in almost all accounts of analogy, but, again, without much attempt at justification. Many accounts, such as Gentner and co-workers' [15] and Winston's [47] require that the mapping be strictly consistent. But others, such as the ACME matcher described in [25], accept that many analogies contain some inconsistencies, and that to insist on strict consistency would considerably restrict generality. In Chapter 1, we saw that simple problem matches such as

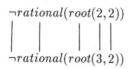

$$\neg rational(root(2,2))$$

$$\neg rational(root(3,2))$$

involve inconsistencies. Kling's matches can have inconsistent predicate mappings, via the default rules in SINGLEMATCH and MULTIMATCH, although this happens rarely in practice.[5] Munyer's matcher pays no explicit attention to consistency, although its reliance on the identical symbols heuristic means that inconsistencies can only be introduced at the adding stage.

So why should we prefer consistent matches at all? Again, by considering automated problem solving, we can understand why we would like matches to be as consistent as possible. In the discussion on the importance of structural similarity in predicting inferences to make on the target problem, we omitted another important feature of unification: it is not only a strict structural match but also a strict match on the identities of predicates, functions and constants. Since, in most interesting analogies there will be non-identical associations, there is a danger that target inferences will fail to go through, not because of structural mismatches but because of symbol mismatches. But if the mapping is consistent we will have greater confidence that this will not happen — if there is a consistent translation of symbols between base and target, where symbols were the same in the base, they will be the same in the target. Although we would like a strictly consistent match for this reason, restricting a matcher to such matches would restrict its generality. More realistically, we would like our match to have as few inconsistencies as possible, but we may have to put up with some.

So we consider the CTH to be strong, but we must be flexible about its application.

Syntactic type heuristic (SyTH)

It is implicit in all existing computational accounts of analogy that syntactic types will be respected by analogy matches — predicates are never associated

---

[5] In fact, inconsistent predicate mappings are rejected by Kling's system ZORBA since the application stage of the system cannot cope with them.

with functions, and propositional connectives are only ever associated with each other. Perhaps even this should not be treated as an absolute criterion — it would be quite possible for a predicate on one side to be associated with a function on the other. But in practice, it seems a reliable heuristic. The application of an analogy which did not respect syntactic types would be difficult. We can therefore consider this to be a strong heuristic.

Argument type heuristic (ATH)

Kling insists that matches preserve the types of the arguments of predicates. Whether or not this is a good heuristic depends on the particular types which are used; with Kling's algebra predicates, the main argument types are *set* and *operation*. We would certainly feel more confident in being able to apply an analogy which matched sets with sets and operations with operations, since the axiomatisations are likely to involve checks on these types. Thus, in this case, we could consider the ATH to be quite strong. However, in some other case, argument types may not be a good clue to analogy at all. Thus, the strength of the heuristic is variable. Brown [3] uses just this notion of type in his matching procedures; however, Brown's matches do not necessarily preserve the types, indicating the variability of the heuristic.

Identical symbols heuristic (ISS)

This heuristic is used heavily in Munyer's matcher, as explained above, but not at all in Kling's. Some accounts of analogy, such as those of Gentner and colleagues ([15]) and Sternberg ([43]) have insisted that all associations between predicates (though not constants) be identical. Munyer's matcher does allow non-identical associations to be added at the adding stage, although, because of the structure of the algorithm, this has limited effect.

While it is clear that most interesting analogies involve a significant proportion of non-identical associations (some authors define analogy as necessarily involving differences in the surface representations), the heuristic nevertheless has some value: we should not forget that the aim of an analogy system is to solve the target problem; it should use the most similar problem which it can find as base. Other things being equal, the presence of identical associations can only be a good thing; it will increase our confidence that we can find structurally similar axioms to apply in the target (the *same* axioms, with luck). Bearing in mind, though, that many examples involve genuine translations, we can only consider the ISS to be relatively weak.

Semantic type heuristic (STH)

The discussion of this heuristic has been left until last because it is the most
problematical to assess. The reason is that it is the only one that requires
extra information to be provided to the analogy matcher, apart from the
problem statements, and other information available in the object language,
such as argument types. Thus we need to assess not only whether the preservation of semantic type is a useful property for an analogy match, but where
the type information comes from and what information it represents.

The term 'semantic type' is taken in AI to refer to groups of symbols
from the object language which are believed to be related to each other in
some (usually unspecified) way.[6] Often, the semantic types are organised
into a **hierarchy**, determined by the subset relations between the groups.
In automated problem solving, type hierarchies have been extensively used
in the field of **inductive generalisation** ([32]), discussed in the previous
chapter. It is generally recognised that semantic types are heuristic devices
rather than conforming to a formal definition; but little attention has been
paid to the origin of the hierarchy, although some work has been done on
modifying the hierarchy over the course of problem solving experience ([45]).

So it is initially unclear what sort of information is being provided to an
analogy matcher in the guise of semantic types. However, by returning to the
automated problem solving argument expounded above, we can identify the
conditions under which a set of semantic types would be *useful* in guiding a
matcher; i.e. conditions on the types which would make the STH successful.
It is clear in the argument that, in order to apply an analogy easily and
successfully, the analogy system needs a structural correspondence not only
between the problem statements, but also between the axioms which were
used in the base proof and other axioms from the axiom base; it is under these
conditions that we can reasonably expect to make a corresponding inference
in the target to one which was made in the base. The partial homomorphism
and consistent translation heuristics tell us nothing about how likely it is
that we will be able to find analogues for the axioms; the identical symbols
heuristic does (if the symbols are the same, we can reasonably guess that
the same axioms will apply), although it handles only the case where most
of the symbols are mapped to themselves. In more interesting cases, such as
Kling's algebra examples, where most of the associations are non-identical,
the heuristics above tell us nothing about potential analogues for the axioms.
For example, given the solution of the equation $a + root(x) = x$ as target

---

[6]In this book, the term 'semantic type' refers only to such aggregations of symbols —
no further interpretation of the word 'semantic' is intended.

problem,[7] we would not be able to distinguish between the following two
potential matches with base equations:

$$root(x) + a = x \qquad a + root(x) = x$$

$$root(x) - a = x \qquad log(a, root(x)) = x$$

That is, in terms of structural correspondence, consistency and the identity or difference of matched symbols, the two matches above are identical.
We call this inability to distinguish between potential matches the **multiple
matches problem**. Intuitively, however, the first of the two seems more
promising; this is because the functions $+$ and $-$ are thought to be more
closely related than are $+$ and log. This feeling is borne out by the fact that
the first two can be solved in similar ways (move the a to the right-hand side,
square to remove the $root$, and solve the resulting quadratic in x), whereas
this simple strategy does not apply to the logarithmic equation. This is
the sort of guidance we would hope to get from the STH; the first match
is chosen because it preserves the type of arithmetic operators, whereas the
second does not.

From the point of view of the analogy system, what makes the first match
above fruitful is the presence of analogues for the axioms used in the solution
of the base equation; in particular, the identity $(x + y) - y = x$ was applied
to move the a to the right-hand side, in the base; the target proof proceeds
analogously in the presence of an analogous identity $(x - y) + y = x$.

In general, we claim

> The extent to which semantic types are useful in analogy
> matching is the extent to which symbols of the same type have
> analogous axioms/theorems associated with them.

To put it another way,

> The extent to which semantic types are useful in analogy
> matching is the extent to which they encode potential analogies
> within or between domains.

This analysis introduces a dilemma: if the types do not encode analogies,
they will not be useful in analogy matching; if they do, their use in analogy
matching is apparently based on a circular argument, i.e. the matcher is
being told, albeit in disguised form, about the analogies which it is supposed
to discover for itself. However, we can avoid the circularity by one or both
of the following means:

---

[7] $\sqrt{}$ is written as *root* to make the syntactic structure clear.

- The semantic types should be used *flexibly* by the matcher, so that it is able to extend and/or override the type information, if other of the analogy heuristics suggest that this is a good thing to do.

- The types could be learnt automatically in some way. Since, as we have seen, useful types encode analogies, the types could represent a succinct summary of the knowledge which the analogy system has gained about analogies within the domain in question. This would provide a means for the analogy system to improve its ability to reason analogically within the domain over the course of its experience. This issue is taken up again in Chapter 7.

  But types could perhaps be derived in some other way as well; while not relating directly to potential analogies, they might nevertheless provide clues to the matcher.

The first alternative really ought to be chosen whether or not the second is pursued: if learnt semantic types are used inflexibly they will never be extended or overridden, which will prevent any further learning from taking place.

Kling's matcher does neither of these things: the types are provided by the user, and they are used inflexibly. Thus the suspicion that Kling's use of semantic types (in his algebra examples, anyway) amounts to a circular argument is confirmed.

In conclusion, the STH can provide useful guidance to an analogy matcher without involving a circular argument. However, it can only be considered as a fairly weak heuristic compared with the partial homomorphism and the consistent translation heuristics from the point of view of the discovery of *new* analogies. From the point of view of finding a successful analogy, whether new or not, the usefulness of the heuristic depends on the reliability of the types. The techniques proposed in Chapter 7 suggest ways of assessing the strength of semantic types; this information could be fed back to the analogy matcher, which would weight the heuristic accordingly.

Summary

All of the heuristics which have been found to underlie the analogy match-ers of Kling and Munyer have validity, and can provide useful guidance to a matcher. The problem with the particular algorithms which we have con-sidered, then, is not the heuristics which they use but the way in which they use them. Each matcher relies far too heavily on the weak heuristic which it uses: the identical symbols heuristic in the case of Munyer, and the semantic type heuristic in the case of Kling; these are used as the source of initial,

plausible associations. The stronger heuristics are used only conditionally
— to propose or retain an association on the basis of an existing association. This strategy for the use of the heuristics restricts the generality of the
matchers considerably — they are only able to find matches which conform
closely to the weak heuristics.

Chapter 4

Flexible matching

The problem with the matchers analysed in the last chapter – too much reliance on weak heuristics – suggests a cure: namely, to use the heuristics, particularly the weak ones, more flexibly, allowing each to be overridden if others suggest that this would lead to a promising match. Furthermore, it is clear from the previous chapter firstly that different people have different ideas about the analogy heuristics that should be used, and secondly that definitive answers as to the relative strengths of the heuristics are hard to come by. Thus as well as making more flexible use of the heuristics, it is desirable to be flexible about which heuristics to use, and what relative significance to give them. The latter two features tend to follow from the former, since, if the heuristics are being used flexibly, this suggests that the design of the matcher is not biased towards particular weak heuristics, and therefore is easy to modify by either changing the heuristics which are used or changing the relative significance of existing heuristics.

We have, then, the following requirements for an improved matcher:

- The matcher should use its heuristics flexibly, rather than being biased in design towards any single weak heuristic.

- It should be easy to modify or extend the matcher on the basis of changing beliefs about the heuristics; this may include tailoring the matcher to a particular domain by the addition of domain-specific heuristics.

- The matcher should accept any terms from the language of the problem solver on which the analogy system is based: Kling's restriction to a subset of first-order logic, containing no functions or constants, would be a severe restriction on a practical analogy system.

In this chapter we describe some recent approaches to matching based around the idea of flexible application of heuristics. In Section 4.1, we describe how heuristics can be used to provide a *specification* for an analogy matching algorithm. In Section 4.2, we describe the kinds of solution method that flexible matchers have used in attempting to meet the specification. In later sections (4.3 and 4.4), we give specific descriptions of the two most promising flexible matchers, ACME and FHM, concentrating on the current author's approach, embodied in FHM ([35]).

4.1   Heuristics as specification

For convenience, we distinguish between the general heuristics, as discussed in the previous chapter, and specific heuristic criteria which are derived from them in a particular matcher. For example, all analogy matchers use the partial homomorphism heuristic strongly, but they tend to do so via different specific criteria: for example, the number of unmatched symbols might be used (negatively) to assess the degree of structural deformation in a match.

The heuristics give a loose specification which an analogy matching algorithm should satisfy. In order to tighten up the specification, two things must be done:

- The heuristics should be refined into precisely defined criteria. Most heuristics will lead naturally to criteria which give degrees of conformance rather than Boolean judgements. Hence, defining a criterion precisely will usually involve coming up with a numerical metric (typically ranging between 0 and 1).

- The relative significance of the criteria must be prescribed in some way. A natural way to do this (and the only one that the current author has seen published) is to give relative weights to the different criteria.

Once we have a precise specification of goodness for analogy matches, we can regard the task of analogy matching as an optimisation problem: *find the match with highest score.* As with many optimisation problems, we would be satisfied with a nearly optimal solution (we would have to be, since the general problem will be extremely hard to solve optimally).

The metrics in the heuristic criteria and the relative weights attached to the criteria only represent approximate judgements (if we give a PHH criterion weight 0.6 while a CTH one 0.4 this reflects a desire to make the PHH significantly though not hugely more important than the CTH — we are not particularly attached to these specific numbers). This means that relentlessly pursuing the optimal match is probably futile anyway, as the difference between its assessment and that of a near-optimal match is probably swamped by the approximation.

A further point to notice is that we might reasonably want to produce more than one match between a given base/target pair. This is because of the heuristic nature of analogy — one match might prove fruitless (i.e. we are unable to use it to solve the target problem), at which point we might wish to try another. This requirement is also psychologically plausible — people are often able to construct a number of analogies between one situation and another.

4.2 Solution techniques

Having defined the problem that flexible matchers are trying to solve, we now describe the sorts of solution technique that flexible matchers have adopted. We first argue that exhaustive search is infeasible, given a flexible notion of match. We then categorise the specific tactical rules which matchers use to develop a match. On the basis of this categorisation, we identify a problem, which we call the **weak heuristic problem**, which flexible matchers must tackle. We then briefly discuss the different **control regimes** by which matchers control the application of the tactical rules, and to what extent different control regimes are able to overcome the weak heuristic problem.

Control is necessary

It is necessary for analogy matching algorithms to use mechanisms to restrict the search through the space of possible analogy matches. This is because the space is usually too large to be searched with the following brute force approach:

> Generate all possible matches between a pair of terms, assessing each and returning the best one or few

i.e. search the space of possible matches exhaustively. Winston ([47]) employs this approach, although he admits that it would be inadequate for examples larger than those which he has considered so far.

Of course, the size of the space of possible matches depends on what *constraints* are imposed on matches. We saw in Chapter 1 that some researchers have used quite restricted notions of analogy match, insisting, for example, on strict consistency and no argument permutation. These restricted definitions of match will lead to much smaller spaces. But Winston's definition of a match is one of the more restrictive, and he accepts that the brute force approach will not scale up.

To reinforce the point, we will consider the size of the space for some small examples, given a more permissive notion of analogy. Consider the following formulae from Boolean algebra:

$$x \cap (y \cup z) = (x \cap y) \cup (x \cap z)$$

$$x \cup (y \cap z) = (x \cup y) \cap (x \cup z)$$

A match is an association between symbols in the two formulae; i.e. a subset of the cartesian product of the sets of symbol occurrences in the formulae. Each formula contains 13 symbols, so the cartesian product contains $13 \cdot 13 = 169$ elements, and thus has 2^{169} subsets. To use the brute force approach, we would clearly need to put restrictions on the types of association acceptable as analogy matches. What restrictions are reasonable?

Winston restricts matches to 1-1 (i.e. consistent) associations of objects in his representation system; but we have seen that consistency can only be used as a relative criterion without restricting the generality of the matcher. Thus, we cannot make this restriction. We have likewise seen that we cannot restrict to identity pairings between predicates and functions.

It would be reasonable to restrict to associations which respect syntactic type; in this case, this restriction would bring the space down to $2^{(12)} \cdot 2^{(12^2)} = 2^{145}$ (the single predicate '=' could only be mapped to itself). We could also restrict to matches which respect the structure of the terms in the following weak sense:

For pairings (a_1, b_1) and (a_2, b_2), if $a_1 \geq a_2$ then $b_1 \geq b_2$

This notion of preservation of structure leaves room for much structural deformation in a match, such as the following matches:

$$even(x) \longrightarrow x = 2 \cdot f(x) \qquad (x + y) - x = y$$

$$odd(x) \longrightarrow x = 2 \cdot g(x) + 1 \quad x \neq 0 \longrightarrow (x \cdot y)/x = y$$

There are degrees of greater structural preservation within this class of matches. Munyer's algorithm can, in theory, construct matches which do not satisfy this restriction. But he gives no real examples of such matches — all of his mathematical examples do satisfy the condition. We regard this as a reasonable restriction for an analogy matcher working within a problem solving system; the matching approach developed in Section 4.4, and embodied in the FHM matcher) produces only matches of this form. It is hard, though, to estimate the reduction in the space of matches produced by this restriction. We can give a worst case analysis for terms of size n (i.e. n symbol occurrences): for given n, two flat terms of size n produce the maximal number of matches, since there is minimal term structure to restrict possibilities; the number is

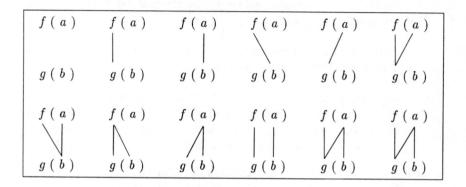

Figure 4.1: Twelve matches between $f(a)$ and $g(b)$

$$2 \cdot \sum_{r=1}^{n} \frac{n!}{r! \cdot (n-r)!} \cdot \frac{n!}{(n-r)!} \; + \; 2 \cdot n$$

So the number of matches is, in the worst case, worse than factorial in the size of the terms. A program which enumerated the possible matches produced 12 possible matches between $f(a)$ and $g(b)$ (shown in Figure 4.1), 88 between $x \cup y$ and $x \cap y$, and ran out of space when called on the terms $x \cap (y \cup z)$ and $x \cup (y \cap z)$. Thus, while we cannot estimate the size of the space of matches between the original terms analytically, it is clear that it will be far too big to be searched exhaustively — apart from enumerating the possibilities, the brute force approach would have to assess each according to the criteria, which in itself requires significant computation (see below).

We can conclude that guidance through the space of possible matches is necessary.

Match development rules

The heuristic criteria that a flexible matcher uses serve to specify its task. We can analyse the way that matchers approach this task as follows. A matcher has a number of **match development rules;**[1] these are successively applied to a developing match until a completed match is produced; they are short-range and tactical in nature; an example of one (from Múnyer's matcher) is:

---

[1] We use the term 'rule' in a general sense, and are not referring to any particular rule formalism.

'if the parent symbols of two paired symbols are both currently unmatched, pair them up'

The match development rules implemented in all matchers published to date fall into one of the following two categories:

Direct support Rules which provide direct support for the presence of particular pairings in a match; for example, the ISS is used to propose initial associations in Munyer's matcher, and the STH directly supports the pairing of symbols of the same semantic type in Kling's matcher.

Relative support Rules which provide support for a pairing given the presence of another one. This is the only way PHH is used in all published matchers, apart from FHM which we describe in Section 4.4. In Munyer's, for example, certain pairings **support** directly dominating pairings, and this is used as reason for maintaining the latter in the match. In almost all cases, the support (or competition) exists between *pairs* of associations, rather than larger sets. For example, there is normally competition between the pair of associations $a \leftrightarrow b$ and $a \leftrightarrow c$ as a result of the CTH.

Hence, all of the control is effected through local support for and interactions between associations. It is not clear whether this is a fundamental feature of analogy or whether it has arisen simply because rules with this property are easier to implement.[2] For example, the neural net approach of [25], which we describe in Section 4.3, implements these sorts of rules naturally (as inputs to and connection strengths between nodes in the net, which represent associations), but would struggle to represent higher-order relative support rules adequately.

An (implausible) example of a higher-order support rule would be a limit, of 3, say, on the number of non-identical pairings in a match — this would be a negative (and asymmetric) dependency between a non-identical pairing and any other two non-identical pairings.

In most matchers, direct support rules are derived from only relatively weak heuristics (according to our analysis of the previous chapter), such as the ISS and STH; relative support rules, on the other hand tend to be derived from strong heuristics, such as the PHH and the CTH. This produces a problem (or challenge) for the designer of a flexible matcher, which we call the **weak heuristic problem**: matchers can easily become dominated by

---

[2]Note that *inherent* computational intractability of the alternative could constitute a fundamental feature — remember that analogy research is directly motivated by human analogical ability, which is some sort of proof of tractability.

weak heuristics, as these underlie the direct support rules which are used first, to start the match off. The strong heuristics, working through the relative support rules, are applied later, and are likely to be unable to correct the mistakes of the weak heuristics. The matchers of Munyer and Kling, for example, were seen in the last chapter to suffer from the weak heuristic problem.

If the weak heuristic problem is not overcome, the matches which are produced will be a long way from the best possible. To illustrate the difficulty, consider the following pair of structurally isomorphic problems and strong analogy match between them:

$$x \cap (y \cup z) = (x \cap y) \cup (x \cap z)$$

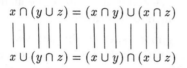

$$x \cup (y \cap z) = (x \cup y) \cap (x \cup z)$$

Here the weak ISS is positively misleading, indicating pairings inconsistent with the strong mapping.

The role of search

Some matchers perform **search**: that is, they develop a number of matches and select between them based on their closeness. A branch in the search space might represent choices in analogues for a given symbol. For example, suppose the current state of matching indicates that there are two plausible analogues for the symbol a – b and c say – with similar levels of support. Rather than choosing one of the plausible pairings arbitrarily, a matcher with search capability might branch the current match development into two, one branch with the pairing $c \leftrightarrow b$ and the other with $a \leftrightarrow c$. The two offspring matches are developed independently and the better one will tend to be chosen. Successive branching can lead to any number of matches being developed at one time.

We can regard the ability to search as providing another direct support rule: the branching process provides direct support for the various pairing options in the respective branches. A branching step might be invoked when matching is bogged down (i.e. the other rules do not clearly suggest more pairings).

An extreme example of a matcher with search is Winston's: search provides the only development rule. Two matchers which mix search with rules based on heuristics are the SME ([15]) and that reported in [35].

Varieties of control

We use the term **control regime** to refer to the way in which the development rules are applied to produce completed matches. It is the job of the control regime to overcome the problem of domination of weak heuristics (the weak heuristic problem).

There are several different control regimes which have been used in matchers to date:

- *Top-down, discrete, no search.* The top levels of the terms being matched are paired up first; matching is then propagated down to the bottom of the terms by relative support rules. Pairings are successively added to the match to produce the final match (or matches). Kling's matcher falls into this category.

  Overshadowing its more specific limitations, the lack of search in Kling's matcher, and the lack of direct support rules based on strong heuristics, cause it to suffer badly from the weak heuristic problem.

- *Top-down, discrete, search.* This regime is the same as the previous one except that search is added. The current author's matcher, FHM, which we describe in detail in Section 4.4, adopts this regime.

  The use of search is one way of overcoming the weak heuristic problem — as explained above, we can think of search as providing a direct support rule which does not depend on weak heuristics.

  FHM also attacks the weak heuristic by introducing a direct support rule based on the PHH, a strong heuristic.

  Top-down analogy matchers can be thought of as loose unification algorithms.

- *Bottom-up, discrete, no search.* Direct support rules are used to construct initial pairings (not necessarily at the upper levels of the terms being matched). Relative support rules are used to add/erase pairings to/from the initial set (or sets) to produce the final match (or matches).

  Munyer's matcher falls into this category, and suffers from the weak heuristic problem, as we might now expect.

- *Bottom-up, discrete, search.* The same as the previous category, except that search is added in order to overcome the weak heuristic problem.

  The current author attempted to add search to Munyer's matcher, but found that the rigid (discrete) nature of the control still succumbed to the weak heuristic problem.

Gentner's matcher falls into this category: in the first stage direct support rules construct all possible pairings; relative support rules are used to group these into final matches. Gentner's notion of a match is more restrictive than that adopted in the other matchers we are discussing in this chapter — no structural deformations are allowed. This allows the application of the relative support rules to be 'all or nothing' — a match either satisfies them, in which case it is constructed, or it does not, in which case it is pruned. Exhaustive search is used to do this. The flexibility in Gentner's matcher comes in the first stage: the direct support rules can be programmed by the user, and hence can be changed to reflect varying contexts.

- *Bottom-up, continuous, no search.* This regime is somewhat similar to the previous one, except that pairings may be partially in and partially out of a match — there is a degree of association which is a number between 0 and 1. Thus, direct support rules can be used more flexibly to favour certain pairings in the first stage. In the second stage, the relative support rules are applied with a spreading activation mechanism (a Grossberg neural net) to update the degrees of association until equilibrium is achieved.

The ACME matcher in PI is of this type; we describe it in Section 4.3. The continuous model can be thought of as another way of overcoming the weak heuristic problem: the initial degrees of association are a long way from being commitments; the spreading activation of the neural net is used to propagate the degrees of association to obtain a good match relative to all the heuristics.

4.3 The ACME matcher

We have already mentioned a number of the features of the analogy matcher of Holyoak and Thagard, called ACME (analogical constraint mapping engine) and described in [25]. In this section we describe it in somewhat more detail.

ACME, like FHM, was designed to make flexible application of a number of possibly competing analogy heuristics. The approach to achieving this is quite different, however. ACME's control regime for matching is the spreading activation of a neural net with Grossberg's update function. Each unit in the network represents the hypothesis that a particular symbol pairing should be made between the base and target. Excitatory and inhibitory connections between units constitute relative support rules. The degree of support (or competition) is represented by the strength of the connection.

Direct support rules are implemented by connections between hypothesis units and special clamped units (i.e. effectively as inputs to the hypothesis units). The network is run until stability is achieved. An analogy mapping is derived from the final state of the network as follows: for each symbol in the target description, find the hypothesis unit involving the symbol with highest activation; map the given symbol to the other symbol in the unit (i.e. accept the hypothesis), as long as the level of activation is above a low threshold. The threshold rule enables symbols to be unmatched. Notice that the matching is therefore asymmetric with respect to the base and target descriptions: we map the target *onto* the base.

4.3.1   Setting up the network

Given the two predicate calculus descriptions to be matched, they are first transformed into function-free descriptions by the same transformation used by Kling for his matcher and described in Section 3.3.2.

Then, hypothesis units are constructed for each **permissible** pairing of symbols between the descriptions. The definition of permissible is as follows: predicates are permitted to pair with other predicates with the same number of arguments; the pairing of arguments to predicates is permitted if and only if the pairing of the respective parent predicates is permitted, and the arguments concerned occupy corresponding argument positions in the predicates. To illustrate, if $p(a,b)$ and $q(c,d)$ are propositions in the base and target descriptions respectively, units for the following symbol pairings between them would be constructed:

$$
\begin{array}{ccc}
p & \longleftrightarrow & q \\
a & \longleftrightarrow & c \\
b & \longleftrightarrow & d
\end{array}
$$

Notice, therefore, that no argument permutation is allowed in matches. While we have seen that this is too restrictive for problem solving analogies, there appears to be no reason why ACME cannot be extended to permit argument permutation, at the cost of increasing the size of the network.

Then connections are set up between units as follows:

- An excitatory connection between a predicate pairing and each of the corresponding argument pairings (this is a relative support rule).

- An excitatory connection between an argument pairing and each sibling argument pairing (i.e. each pairing with the same parent predicates) (also a relative support).

- An inhibitory connection between any pair of units that represent alternative mappings for a symbol (relative inhibition).

- An excitatory connection between any unit which pairs semantically similar symbols and a distinguished 'semantic' unit, which is always clamped to the maximum value (direct support).

- Similarly, an excitatory connection between any unit which involves a symbol deemed to be 'important' and a distinguished 'pragmatic' unit, which is likewise clamped to the maximum value (also direct support).

The semantic similarity judgements and the importance judgements are part of the input to the matcher from its context. Note that the semantic and pragmatic influences on a unit provide the unit with a fixed contribution to its excitatory input.

Each symbol pairing is only represented in one unit. This will cause difficulties with matches such as

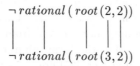

where different occurrences of 2 on one side are mapped to different symbols on the other; an inconsistent mapping may be produced but nothing would tell us which occurrence was paired with which symbol; this might be important for the later stages of analogy. As above, ACME could easily be extended to use different nodes for different symbol occurrences, once again at the cost of an enlarged network.

4.3.2 Heuristics used

The central heuristics used are the PHH and the CTH. The PHH is used in restricting permissible argument pairings to be the daughters of permissible predicate pairings, and then in making 'syntactically adjacent' pairings support each other. The CTH is used in making alternative mappings for a symbol mutually inhibitory. These uses of the PHH and the CTH are programmed into ACME.

The SyTH is also used in restricting permissible pairings to those between symbols of the same syntactic type.

The STH is used to effectively provide direct support to a pairing hypothesis; the judgements of semantic similarity, and the degree of support, can be set by the user. Similarly, the user can specify symbols which are

important in much the same way that Winston's matcher allows. ACME responds by giving direct to support to all pairings which involve an important symbol.

4.3.3 Performance

Holyoak and Thagard [25] reports impressive performance for ACME. Examples are given which indicate that a variety of matches of different types can be constructed. In particular, there are some examples of purely structural matches, which do not involve semantically similar symbols. As we have seen, most matchers are not able to construct such matches.

The theory of neural nets states that the net will stabilize at a (possibly local) minimum of the energy function:

$$G = \sum_i \sum_j w_{ij} \cdot a_i \cdot a_j$$

where a_i is the activation level of unit a_i at equilibrium and w_{ij} is the connection strength between units i and j. Therefore, G represents, for ACME, the strength of the mapping inferred from the network. A frequent problem with neural nets is that the local minimum found is much weaker than the global minimum. However, [25] does not report any problems with this phenomenon.

A detailed empirical comparison between ACME and FHM would be interesting. ACME has the advantage of having a much simpler design than FHM. FHM, on the other hand, is capable of constructing more than one coherent mapping and appears easier to enhance with the sort of re-expression capabilities that we describe in the next section.

4.4 FHM — a flexible top-down matcher

In this section we step through the development of a flexible top-down matcher with search capability. We call the matcher FHM — flexible heuristic matcher. We develop the design from initial guidelines through to a complete algorithm. This style of presentation will emphasise two points:

- While the final algorithm is quite complex, it is derived in a natural way from intuitive guidelines.

- The specific algorithm produced is just one of many that can be produced by using different heuristic criteria and development rules; the matcher lends itself to modification.

Guidelines

We repeat the requirements for a flexible matcher which were stated at the beginning of this chapter:

- The matcher should use its heuristics flexibly, rather than being biased in design towards any single weak heuristic.

- It should be easy to modify or extend the matcher on the basis of changing beliefs about the heuristics; this may include tailoring the matcher to a particular domain, by the addition of domain-specific heuristics.

- The matcher should accept any terms from the language of the problem solver on which the analogy system is based: Kling's restriction to a subset of first-order logic, containing no functions or constants, would be a severe restriction on a practical analogy system.

The above constitute most of the guidelines for the development of FHM. The other guideline is that the control regime of the matcher should be top-down, in the sense described in the previous section. This guideline is not based on a belief that top-down control is necessarily the best, but that there is much more potential in top-down matching than is exploited in Kling's algorithm.

Matching as problem refinement

One part of Kling's matcher which is promising is his pairing up of the arguments to logical conjunction, which are always atoms in his restricted syntax. Although he relies too heavily on semantic templates to suggest the pairings, which contributes to the overall inflexibility of his matcher, the associativity and commutativity of conjunction are implicit in the process, so that there are no preconceptions as to which atoms are paired with which — the pairings are determined by analysing the atoms using heuristics. By contrast, Kling's procedure ATOMMATCH, for extracting variable associations from a pair of atoms which have been associated, is based on arbitrary preservation of argument order, which is totally unsatisfactory.

FHM makes the following generalisation of the promising part of Kling's algorithm: a flexible, heuristic analysis of possible argument (or subterm) pairings should be done at *every* stage of matching, whether at the propositional or functional level. This generalisation will enable FHM to work with an unrestricted syntax (one of the guidelines).

The analysis is done with match development rules based on the analogy heuristics (as discussed above). The development rules make suggestions about how the current match should be extended which are co-ordinated flexibly, by the control regime, to produce subterm pairings. For example, if the following (sub)terms are to be matched, FHM might make the argument pairings shown:

$$f(f(a_1, b_1), c_1)$$

$$g(c_2, g(b_2, a_2))$$

In general, a given set of argument or subterm pairings will lead to a corresponding set of **matching subproblems**. If, for the moment, we represent a matching subproblem as a pair (t_1, t_2) of subterms to be matched, the argument pairings shown above cause the matching problem

$$(\ f(f(a_1, b_1), c_1),\ g(c_2, g(b_2, a_2))\ )$$

to be replaced by the two subproblems

$$(\ f(a_1, b_1),\ g(b_2, a_2)\ ) \quad \text{and} \quad (\ c_1,\ c_2)$$

So we are led to a **problem refinement** view of analogy matching: the initial problem is to match the two terms or formulae which are given; as matching proceeds, subproblems, to match pairs of subterms of the original terms, are produced, and recursively refined. Subproblems are solved without producing more subproblems when one of the subterms in question is a constant or a variable, or when no pairings are suggested by the refinement procedure. Thus, instead of Kling's one-pass matching procedures, the whole matching process needs to be recursive, calling the same procedure on subterms which have been associated.

An evolving mapping

As matching proceeds, symbolic associations will be made (between the head function/predicate symbols (hfs's) of subterms which are associated); these associations will be added to an evolving **mapping**, which will in turn be used to make new refinements. In the example above, the association[3]

$$(f, g, [(1, 2), (2, 1)])$$

---

[3]Recall that we can write an association either in the form $f \leftrightarrow g$ or in the form (f, g, p) (sometimes omitting the third argument from the latter); p contains elements of the form (i, j) meaning that the ith argument of f is paired with the jth argument of g. In this chapter, we tend to use the second form because we are usually interested in the argument pairings.

would be added to the mapping when the argument pairings are made.

Notice that this approach to matching will only produce matches which satisfy the structural preservation constraint discussed earlier:

$$\text{for pairings } (a_1, b_1) \text{ and } (a_2, b_2), \text{ if } a_1 \geq a_2 \text{ then } b_1 \geq b_2$$

This constraint thus represents an assumption behind the approach to matching which is developed in this section. The **partial homomorphism heuristic** is therefore built into the structure of the algorithm. However, as noted above, the restriction still allows considerable scope for structural deformations, which encompassess the types of structural mismatch which have been suggested by example.

Flexible control with an agenda

It is important to realise that, in contrast to unification algorithms, it cannot be predicted on which of the subproblems progress can next be made. Thus a fixed flow of control (for example, top-down left-to-right), in which each matching subproblem is either successfully refined or the whole match fails, is not suitable for a heuristic analogy matcher.[4] This suggests that the matching subproblems should be organised as an **agenda**; if no refinement is suggested for a subproblem, it should be moved to the end of the agenda, and the next subproblem analysed. Matching should terminate only when no progress can be made on any of the subproblems on the agenda. When a subproblem is successfully refined, the sub-subproblems which are produced are added to the front of the agenda. Since the existing mapping is used by the refinement procedure, we may (and often will) find that a matching subproblem which had been analysed without success previously will be returned to with an extended mapping and will be refined successfully. This is the benefit of the agenda-based refinement.

The agenda of matching subproblems in a partial match are conjunctive subproblems — that is, they represent parts of a single match, and we hope to be able to solve them all together with a common mapping. We call this kind of agenda an *and*-agenda, to contrast it with the alternative type (*or*-agenda) which will be introduced below.

Agendas are often used to give control strategies for applications where there is no pre-specified algorithm for the task at hand. Examples are the discovery system AM of Lenat ([30]), planning systems and real time control expert systems.

---

[4] Kling's matcher was criticised in the previous chapter for its inflexible co-ordination of the procedure MULTIMATCH1 within MULTIMATCH.

The need for search

The second observation is that the heuristic analysis of a subproblem from
the agenda may suggest more than one way of refining the subproblem, i.e.
more than one set of subterm pairings. Each such set can then be investigated separately. Therefore, whenever this happens the entire agenda should
branch into a set of new agendas, each arising from one set of pairings. That
is, the matcher should be able to **search** a space of plausible matches.

For example, on the following problem:

$$f(x, f(y, z)) = f(f(x, y), z)$$

$$g(x, g(y, z)) = g(g(x, y), z)$$

FHM might decide to make the two sets of argument pairings $[(1,1),(2,2)]$
and $[(1,2),(2,1)]$; the partial match would be split into two, containing the
new sets of subproblems

$$\{ \, (\, f(x, f(y, z)), \, g(x, g(y, z)) \,), \; (\, f(f(x, y), z), \, g(g(x, y), z) \,) \, \}$$

and

$$\{ \, (\, f(x, f(y, z)), \, g(g(x, y), z) \,), \; (\, f(f(x, y), z), \, g(x, g(y, z)) \,) \, \}$$

respectively. Thus, the current state of matching between a pair of terms
involves, in general, a *set* of partial matches, each represented as an and-
agenda together with an evolving mapping. In the current example, the
mappings associated with the offspring partial matches would be produced
by adding to the previous mapping the associations

$$(f, g, [(1, 1), (2, 2)])$$

and

$$(f, g, [(1, 2), (2, 1)])$$

respectively.

Top-level structure

As we shall see, each partial match can be assessed as to its promise, via
its mapping. Since we are looking for strong matches, we develop the most
promising of the partial matches first. After the strongest has been developed
a certain amount, we reassess its mapping, compare it with the rest, and
develop the (possibly) new strongest partial match. Thus the set of partial
matches between terms is handled as an agenda as well; this agenda is an

or-agenda, since we only need a single match between the terms in order to progress to the later stages of the analogy process; the partial matches on the top-level or-agenda do not share any information.

Thus, the overall structure of FHM will be an *or-agenda*, which consists of *partial matches* between the terms, each of which itself consists of an *and-agenda* of pairs of subterms still left to be matched coupled with an evolving *mapping*.

While this structure may seem rather complex at first sight, it has been derived from some simple and natural properties that an analogy matcher should have. We emphasise this basic simplicity as an attractive feature of the approach to matching which we are taking. In the next two sections we add detail to the structure: in Section 4.4.1 we describe the procedures involved in refining a partial match; in Section 4.4.2 we describe how matching is co-ordinated *between* partial matches, i.e. how the top-level or-agenda is developed.

4.4.1 The development of a partial match

In this section we describe how a given partial match is developed — that is, how one or more of the matching subproblems which make up the partial match is refined, and how offspring partial matches are constructed from a refinement. Specifically, we describe:

- The match development rules which are used to propose argument or subterm pairings.

- How the suggestions made by the rules are evaluated to decide on which pairings to make.

- How offspring partial matches are constructed once the pairings are decided on.

It is an important feature of FHM that the development rules are separate from the procedures that make use of them. This separation facilitates modification of FHM, by introducing new rules (possibly based on new heuristics), adjusting the relative importance of existing rules, or altering the strategy for co-ordinating the rules.

Development rules

The development rules perform tests on the two terms involved in a matching subproblem and make 'suggestions' for pairings of arguments.

We list the rules which are used in FHM below, together with examples of their use. We then discuss each, and say which analogy heuristic it is based on. All but one of the rules are completely specified; one however, rule 3, is only partially specified, and will be described in detail in the remarks which follow.

> *Given a matching subproblem, consisting of a pair of terms*
> *to be matched, and the existing mapping:*

1. Suggest pairs of arguments to the terms which have hfs's which are associated in the existing mapping.

   For example, if the existing mapping contained the association

   $$(\cup, \cap, P)$$

   this rule would suggest the pairing (2,2) on the following subproblem[5]

$$x \cap (y \cup z)$$
$$|$$
$$|$$
$$|$$
$$x' \cup (y' \cap z')$$

2. If the hfs's of the terms are associated in the existing mapping, suggest the previous argument pairings. If either of the hfs's in question is commutative, return all possible argument pairings (i.e. $\{(i,j)| \text{ any } i,j\}$).

   For example, suppose the existing mapping contains the association

   $$(f, g, [(2,1), (1,2)])$$

   Then the pairings
   $$\{(1,2), (2,1)\}$$

   would be suggested on the following subproblem:

$$f(a_1, b_1)$$
$$\begin{array}{c} \backslash \ \ / \\ \times \\ / \ \ \backslash \end{array}$$
$$g(b_2, a_2)$$

---

[5]We are using the convention that the upper formula in a diagram corresponds to the left element in associations, and the lower corresponds to the right. Pairing suggestions are illustrated with dashed lines, in this section, to distinguish them from actual pairings.

3. Suggest pairs of arguments to the terms in the match which have *similar syntactic structure*, as long as almost all of the arguments can be paired in this way.

   This rule is further specified and discussed below, where an example is given.

4. Suggest pairs of non-head symbols in the arguments of the terms which are associated by the existing mapping.

   If $(x, x, term) \in \alpha$,[6] the pairing ([2,1],[1,2,1]) would be suggested on the following subproblem

   $$2 \cdot f(x)$$
   $$/$$
   $$/$$
   $$/$$
   $$2 \cdot g(x) + 1$$

   Note that the complete subterm positions at which the symbols occur are retained in the pairing suggestion; this is so that the rule can be used to suggest pairings other than argument pairings.

5. Suggest pairs of arguments of the terms which have the same hfs.

   The suggestions $\{(1,1),(2,2),(2,3)\}$ would be made by this rule on the subproblem

   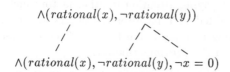

   $$\wedge(rational(x), \neg rational(y))$$

   $$\wedge(rational(x), \neg rational(y), \neg x = 0)$$

6. If the terms have the same hfs, the same number of arguments, and the hfs is not known to be commutative, suggest argument pairings which respect argument order (i.e. the pairings $\{(1,1),(2,2)\dots(n,n)\}$); if they have the same hfs which is known to be commutative, suggest all argument pairings (i.e. pairings (i,j) for all possible i and j.

   On the (schematic) subproblem

   $$A \longrightarrow B$$
   $$A' \longrightarrow B'$$

---

[6]The current mapping is referred to as α throughout this chapter. The expression *term* in the argument pairing slot of an association indicates that the symbols have no arguments paired, i.e. the association is terminal in the match. This will usually be because at least one of the symbols in question is atomic and thus has no arguments.

this rule would suggest the pairings $\{(1,1),(2,2)\}$.

Remarks on the development rules:

1. This rule, a relative support rule, is based on the **consistent transla-tion** heuristic (CTH); argument pairings are suggested which, if made, would maintain the consistency of the existing mapping. If pairings suggested by this rule are overruled, the mapping is very likely to be-come inconsistent. Thus, we regard this as a strong rule. Kling uses similar rules in SINGLEMATCH and MULTIMATCH.

2. Again this is based on the CTH, and is also a relative support rule; an association of predicates or functions which is repeated in a match with *different* argument pairings is regarded as a (mild) form of in-consistency. If either of the symbols in question is commutative, the particular pairings used before are not relevant, so all possible pairings are suggested. It would be possible to make no suggestions in this case, and this was done with an earlier version of the rule, but this had the effect of discriminating against commutative functions and so it was replaced with the present version.

3. This direct support rule is based on the **partial homomorphism** heuristic: pairings are suggested which would allow a close structural match, not paying attention to other factors such as consistency. This rule was added to FHM after the others had been implemented, and the resulting matcher found to suffer from the weak heuristic problem discussed in the previous chapter.

So far, we have only specified the *intention* of the rule: to look for structural similarity between arguments. The following other consid-erations motivated the design of the syntactic structure rule:

- If arguments can be unambiguously paired by analysing their syn-tactic structure to a certain level, there is no point in analysing them any further, at that stage. For example, in matching $x \cap 1 = x$ and $x \cup 0 = x$, analysis at level 1 (i.e. just arities) indicates the pairings (1,1) and (2,2), so the rule need go no further.

- Unless almost all of the arguments of the terms can be paired off on the basis of syntactic structure, no pairing suggestions should be made at all. This is because, even between terms with little overall syntactic similarity, there are likely (by coincidence) to be some pairs of arguments with the same structure; this should not be regarded as evidence for their pairing.

The rule which has been implemented is given below, and is illustrated on the subproblem

$$\wedge(rational(x), \neg rational(y))$$

$$\wedge(rational(x), \neg rational(y), \neg x = 0)$$

Syntactic structure rule. Sort the arguments of each of the terms into blocks of equal arity; then pair up the arity blocks on one side with those of the same arity on the other; on the example we would get[7]

$$\{([1,2],1)\}$$

$$\{([1,2,3],1)\}$$

For each pairing of blocks, if each block contains just one argument mark these as paired (this does not apply in the present case); if the blocks contain more than one argument, attempt to pair up the arguments within the blocks on the basis of the arities of *their* arguments; with each argument in a block associate the bag of the arities of its arguments, and mark as paired each pair of arguments within the given blocks with the same bag of arities. In this case, we get

$$[(1,[0]),(2,[1])]$$

$$[(1,[0]),(2,[1]),(3,[2])]$$

If, by the above procedure, all of the arguments to the terms can be paired up (perhaps ambiguously), except for at most one argument on one side, then return the pairings as suggestions. If not, return no suggestions. In the present case, there is just one unpaired argument, so the pairings $\{(1,1),(2,2)\}$ are returned.

This rule only looks to depth two; if there are sets of arguments which have the same structure at this level, but which could be differentiated at a deeper level, the pairings are still made.

The above is just one way of implementing a syntactic structure rule, and is not meant to be taken as the definitive version. Experience with

---

[7]I.e. both the arguments of the first term have arity 1 as do all those of the second term.

FHM without it has indicated the need for *some* syntactic structure
rule.

4. This relative support rule is based on the CTH, and is a weaker form
   of rule 1. It is weaker because the symbols which are associated by the
   existing analogy may not be in corresponding positions in the arguments, and thus we are not so sure that the argument pairings which
   are suggested would lead to preservation of the consistency of the mapping. This rule is designed to be a cheap form of look-ahead. Kling
   uses a similar pairing rule as the basis of MULTIMATCH1. This rule
   may be used to suggest structural mismatches, such as that shown
   above, as well as argument pairings.

5. This direct support rule is based on the **identical symbols heuristic**;
   we propose argument pairings which will lead to identical associations
   being added to the mapping. Just as the identical symbols heuristic
   was seen to be a weak heuristic, this rule is a weak rule, compared to
   those discussed above.

6. This direct support rule is again based on the **identical symbols**
   heuristic, and thus is also a weak rule; 'identical association' in the
   context of an analogy mapping means having identical argument pairings as well. If the hfs is known to be commutative, there should obviously be no inclination towards identical pairings, and so all pairings
   are suggested. Kling uses a similar rule, as the basis of ATOMMATCH,
   but for *all* pairs of predicates, not just identical pairs.

General remarks on rules   Note that there is no rule based on the semantic type heuristic; as discussed in the previous chapter, there are problems of
circularity associated with the use of this heuristic. While the heuristic may
be used to give FHM clues to analogies, it is important for the matcher to be
able to work without any type information. It would be easy to add a rule,
similar to rule 5, which would find arguments whose hfs's have the same (or
similar) type. The use of the semantic type heuristic, being weak, could also
be restricted to the assessment stage of matching; this use for the heuristic
is also suggested by the fact that the types would, in general, be organised in
a **hierarchy**, and the semantic judgement between a pair of symbols would
be a degree of semantic closeness, rather than an all or nothing judgement.

The co-ordination of the rules in making pairings

We now describe how the rules are co-ordinated across a partial match to
make a refinement. Recall that a partial match is an and-agenda of matching

subproblems, together with a mapping. We need to decide

1. Which subproblem to apply the rules to.

2. Given pairing suggestions, how to derive the pairings which are actually made.

3. Given the pairings which are made, how to update the partial match to produce offspring matches (including perhaps some complete matches).

At any stage, the answer to 1 is simple — choose the subproblem at the top of the agenda; the order of the agenda is a consequence of the procedures described below. The following procedure would be an obvious way of tackling 2:

> Apply all of the rules to the subproblem. Put all of the evidence together to get a measure of strength (weighted according to the strength of the rules) for each suggested argument pairing. Find consistent (1-1) subsets of the pairings which are relatively strong, the strength of a subset being the sum of the strengths of its elements. Return these strong subsets as the plausible argument pairings.

A control strategy such as this would have the following deficiencies:

- Some of the rules are considerably stronger than others; if strong rules suggest argument pairings unambiguously, there would be no point in applying the weaker rules, since, in this case, they would not affect the overall judgement about pairings; doing so would be wasteful, particularly considering that one of the weaker rules, rule 4, will involve considerable computation.

- If only weak rules suggest pairings, or if the strong rules are ambiguous, it may be wise to suspend the current subproblem, making no pairings and moving it to the back of the and-agenda; stronger rules may be active and unambiguous at another subproblem. The pairings suggested at the other subproblem would be more reliable, and, once made, the associations added to the mapping might lead to clearer pairing information at the original subproblem. The simple control strategy does not allow this flexibility.

- It would be sensible to delay splitting a partial match as long as possible; i.e. to see if a single set of pairings is suggested at any subproblem, before splitting the match. This would avoid the proliferation of weak partial matches in the top-level or-agenda. Again, the simple control strategy would not be able to do this.

These factors suggest a control regime for match development under which stronger rules are considered first throughout the agenda before the weaker rules are considered anywhere. Furthermore, the weak rules would be considered at all subproblems before any splitting of the partial match was done. Thus we are led to to a three-level organisation of rules:

Level	Rules
1	1,2,3
2	(1,2,3),4,5,6
3	(1, .., 6), splitting

Thus we deem rules 1,2 and 3 to be stronger than the others; this judgement is based on the strength of the heuristics on which the rules are based. The only exception is rule 4 which, although based on a strong heuristic, the consistent translation heuristic, is put in at level 2; this is because, as explained above, the rule is based more loosely on the heuristic than is so with the other rules.

To develop a match, we first attempt to make a refinement at level 1; if successful, the and-agenda and mapping are updated according to the new subterm pairings; if unsuccessful (i.e. no clear pairings can be made at any matching subproblem at level 1), we attempt a refinement at level 2; similarly, if this is successful, the agenda and mapping are updated; if not, an attempt is made to refine at level 3.

Thus, there are two possible results to developing a partial match: (1) a refinement is made at some level, and new matches are produced as a result; some of these may be complete, having empty and-agendas, and some still partial; each new partial match would then be available for further development (2) no refinement is made, in which case matching terminates; any subproblems remaining on the agenda are transferred to the mapping, i.e. we regard the entire subterms as being associated as wholes.

Pairing evaluation   We now describe how the pairing suggestions made, at a level, are analysed to find clearly suggested pairings.

Level 1. Firstly, some weakly suggested pairings are removed from the list obtained from rules 1 2 and 3 — those that share an argument position with another pairing which is suggested by a larger set of rules.[8] Those pairings

---
[8] By larger set, we mean strict superset.

which remain and are now **unambiguous** (i.e. do not share arguments with others that remain) are returned as the clearly suggested pairings.

The rationale behind this procedure is as follows. The rules which are being used often suggest many different argument pairings; those which are less well suggested than others with which they compete are removed to cut down the level of 'crosstalk'. After this has been done, any which remain and do not compete with any other which remain, may be taken to be reliable (clearly suggested) pairings, and should thus be made. Note that the pairings made here may not be complete, i.e. there may be arguments left in the terms which have not been paired.

If terms in the subproblem each have all but one of the arguments paired, the remaining two are also paired. This is a default rule, similar to rules used by both Kling and Munyer.

If there are no clearly suggested pairings, the subproblem is put at the back of the agenda, the next is chosen, and the procedure is repeated. This continues until either some clear pairings are found (a refinement is made), or all subproblems have been analysed at level 1 (no refinement is made).

Level 2. The level 2 procedure is an extension of that at level 1; pairing suggestions from rules 4, 5 and 6 are added to any remaining from level 1 (multiple suggestions from rule 4 are counted multiply). The main procedure is exactly that for level 1. To illustrate, suppose we had the following subproblem, with pairings labelled with the sets of rules suggesting them:

$$even(x) \wedge even(y)$$

$$[1,3] \quad [1,3,4] \quad [1,3]$$

$$[1,3,4]$$

$$odd(x') \wedge odd(y')$$

The first stage removes the pairings (1,1) and (2,2), leaving

$$even(x) \wedge even(y)$$

$$odd(x') \wedge odd(y')$$

The two remaining pairings are both unambiguous and so would be returned as the clearly suggested pairings.

Again, a refinement is initiated when new pairings are suggested by the evaluation routine at some subproblem. Otherwise, the match passes to level 3.

Level 3. Level 3 involves no further calculation of rules; the first subproblem (if any) which contains pairing information from levels 1 and 2 is

taken from the agenda; the suggested argument pairings are split up into
maximally consistent subsets.[9] Only those subsets having maximal size are
retained, each of these producing a set of argument pairings. If there is no
pairing information at any subproblem in the agenda, no refinement is made.

Updating the agenda and the mapping, given pairings

When the procedures just described result in pairings being made at a subproblem in a match, the pairings made are used to update the and-agenda
and mapping of the match. We describe these procedures now.

When more than one set of pairings is made, the updating procedures
described below are called on each such set in turn, to produce a corresponding set of offspring matches.

The agenda
Given a set of pairings, the agenda is updated in the following two ways:

- New subproblems may be added to the front of the agenda, corresponding to the subterms which are paired. A new subproblem is added for
  each new pairing of *compound* subterms. If one or both of the subterms
  in a pair is atomic, the association between them is added directly to
  the mapping, as described below, and no new subproblem is put on the
  agenda; this is because there is no more matching to be done between
  these subterms.

- The subproblem at which the pairings were made may be removed from
  the agenda. This happens if the pairings made are **complete** — that
  is, one of the terms in the subproblem has all its arguments paired, or
  if there is a structural mismatch. If the pairings are incomplete, it is
  retained, to be analysed again at a later time in the hope of being able
  to complete the pairings; in this case, the pairing suggestions made for
  the subproblem are retained for analysis at lower levels.

The mapping
If the subproblem giving rise to the pairings is having its first argument pairings made, the association between the hfs's of the terms in the subproblem
is added to the mapping together with the argument pairings which are being made. We could add the association as soon as the subproblem is put
on the agenda, rather than waiting for pairings to be made; we do not do

---

[9]By consistent, we mean that each argument is paired with at most one argument from
the other term.

this for two reasons. Firstly, the subproblem may lead to a structural mismatch, which does not involve an association between the hfs's of the terms. Secondly, the terms of the subproblem might not match syntactically at all, and would be shifted directly to the mapping when matching terminates (i.e. they would be considered part of the difference between the original terms in the analogy).

If the subproblem has already had some pairings made, and more are being added, the association between the hfs's will already be in the mapping, and is merely updated with the extra argument pairings.

The mapping is also extended whenever subterms are paired at least one of which is atomic; the association is simply that between the subterms, with no argument pairings (i.e. with *term* in the pairing slot).

Completed matches There are two situations under which an offspring match is deemed to be complete:

- If the and-agenda is empty after it has been updated. This is the 'better' form of completion, as it means that the original formulae have been completely matched.

- If no pairings are made at the previous stage, i.e. no further matching is suggested between subterms which remain on the agenda. In this case, if we are to regard the original formulae as analogous, we must regard the remaining subterms as being associated as wholes, without further decomposition of their association. The subproblems which remain on the agenda are therefore transferred to the mapping as associations.

4.4.2 Co-ordination of matching over partial matches

In the previous section, we looked in detail at how a given partial match is refined, producing, in general, a set of new partial matches. We now describe the top level of the matching algorithm — how the development of the various partial matches is co-ordinated. We have already explained that the various partial matches being developed are organised in an or-agenda. The ordering of the agenda is based on an assessment of the promise of the matches — the assessment procedure is described below.

Assuming the assessment procedure, the development of the or-agenda of partial matches is straightforward: the top match (i.e. the most promising one) is taken from the agenda; the match refinement procedure is called to make a refinement to the match, producing a set of offspring matches. Each of the offspring matches is then developed as far as possible at level 1. The resulting matches, some complete and some still partial are assessed;

the partial ones are **merged** with the or-agenda (i.e. inserted in order of
strength); the complete ones are kept in a separate list; the set of matches
(both complete and partial) is then pruned by removing all matches with
strength less than a dynamic threshold — the threshold is calculated by
subtracting a fixed number (0.125 in the current version) from the strength
of the strongest complete match.

The above procedure is repeated until the or-agenda becomes empty.
One aspect of the procedure requires further explanation — the further
development of offspring matches at level 1, after the initial refinement has
been made. A single stage of development of a match may thus consist of
more than one refinement. The reason for this is that a refinement at level
1 can be thought of as an inevitable consequence of the initial refinement,
and involves no further splitting of the match; it is thus sensible to perform
all such refinements before reassessing the match. This is not an important
feature, but does limit the amount of time spent processing the top-level
agenda and in match assessment.

Match assessment

The assessment of a match is done using its associated mapping, and is based
directly on the analogy heuristics. For a completed match, this gives the
specification of goodness for the match which was discussed in Section 4.1.
For a partial match, it is an estimate of the assessment of complete matches
which it might lead to. The mapping is assessed according to each heuristic
separately, and the overall assessment is determined from the individual
assessments. More specifically, the mapping is rated according to its degree
of conformation with a heuristic on a scale of 0 to 1. The overall assessment
is a weighted average of these numbers; the weights determine the relative
significance given to the heuristics. The heuristics which are incorporated
into the current assessment procedure are the following:

1. *Partial homomorphism.* As explained earlier, a degree of structural
   preservation is ensured by the design of FHM, but there is still scope
   for significant variation within this — individual symbols or entire
   subterms may be unmatched. The proportion of symbols which have
   been matched to symbols which have been left unmatched is taken as
   a measure of the structural closeness of the match.

2. *Consistent translation.* We assess the degree of consistency of a mapping by counting the number of inconsistencies as a proportion of the
   size of the mapping and scaling the answer so that it lies between
   0 and 1. If l is the length of the mapping and n is the number of

inconsistencies the assessment is

$$\frac{1}{1 + 3 \cdot (n/l)}$$

Inconsistencies such as $\{a \leftrightarrow b, a \leftrightarrow c\}$, where a, b and c are atomic and distinct, in a mapping are easy to count. It is more difficult if compound terms are involved in the associations, which, as explained above, can happen. The general definition of an inconsistency which is used by the current assessment procedure is as follows:

> The distinct associations
>
> $$s_1 \leftrightarrow t \text{ and } s_2 \leftrightarrow v$$
>
> where s_1, s_2, t and v are possibly compound terms, are regarded as inconsistent (from left to right) if t and v are distinct and s_1 and s_2 share at least one symbol. Inconsistency from right to left is defined analogously.

This definition of an inconsistency, which subsumes the normal one for atomic associations, is perhaps rather strict; we might find that some mappings are penalised more than they intuitively ought to be, although this problem has not yet arisen in practice with FHM.

When an association in the mapping involves unmatched arguments, these are taken into account when counting inconsistencies: if a symbol occurs in an unmatched term, and is also associated in the mapping, we regard this as a mild form of inconsistency; half an inconsistency is added for each such situation.

3. *Identical symbols.* The proportion of the associations in the mapping which link identical symbols is computed as the extent to which the mapping conforms to the identical symbols heuristic.

The overall assessment of a mapping is given by

$$\alpha \cdot PH + \beta \cdot CT + \gamma \cdot IS$$

where PH, CT and IS are the contributions from the partial homomorphism, consistent translation and identical symbols heuristics respectively, and

$$\alpha + \beta + \gamma = 1$$

In the current version, $\alpha = 0.5$, $\beta = 0.4$ and $\gamma = 0.1$. These numbers reflect the relative significance attached to the corresponding heuristics.

Examples of assessments of matches are given in Section 4.4.2.

Summary of FHM

We have now completed the description of FHM. Since we have chosen to introduce the features gradually, with explanation and examples, the description has been rather spread out. Therefore, we give here a concise summary of the structure of FHM.

Data structures

State of matching. A pair (C,O), where O is an or-agenda whose nodes are *partial matches*, ordered by their assessments, and C is a list of *completed matches*, again ordered by their assessments.

Partial match. A quadruple (A,M,L,S), in which A is an and-agenda of *matching subproblems* (ordered by (1) recency of addition and (2) success/failure of refinement); M is a *mapping*; L is a level (1, 2 or 3); S is the assessment of the partial match.

Completed match. A pair (M,S), where M and S are as above.

Matching subproblem. A quadruple (T1,T2,P,I), where T1 and T2 are the subterms to be matched, P records argument pairings of T1 and T2 which have already been made and I records any pairing information which has been passed down from analysis of the node at higher levels.

Mapping. A list of pairs (F1,F2,P), where F1 and F2 are symbols from the terms, and P gives pairings of the arguments to F1 and F2.

Initialisation

Initially, *state of matching*=$(\phi,\{(\{(T1,T2,\phi,\phi)\},\phi,1,u)\})$, where T1 and T2 are the entire terms to be matched; i.e. there is one partial match, which consists of a single subproblem (the entire problem), empty mapping and no assessment; the initial level is 1.

Algorithm

Repeat *main cycle* until *state of matching*=(C,ϕ); return the completed matches C as the result of the procedure.

Main cycle *(given state of matching, (C,O), returns new state of matching (C',O'))*. Remove top partial match, (A,M,L,S) from O; call the *development routine*, producing sets of daughter matches (C'',N''), C'' complete and N'' partial; assess these (as described above), and merge them with (C,O), adding any completed daughters to C and the rest to O; compute the strongest completed match, and remove all matches (complete or partial) having strength more than a preset threshold below the strongest; return new state of matching (C', O').

Development routine *(given partial match, (A,M,L,S), returns new sets of matches (C,N), where C are complete and N are partial).* Attempt to make a refinement to the partial match, calling the *refinement procedure* at decreasing levels starting at L, until either a refinement is made at some level or the levels are exhausted; if a refinement is made, producing sets of new matches (C', N'), C' complete and N' partial, call the *refinement procedure* at level 1 repeatedly on each partial match from N', until either the match becomes complete or no more progress can be made at level 1; return the resulting sets of complete and partial matches as (C, N); if no refinement is made, move the nodes from A to the mapping M and return $(\{(M', S)\}, \phi)$ as (C, N), where M' is the extended mapping; that is, mark the match as complete.

Refinement procedure *(given partial match (A,M,L,S), returns new sets of matches (C,N), where C are complete and N are partial).* Attempt to make a refinement to (A, M, L, S) by calling the *subproblem analysis procedure* repeatedly on subproblems from A (from the top), until either new pairings are made at some subproblem or all subproblems from A have been tried; if new pairings are made at some subproblem, call the updating procedures (as described above) on each set of new pairings, producing new sets of complete and partial matches (C, N); if no new pairings are made at any subproblem, return $(\phi, \{(A', M, L, S)\})$, where A' is the agenda updated by any pairing information at level L.

Subproblem analysis procedure
(given matching subproblem $(T1, T2, P, I)$, mapping M and level L, returns a set of sets of new argument pairings S). Call the pairing rules associated with L on those arguments of $T1$ and $T2$ not already paired according to P; add pairing information obtained to that in I and pass to the pairing evaluation procedure associated with L (as described above); if new pairings are suggested, return these as S; if not, return ϕ.

Additional features

- If we already know some associations that we want to be in the mapping between a pair of terms, we can start the matching with a non-empty mapping slot, containing the associations which we want to appear in the match. This facility allows guidance to be given to FHM, and will prove useful in later stages of the analogy process (see Chapter 5).

- If the propositional structures of the terms being matched are not the same, they are both rewritten into conjunctive normal form (i.e. each term is transformed into an equivalent one which is a conjunction of disjunctions of literals), and matching proceeds on the normal forms. The idea behind this is that a potential analogy may be obscured by superficial differences in the propositional presentation of formulae; if both formulae are normal-formed, such differences will be removed. Other kinds of superficial difference between formulae are considered in Section 4.5.

- When FHM produces multiple matches between a pair of terms, some of them may be trivial variants of each other: for example, the following two matches

$$x \cap y \qquad x \cap y$$
$$\big| \big| \big| \qquad \big\Vert$$
$$x \cup y \qquad x \cup y$$

differ only in their association of variables and the argument pairings to the association $\cap \leftrightarrow \cup$. But the variable associations are equivalent up to renaming of variables (i.e. are α-variants of each other) and the functions $\cap$ and $\cup$ are known to be commutative; the argument pairings are irrelevant therefore and only one of the matches need be retained.

Generally, two matches are considered variants of each other if: (1) their variable associations are α-equivalent, and (2) their non-variable associations are identical modulo commutativity. After two terms are matched, the set of matches which has been produced is analysed, and any variants are removed.

- The top-level or-agenda allows partial matches between a problem and a number of other problems to be considered alongside each other. The initial agenda contains a node for each of the other base problems. As matching proceeds, the promising matches with the promising base problems will tend to rise to the top of the agenda; the rest will fall to the bottom, and may well be cut off by the threshold. Thus it will not be necessary to match each candidate base problem to completion in order to find the best.

Performance

We illustrate the performance of FHM on some examples.

Example 1   Formulae to be matched:[10]

$$rational(x) \ \wedge \ \neg rational(y) \longrightarrow \neg rational(x + y)$$

$$rational(x) \ \wedge \ \neg rational(y) \ \wedge \ \neg x = 0 \longrightarrow \neg rational(x \cdot y)$$

The matcher starts with a single node, containing the whole formulae. The level 1 rules are first checked; none of these makes any suggestions, so the match goes to level 2. Of the level 2 rules, both 5 and 6 suggest the argument pairings (1,1) and (2,2). These suggestions are undisputed, so the argument pairings are made; two new nodes are added, containing the hypotheses and the conclusions respectively, and the original node is deleted, having had complete pairings made; the association $(\longrightarrow, \longrightarrow, [(1,1),(2,2)])$ is added to the mapping, and the match returns to level 1.

The hypotheses node is analysed first at level 1; rule 3 suggests the pairings $[(1,1),(2,2)]$, which are undisputed and therefore made; two new nodes are added to the agenda, and the hypotheses node is deleted, as one side has had all its arguments paired; the association

$$(\wedge, \wedge, [(1,1), (2,2), (u, p(3, \neg x = 0))])$$

is added to the mapping,[11] and the match stays at level 1.

The new node

$$(rational(x), rational(x))$$

is analysed next: rule 3 suggests the undisputed pairing $[(1,1)]$, which is made; the node is deleted, and associations

$$(rational, rational, [(1,1)]) \text{ and } (x, x, term)$$

are added to the mapping, the latter arising automatically from an atomic node. In a similar way, the hypotheses $\neg rational(y)$ and $\neg rational(y)$ are paired up using rules 1, 2 and 3, and adding the associations $(\neg, \neg, [(1,1)])$ and $(y, y, term)$ to the mapping.

On the conclusions, still at level 1, refinement proceeds via rules 1 and 3. On the node $(x + y, x \cdot y)$, rule 1 suggests $[(1,1),(2,2)]$, on the basis of

---

[10]The hypothesis of the second formula is written with $\wedge$ as an infix operator for the sake or readability; the term presented to FHM is actually

$$\wedge(rational(x), \neg rational(y), \neg x = 0)$$

This convention is repeated elsewhere.

[11]When the argument pairing list contains a pair of the form $(u, p(I, T))$, this means that the ith argument of the right symbol, T, was unmatched; similarly, the notation $(p(I, T), u)$ refers to the left symbol having an unmatched argument.

the existing variable associations, and rule 3 suggests [(1,1),(1,2),(2,1),(2,2)]: the more weakly suggested pairings, (1,2) and (2,1) are removed, and the remaining ones are made, which completes the matching.

Thus, the following single match is found:

$$rational(x) \wedge \neg rational(y) \longrightarrow \neg rational(x + y)$$

$$rational(x) \wedge \neg rational(y) \wedge \neg x = 0 \longrightarrow \neg rational(x \cdot y)$$

Assessment: 0.850

Example 2 Formulae to be matched:

$$\sqrt{x} + a = b$$

$$\sqrt{x+1} + a = b$$

This example was used, in the last chapter, to illustrate the inflexibility of Kling's matcher.

Firstly, at level 1, the initial node has pairings [(1,1),(2,2)] made by rule 3, adding the association $(=,=,[(1,1),(2,2)])$. The (2,2) pairing yields an atomic association $(b, b, term)$, which is added to the mapping. The node arising from the (1,1) pairing has pairings [(1,1),(2,2)] made by rule 3 again, adding the association $(+,+,[(1,1),(2,2)])$ to the mapping. The (2,2) pairing yields another atomic association $(a, a, term)$. The other new node, $(root(x), root(x + 1))$, leads to no suggestions at level 1. Therefore, since it is the only node left, the match goes to level 2; the same node is analysed by the level 2 rules, of which rule 6 suggests the pairing (1,1), which is made, yielding an atomic association $(x, x + 1, term)$, which completes the matching.

Thus, the following single match is produced:

$$\sqrt{x} + a = b$$

$$\sqrt{x+1} + a = b$$

Assessment: 0.795

On the two examples considered so far, most of the matching takes place at level 1, with rule 3 doing most of the work. This is because there is a close structural correspondence in each case. However, with rule 3 removed from FHM, the same matches would have been produced. In this case, most of the matching would be done at level 2, with applications of rules 5 and 6 replacing those of rule 3.

In the next example, the structural correspondence is not so close.

Example 4

HYPOTHESES	HYPOTHESES
$group(g, *)$	$ring(r, *_1, +)$
$propernormal(m, g, *)$	$properideal(n, r, *_1, +)$
$factorstructure(x, g, m)$	$factorstructure(y, r, n)$
$simplegroup(x, *)$	$simplering(y, *_1, +)$
CONCLUSION	CONCLUSION
$maximalgroup(m, g, *)$	$maximalring(n, r, *_1, +)$

This is one of Kling's algebra examples. As explained in the previous chapter, Kling's matcher leans heavily on the semantic templates to match up these formulae.

The matching with FHM proceeds as follows: no pairings are suggested for the initial node at level 1, so the matcher goes to level 2. Rule 5 suggests the pairing $(1,1)$, and rule 6 the pairings $[(1,1),(2,2)]$. Thus, these pairings are made, and the matcher returns to level 1.

No progress is made on either of the two new nodes at level 1 (on the conclusion node, rule 3 suggests all possible pairings, but there are no undisputed ones), so the matcher goes back to level 2. On the hypotheses, rule 5 suggests the pairing $(3,3)$, and rule 6 suggests all possible pairings, since conjunction is commutative (symmetric); the assessment procedure removes the more weakly suggested pairings that compete with $(3,3)$; of the remainder, $(3,3)$ is the only undisputed pairing and is therefore made. The hypothesis node is retained on the agenda, since it has not had complete pairings made. The match goes to level 1, but, again, no progress is made there, so it returns to level 2. Rule 6 suggests the pairings

$$[(1,1),(2,2),(3,3)]$$

at the node

$$(factorstructure(x, g, m), factorstructure(y, r, n))$$

These suggestions are assessed along with those remaining at the node from rule 3, which had suggested all possible pairings; the pairings

$$[(1,1),(2,2),(3,3)]$$

being the more strongly suggested, are made, and lead to atomic associations, (x,y), (g,r) and (m,n), which are added to the mapping. The match returns to level 1, where the conclusion node

$$(maximalgroup(m,g,*), maximalring(n,r,*_1,+))$$

has pairings [(1,1),(2,2)] made by rule 1 (rule 3 again suggests all possible pairings). No further progress is made at level 1.

At level 2, the hypothesis node is analysed again: rule 6 again suggests all possible pairings. Rule 4 suggests the pairings

$$[(1,1),(1,2),(2,1),(2,2),(2,2),(4,4)]$$

on the basis of the existing variable associations (note that (2,2) is suggested twice by rule 4). After weakly suggested pairings have been removed, the pairings

$$[(1,1),(2,2),(3,3)]$$

remain, and, being mutually consistent, are made (the structural mismatch rule does not fire). The new node,

$$(simplegroup(x,*), simplering(y,*_1,+))$$

is analysed at level 1, and the pairing (1,1) is made on the basis of rule 1 (rule 3 again suggests all possible pairings); similarly, the other new nodes,

$$(propernormal(m,g,*), properideal(n,r,*_1,+))$$

and

$$(group(g,*), ring(r,*_1,+))$$

are refined at level 1 by rule 1; no further progress is made at level 1.

At level 2 the five remaining nodes, are reanalysed, but there are no clearly indicated pairings. The match therefore goes to level 3; the match is split up on the basis of the node

$$(group(g,*), ring(r,*_1,+))$$

the pairing (1,1) has already been made; the remaining possible pairings, (2,2) and (2,3), are both suggested by rule 3; each of these pairings leads to a new match.

Each of these new matches is developed further. In each case, the matching is completed at level 1 by rule 1. Therefore, two matches are constructed, which are shown below.

$$\wedge(\, grp(g,*),\, pnorm(m,g,*),\, fstx(x,g,m),\, sgrp(x,*)\,) \longrightarrow mgrp(m,g,*)$$

$$\wedge(\, rg(r,*_1,+),\, pidl(n,r,*_1,+),\, fstx(y,r,n),\, srg(y,*_1,+)\,) \longrightarrow mrg(n,r,*_1,+))$$

Assessment: 0.935

$$\wedge(\, grp(g,*),\, pnorm(m,g,*),\, fstx(x,g,m),\, sgrp(x,*)\,) \longrightarrow mgrp(m,g,*)$$

$$\wedge(\, rg(r,*_1,+),\, pidl(n,r,*_1,+),\, fstx(y,r,n),\, srg(y,*_1,+)\,) \longrightarrow mrg(n,r,*_1,+))$$

Assessment: 0.935

The only difference between the two matches which are produced is that, in one, the group operator is associated with the ring addition, whereas, in the other, it is associated with the ring multiplication. FHM cannot distinguish between these possibilities and gives them the same assessment (0.935).

It is interesting that this example does not actually need the semantic templates in order to be matched. On other of Kling's algebra examples, FHM produces more than two consistent matches; in some of these, set variables are matched with operator variables. Kling avoids these by insisting, in ATOMMATCH, that argument pairing respects argument types. The argument type heuristic is not used in the present version of FHM; it could be added as a development rule to prune matches which do not preserve the argument types; alternatively, it could just be added to the assessment phase, so that the type-respecting matches are preferred.

Assessment of FHM

The performance of FHM demonstrates its flexibility with respect to the analogy heuristics. It is able to construct a wide range of match types:

- Matches which are structurally close but with few initial clues from weak heuristics as to which pairings should be made:

$$even(x) \wedge even(y) \longrightarrow even(x \cdot y)$$

(number theory)

$$odd(x) \wedge odd(y) \longrightarrow odd(x \cdot y)$$

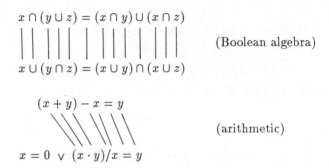

$$x \cap (y \cup z) = (x \cap y) \cup (x \cap z)$$

(Boolean algebra)

$$x \cup (y \cap z) = (x \cup y) \cap (x \cup z)$$

$$(x + y) - x = y$$

(arithmetic)

$$x = 0 \ \lor \ (x \cdot y)/x = y$$

- Matches involving permutation of arguments to functions, such as the following one from Boolean algebra:

$$x \leq x \cup y$$

$$x \cap y \leq x$$

FHM can be thought of as a generalisation of Kling's: it shares the basic top-down approach to matching. It is a generalisation in that it accepts an unrestricted syntax, removes arbitrary restrictions of Kling's matcher as explained above and makes more flexible use of the analogy heuristics. Furthermore, the agenda-based refinement architecture of FHM makes it more persistent, and therefore powerful, in matching than Kling's matcher.

An important feature of FHM is that it is easy to change — the development rules being separate from the control structure. We will demonstrate this in the next section, when new criteria are introduced which involve aspects of the matching context into the matching algorithm.

4.5 More powerful matching

In this section, we describe the need, and some outline mechanisms, for analogy matchers to find a wider range of intuitively easy analogies. Some of the examples we consider were used as motivating examples in Chapter 1. We discuss the extensions in terms of FHM. The need for the extensions, however, applies to analogy matchers in general. The extensions have a common theme: the need to take a more global view of the terms (or subterms) which are being matched. Some of what we propose is purely syntactic analysis (for example, reasoning about the respective numbers of variables in a term which is being matched), but much of it uses aspects of the **meaning** of the symbols in the terms.

4.5.1 Variable analysis

In problem solving, the number of variables, and occurrences of variables, which an expression contains can be very important to its role in a solution to the problem. Analogy matches in which expressions containing different numbers of variables are paired are not promising ones. Conversely, suppose we are trying to match two terms for which there is no clear way of developing the match (in terms of the matcher's development rules), such as

$$2 \cdot f(x)$$

$$2 \cdot g(x) + 1$$

The fact that the terms each contain a single variable x suggests that we add the association $x \leftrightarrow x$ to the match. That is, we can regard the terms as different expressions of an analogous variable:

$$E_1[x]$$

$$E_2[x]$$

Hence, we should also add the association:

$$E_1 \longleftrightarrow E_2$$

to the match, where

$$E_1[<v>] = 2 \cdot f(<v>)$$
$$E_2[<v>] = 2 \cdot g(<v>) + 1$$

This association indicates that the analogue of an expression of the form

$$2 \cdot f(<v>)$$

should be

$$2 \cdot g(<v>) + 1$$

Just pairing the entire original subterms would not naturally give this behaviour.

This situation occurs in attempting to match up the definitions for *even* and *odd*:[12]

---

[12]These are skolemised existential definitions, of the kind used by resolution systems: instead of using an explicit existential quantifier to state that there is an a such that $x = 2 \cdot a$ for each x, a function, f, of x is introduced which picks out the a for each x. The variable x is universally quantified in each sentence.

HYPOTHESES
point(*x*) ∧
point(*y*) ∧
point(*z*)

CONCLUSIONS
point(*o*(*x, y, z*)) ∧

lies_on(*o*(*x, y, z*),
     line(*z, midpt*(*x, y*)))) ∧

lies_on(*o*(*x, y, z*),
     line(*x, midpt*(*y, z*)))) ∧

lies_on(*o*(*x, y, z*),
     line(*y, midpt*(*z, x*))))

HYPOTHESES
point(*x*) ∧
point(*y*) ∧
point(*z*) ∧
point(*w*)

CONCLUSIONS
point(*p*(*x, y, z, w*)) ∧

lies_on(*p*(*x, y, x, w*),
     line(*w, orth*(*x, y, z*)))) ∧

lies_on(*p*(*x, y, z, w*),
     line(*x, orth*(*y, z, w*)))) ∧

lies_on(*p*(*x, y, z, w*),
     line(*y, orth*(*w, z, x*)))) ∧

lies_on(*p*(*x, y, z, w*),
     line(*z, orth*(*w, x, y*))))

Figure 4.2: Geometry theorems

$$even(x) \rightarrow x = 2 \cdot f(x)$$

$$odd(x) \rightarrow x = 2 \cdot g(x) + 1$$

This occurs in the application of one the examples of Chapter 1.

4.5.2   Introducing sets and symmetries

A more ambitious challenge for variable analysis is set by the geometry example discussed in Chapter 1. The formal presentation of the theorems is repeated in Figure 4.2.

The two formulae of Figure 4.2 represent the theorems:

> The three lines joining the vertices of a triangle to the midpoints of the opposite sides meet at a point (the orthocentre).

> The four lines joining the vertices of a tetrahedron to the orthocentres of the opposite faces meet at a point.

There is a clear analogy between these theorems which is obscured by their syntactic presentation above. We sketch mechanisms by which the formulae can be re-expressed in such a way that there is a close syntactic analogy between them.

If the matcher performed variable analysis, problems could be anticipated from the beginning: the base problem contains four variables, three universally and one existentially quantified while the target contains five, four universal and one existential. Such analysis could be performed at the outset, or, alternatively, delayed until the matcher got 'bogged down', i.e. the development criteria did not suggest further clear pairings. The mismatch in numbers of variables indicates that the method adopted above would not work in this case.

Given such a situation, we suggest that a matcher would have at its disposal various *re-expression* methods, which it would activate in an attempt to rewrite the base and/or target theorem to make them syntactically analogous.

The key to this example appears to be the ability to re-express both base and target so that they each talk about a *set* of points, rather than mentioning isolated points. This has the potential to remove the discrepancy between the numbers of variables by collapsing them into sets.

Grouping isolated variables into sets essentially involves determining symmetries. Determining that the base problem is symmetric with respect to x, y and z (i.e. that it is invariant under any permutation within these three variables) involves a small amount of logical and domain knowledge: the associativity and commutativity and logical conjunction and the function *midpoint* — the problem is not strictly syntactically symmetric.

We assume that the matcher can call on a symmetry detector good enough to detect the symmetry between $\{x, y, z\}$ in the base, and $\{x, y, z, w\}$ in the target. From these symmetries, it is simple to produce the following re-expressions of the two problems, which now match closely:

$$\bigwedge_{s \in S} pt(s) \longrightarrow pt(o(S)) \wedge \bigwedge_{s \in S} lies\_on(o(S), line(s, midpt(S \backslash \{s\})))$$

$$\bigwedge_{s \in S'} pt(s) \longrightarrow pt(o(S')) \wedge \bigwedge_{s \in S'} lies\_on(o(S'), line(s, orth(S' \backslash \{s\})))$$

where $S = \{x, y, z\}$ and $S' = \{x, y, z, w\}$. These set-based expressions express directly our intuitions about *how* these problems are analogous.

4.5.3 Introducing lists

The block stacking example which we discussed in Chapter 1 indicates re-expression techniques similar to those just discussed, but ordered lists are

	START	GOAL
BASE	$on(B,C)$ $on(C,table)$	$on(C,B)$ $on(B,table)$
TARGET	$on(A,B)$ $on(B,C)$ $on(C,table)$	$on(C,B)$ $on(B,A)$ $on(A,table)$

Figure 4.3: Stack-reversing problems

introduced, rather than unordered sets; and the validity of the re-expression depends not on the determination of symmetries, but on the derivation of recursive templates. The example, in English, involves reversing a stack of three blocks by analogy to the known procedure for reversing a stack of two. Figure 4.3 gives the formal version of the base and target problems.

Once again, variable analysis can be used to indicate the need for re-expression: the base contains two variables and the target three. But the symmetry mechanisms would fail to find any symmetries in either the base or the target, since there are none. Another method of re-expression is to abstract the problems in terms of recursively defined templates applied to *lists* of variables.

Consider the subexpressions (the start states)

BASE $on(B,C) \wedge on(C,table)$

TARGET $on(A,B) \wedge on(B,C) \wedge on(C,table)$

The above pair of descriptions are subdescriptions of the base and target problems respectively. Partial matching between the base and target problems would lead to these terms occurring in a matching subproblem. But normal match development would become bogged down at this stage, as there is no clear way to refine the subproblem in its current form. Thus re-expression methods would be invoked. We assume a method for proposing recursive templates which would find that the following template P instantiates to both expressions (as $P([B,C])$ and $P([A,B,C])$ respectively)[13]

$$P([X]) \quad = \quad on(X,table)$$
$$P([X,Y|Z]) \quad = \quad on(X,Y) \wedge P([Y|Z])$$

------

[13] We use standard Prolog list notation here, where $[A|B]$ stands for the list with head A and tail B.

The goal states would be found to match with $P([C, B])$ and $P([C, B, A])$ respectively. To obtain the final re-expression, we need to observe that $[C, B]$ is $[B, C]$ reversed and likewise for $[C, B, A]$ and $[A, B, C]$.

Putting this together, we obtain the re-expressions, and hence the close match:[14]

$$
\begin{array}{ccc}
 & \text{START} & \text{GOAL} \\
\text{BASE} & P(L_1) & P(rev(L_1)) \\
 & | \; | & | \; | \; | \\
\text{TARGET} & P(L_2) & P(rev(L_2)) \\
\end{array}
$$

We have avoided important issues of control in the above discussion. But notice how, once again, the new forms of the problems express more directly our intuitions about the the nature of the task represented, and the similarity between them.

4.5.4   Known analogies and semantic types

It is widely accepted that judgements of similarity between symbols are relevant to finding analogies: we should prefer to pair symbols of similar semantic type — this is the semantic type heuristic. Incorporating the heuristic into the FHM and ACME matchers is not difficult. We mention it here because it is an example of the use of contextual information.

For example, the STH would be used to prefer the first of the following two matches to the second, on the basis that $+$ and $-$ are of closer semantic type than $+$ and log:

$$
\begin{array}{cc}
root(x) + a = x & a + root(x) = x \\
| \; | \; | \; | \; | \; | \; | & \text{\textbackslash}/ | \; | \; \text{\textbackslash} \\
root(x) - a = x & log(a, root(x)) = x \\
\end{array}
$$

When searching for an analogue in a large knowledge base of solved problems, this problem could occur often. In computational analogy research to date, the STH has not become important as the base of solved problems has never been very large.

Gentner and co-workers ([15]) argue that the primary use of the STH is in the filtering stage, where it is used to cut down the number of problems to be fully matched.

---

[14]*rev* is our notation for the list reversing function.

Closely related to semantic types, known, strong analogies can be used to enhance matching in a similar way: if two symbols have proved successful analogues for each other in the past, we consider them to be plausible analogues now. In Chapter 7 we discuss in detail how successful instances of Basic APS can lead to the construction and exploitation of global analogies.

4.5.5 Matching modulo a theory

We consider lastly how axioms/definitions/operators from the current domain may be important in perceiving an analogy which is obscured syntactically. Consider the following pair of problems from elementary number theory:

$$even(x) \longrightarrow even(x^2)$$

$$odd(x) \wedge odd(y) \longrightarrow odd(x \cdot y)$$

There is an intuitively clear analogy between these two, on the basis that the first is (equivalent to) the special case of the second when the two numbers concerned are equal. However, a syntactic matcher would not be able to find any close syntactic analogy between these two. The matcher needs to have access to the facts

$$A \wedge A \leftrightarrow A \qquad\qquad x^2 = x \cdot x$$

in order to be able to re-express the first problem to form the close match:

$$even(x) \wedge even(x) \longrightarrow even(x \cdot x)$$
$$odd(x) \wedge odd(y) \longrightarrow odd(x \cdot y)$$

But how could the application of the domain knowledge be controlled? Firstly, variable analysis would suggest the need for re-expression: for example, x^2 contains just one variable occurrence while $x \cdot y$ contains two. One directed tactic for re-expression would be to apply known operators which change the number of occurrences of variables; for example

$$x^2 = x \cdot x$$

Winston ([47]) suggests the use of taxonomic knowledge to perform rewriting in matching, a kind of domain knowledge. For example,

$$is(ROMEO, MAN)$$

matches well with

$$is(CHARMING, PRINCE)$$

because all *PRINCES* are *MEN*.

Generally, the problem of controlling the use of domain knowledge is a challenging one for future research.

4.5.6 Summary

Most of the extensions to syntactic matching we have discussed have been techniques of re-expression, applied to remove superficial syntactic differences between base and target. This appears to be a crucial facility for a genuinely useful analogy matcher to have — constructing an analogy often involves finding the right level of expression at which the base and the target are similar.

We have described how, in some cases, the failure of a straightforward syntactic match can be used to instigate and direct the methods of re-expression.

Chapter 5

Plan construction

5.1 Introduction

The previous chapter was concerned with finding analogies via analogy matching. In this chapter we consider the next stage of the analogy framework which was described in Chapter 1 — the construction of a plan for the solution of the target problem, given a match with a base problem, and the solution to the base problem. We can think of plan construction as the **prediction** part of Basic APS: we are predicting the form of the solution to the target problem by analogy.

We can think of the plan construction phase as being separate from the plan application phase, described in Chapter 6 — given a match with a base problem we could construct a complete plan before trying to apply any of it. However, we will see that, in practice, it may be wise to interleave the construction and application stages, constructing a part of the plan, attempting to apply it, then constructing some more, and so on. Therefore, in this chapter we describe the procedures for constructing individual parts of the plan, and leave the discussion of how the procedures are co-ordinated with the application of the plan until Chapter 6.

As we explained in Chapter 1, different analogy researchers have used different notions of plan in their systems. For example, in Kling's system ZORBA ([29]) plans are just sets of axioms to try in the target proof (we are stretching the term plan here); and in Munyer's planning system ([33]), plans are sequences of intermediate steps. In the next chapter we will try out various possible notions of plan. For now, we will assume we might want to use any information in the base proof in constructing a plan.

We can distinguish three types of object within the proofs produced by automated problem solving systems:

- *Goal statements.* These are the statements which represent the goal of

123

the problem solver, i.e. what is being proved. In a planning system, these would be start-state/goal-state pairs; in a natural deduction system the goal would be a literal statement of the theorem to be proven. In a resolution system, the goal clauses would be produced by negating, normal-forming and skolemising the conjecture which is being proved.

- *Intermediate steps.* These are statements which are produced by successive application of axioms, operators or inference rules to goal statements. They describe the 'path' that problem solving has taken. Certain steps are distinguished as solution states: in a natural deduction system these might be sequents of the form

$$A \vdash A,$$

depending on the presentation being used; in resolution there is a single solution state, the empty clause *nil*; in a planning system, a solution state would be the goal state described in the problem statement.

- *Axioms/operators.* These are the facts about the domain which are applied to construct new steps from old ones.

In some systems (such as resolution and planning-type systems) there may be more than one way to apply an axiom/operator to an intermediate step. In such cases, the base proof records the **inference positions** of the inferences which were made, i.e. to which part of the intermediate step was the axiom/operator applied.

We therefore describe how to map over each of the above kinds of information about the base proof, including the inference positions.

Goal statements

Since we already know the target goal statements, we do not need to guess at them. In systems, such as resolution, where there may be more than one goal clause, the target goals are paired up with the base goals via the mapping between the problems.

Intermediate steps

For the intermediate steps, we want to construct their analogues as best we can according to the current match; there is no *a priori* restriction on the form of the analogues; i.e. we are solving problems of the form

$$A \text{ is to } B \text{ as } C \text{ is to } X$$

where A and C are the problem statements,[1] B is an intermediate step in the base solution, and X is the (unconstrained) unknown. Given the existing match between A and C, we *apply* the match to B to get X. This application is done by the **analogue construction rule** (ACR) described in Section 5.3.

Axioms/operators

For the axioms, we have a similar problem to the one above, except that X is constrained to be an axiom (or theorem) from the knowledge base. The 'free' application of the ACR is not guaranteed to result in an axiom, so we need some way of finding the axiom, or axioms, which is closest to being the analogue of B. This is done by the **analogous operator identification** routine (AOI), described in Section 5.4.

In the next section, we take care of an issue that only arises in refutation systems, such as resolution — the fact that the problem statements are negated and skolemised before the proof begins.

5.2 Negating and partitioning the mapping

Refutation problem solving systems, such as resolution, prove that a conjecture follows from some axioms by showing that, in the presence of the axioms, the negation of the conjecture leads to a contradiction. The initial match between problems is between the skolemised forms of the *un*-negated conjectures; the goal clauses, being skolemised forms of the negated base conjecture, will contain skolem terms where the matched clause contains variables, and vice versa. Thus, the initial mapping will not apply directly to the goal clauses. The same is true of the intermediate steps, which will contain skolem constants and variables introduced by the goal clauses. However, the negated forms may be obtained from the positive forms by a consistent replacement of variables and skolem terms by skolem terms and variables respectively: for example, if the positive form is

$$p(x_0, y, z_0(y))$$

where x_0 is a skolem constant and $z_0(y)$ is a skolem function, arising from the unskolemised conjecture

$$\exists x\, \forall y\, \exists z\ p(x, y, z)$$

---

[1] More generally, A and C may stand for whatever has been matched so far to produce the current mapping — this may include previous axioms and intermediate steps as well as the original problem statements.

then the negated form is

$$\neg p(x, y_0(x), z)$$

arising from the negated conjecture

$$\forall x \, \exists y \, \forall z \ \neg p(x, y, z)$$

The associated replacement substitution is

$$\begin{array}{ccc} x_0 & \longmapsto & x \\ z_0(y) & \longmapsto & z \\ y & \longmapsto & y_0(x) \end{array}$$

By composing with the replacement substitutions for the base and target conjectures, we transform the initial mapping between the positive forms into a negated mapping between the negated forms, as shown below:

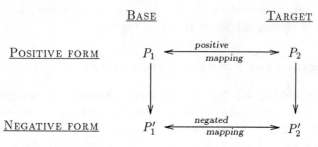

It it is the negated mapping which is used in mapping the goal clauses and intermediate steps. For example, if the positive base and target conjectures (from Boolean algebra) were

$$x \cup x = x \quad \text{and} \quad x \cap x = x$$

respectively, the initial mapping between them was

$$\{x \leftrightarrow x, \ \cup \leftrightarrow \cap, \ = \leftrightarrow =\}$$

and the negated forms were

$$\neg a \cup a = a \quad \text{and} \quad \neg b \cap b = b$$

the replacement substitutions would be

$$\{x \longmapsto a\} \quad \text{and} \quad \{x \longmapsto b\}$$

and the negated mapping would be

$$\{a \leftrightarrow b, \ \cup \leftrightarrow \cap, \ = \leftrightarrow =\}$$

The part of the initial mapping which is transformed by the above procedure, that involving variables and skolem terms, is relevant for mapping goal clauses and intermediate steps, but not base axioms. Therefore, the negated mapping is partitioned into two subsets, one containing associations free of skolem terms and variables, and the other containing all other associations. In the above example, we would have

$$\{\cup \leftrightarrow \cap, \ = \leftrightarrow = \}$$

and

$$\{a \leftrightarrow b\}$$

An alternative to negating and partitioning the mapping would be to negate and skolemise the problem statements before matching them. We do not do this for two reasons: firstly, it is much easier for a user to interpret a match between positive forms of the problem statements, since these directly express what is being asserted; secondly, and more importantly, if an analogy is successful we may wish to store the match for later use in guiding other analogy attempts (Chapter 7 discusses this in detail); the match would be used in its positive form; thus, we would have to invert the mapping at some stage anyway.

5.3   The analogue construction rule

As explained in the introduction to this chapter, the ACR is given the existing match, and a clause from the base proof, and has to construct the (best guess at the) analogue of the clause according to the mapping.

The basic idea behind the ACR is simple: view the existing match as a mapping from base to target, and apply the mapping to the clause to get its analogue. For example, supposing the match contained the associations[2]

$$(\cup, \cap, id), \ (\cap, \cup, id), \ (\leq, \leq, [(1,2),(2,1)]),$$
$$(=,=,id), \ (a,b,term) \text{ and } (0,1,term)$$

and the clause from the base proof to be mapped was

$$a \cup (a \cap 0) = a$$

---

[2] Recall that the third component of the associations give argument pairing information about the symbol pair; '*id*' (short for identical) means that argument order is preserved, '*term*' (short for terminal) that there are no arguments to be paired, and otherwise the pairing is given by a list of pairs (i,j), meaning that argument i on the left is paired with argument j on the right.

Then the correct analogue would be

$$b \cap (b \cup 1) = b$$

If the base clause was

$$a \leq a \cup a$$

then the analogue would be

$$b \cap b \leq b$$

However, the following cases may arise, which the ACR will have to cope with:

1. The base clause contains symbols which are not mapped in the existing match. This will happen often, as proofs almost always contain symbols which do not occur in the original problem statement. When we make our prediction about what the target proof will be like here, we should have some way of expressing our uncertainty as to what symbols should be at these positions.

2. The base clause contains a symbol which is mapped to more than one other by the existing match (i.e. the match is inconsistent with respect to this symbol). Again, we want to represent uncertainty in the term that we predict — that the corresponding symbol in the target proof might be any of the possible analogues.

The ACR which we develop in this section treats these cases as follows:

1. The symbols are copied over to the target, with identical pairings if they are not atomic. The results are flagged as being default symbols, as this fact is relevant for plan application. For example, with the mapping used above, the analogue of the clause

$$a \cup \bar{a} = 1$$

   would be

$$b \cap def(\bar{b}) = def(1)$$

The unary function symbol def is special syntax introduced to flag symbols which have been mapped by default; $def(T)$, for some term T, indicates that the head function symbol of T has been mapped by default. Depending on how the plan application procedures treat the default symbols in a plan, their use may involve an application of the **identical symbols heuristic**.

2. All analogues are constructed and are returned either as a list or as a more compact notation, if this is possible (see below). The list can be thought of as a disjunction of possibilities, and the plan application procedures of the next chapter treats it in this way. For example, if the mapping used above in addition contained the association $(a, c, term)$, the analogue of

$$a \cup (a \cap 0) = a$$

would be

$$[b, c] \cap ([b, c] \cup 1) = [b, c]$$

We next give the formal definition of the ACR which has the behaviour called for above. The definition is by recursion on the structure of the term whose analogue is being constructed. Firstly, some notation used in the definition: for a term or symbol T and a match α, let

$$T_\alpha = \{V | (T, V, term) \in \alpha\}$$

i.e. T_α is the set of terms to which T is directly mapped by α.

Analogue construction rule

Given a term T and a mapping α, ACR produces the result of applying the mapping to the term, T^α.

Base case. T is atomic: if $T_\alpha \neq \phi$ then $T^\alpha = T_\alpha$ (if T^α contains just one element, it is represented as the element, to improve readability); if $T_\alpha = \phi$ then $T^\alpha = def(T)$.

Recursive case. T is not atomic, $T^\alpha = T_\alpha \cup {}_\alpha T$, where ${}_\alpha T$ is as defined below[3] (again, if T^α contains just one element, it is represented as the element): if

$$T = f(a_1, a_2, \ldots a_n)$$

let $a_1^\alpha, a_2^\alpha, \ldots, a_n^\alpha$ be the results of the recursive calls to the ACR. There are three subcases to the recursive case:
(a) If $f_\alpha = \phi$ then

$${}_\alpha T = \{def(f(a_1^\alpha, a_2^\alpha, \ldots a_n^\alpha))\}$$

---

[3] T_α is the direct analogue, if any, of T, and ${}_\alpha T$ is the composite analogue, formed from the analogues of the constituents of T.

(b) If f_α contains just one element, g, where $(f, g, P_{fg}) \in \alpha$, then

$$_\alpha T = \{g({a_{\sigma(1)}}^\alpha, {a_{\sigma(2)}}^\alpha, \ldots {a_{\sigma(n)}}^\alpha)\}$$

where σ is the argument mapping implied by P_{fg}.[4] If the previous argument pairings of f and g, P_{fg}, leave an argument unmapped on the left (represented as $(p(i, t'), u)$ in P_{fg}, meaning that the ith argument, t', was unmatched previously), then for any j such that a_j unifies with t', a_j^α is flagged in $_\alpha T$ in the form $bdef(a_j^\alpha)$ to signify the fact that it may need to be omitted; in addition, if f is not known to be commutative, $bdef(a_i^\alpha)$ is added as a final argument to $_\alpha T$ (it would otherwise be erased by the above definition); if argument i is unmapped on the right (represented as $(u, p(i, t'))$ in P_{fg}), then the term t' is introduced in the ith argument position of $_\alpha T$; again, it is introduced in the form $bdef(t')$ to signify its special status. (These complicated conditions involving $bdef$ are explained in the remarks below.)

(c) If f_α contains more than one element, say $[g_1, g_2, \ldots]$, the pairings of f with each of the gs are checked to see if they are consistent; if they are, then

$$_\alpha T = \{poss([g_1, g_2, \ldots], [{a_{\sigma(1)}}^\alpha, {a_{\sigma(2)}}^\alpha, \ldots])\}$$

where σ is the (consistent) argument mapping derived from the P_{fg}s. This is the compact notation referred to above (the meaning of $poss$ is explained in the remarks which follow). If the pairings are not mutually consistent,

$$_\alpha T = \{\ g_1({a_{\sigma_1(1)}}^\alpha, {a_{\sigma_1(2)}}^\alpha, \ldots {a_{\sigma_1(n)}}^\alpha),$$
$$g_2({a_{\sigma_2(1)}}^\alpha, {a_{\sigma_2(2)}}^\alpha, \ldots {a_{\sigma_2(n)}}^\alpha), \ldots \ldots\}$$

i.e. just the set of the individual analogues. The same conditions on unmatched arguments in (b) apply to this case as well.

Remarks

- For most composite terms, $T_\alpha = \phi$; i.e. it is rare for composite terms to have direct analogues in the mapping. Thus, usually $T^\alpha = {_\alpha T}$. Where a composite term does have direct analogues, these are considered to be alternatives to the composite analogues derived by recursion on the structure of T, and so the union of the possibilities is taken.

---

[4] If the previous occurrences of the (f, g) association have consistent argument pairings, σ is derived from these; if the previous occurrences are inconsistent, the first set of pairings in P_{fg} is used for σ.

- $poss(L, Args)$, where L is a list of function or predicate symbols stands for the list of terms constructible from symbols in L applied to $Args$; the notation is more compact that the list of the possibilities, and makes the analogue easier to interpret.

- The treatment of associations which include unmatched arguments is illustrated by the following example: Suppose the terms

$$angle(a, b, c) \quad \text{and} \quad segment(a, c)$$

have been matched together previously (say, within the problem statements), and have given rise to the association

$$(angle, segment, [(1, 1), (p(2, b), u), (3, 2)])$$

in the existing match; if, later, we want to construct the analogue (from left to right) of the term

$$angle(d, b, e)$$

the ACR would produce

$$segment(d, e, bdef(b))$$

If we wanted to construct the analogue (from right to left) of

$$segment(x, z)$$

the ACR would produce

$$angle(x, bdef(b), z)$$

Terms headed by the unary $bdef$ function symbol should be thought of as optional. This means that they are deemed to unify with another term if they unify (in the normal sense) either with or without the term inside the $bdef$. The motivation behind the conditions involving $bdef$ is that we want to allow arguments to be erased or introduced again, where this has happened before. However, it would be hard to be confident as to just when arguments would be introduced or erased; the symbol $bdef$ is introduced and interpreted to allow flexibility — i.e. arguments may or may not be unmatched again. For a non-commutative symbol, an argument position which has been unmatched in the past is a candidate for being erased by the ACR, so $bdef$ is used for such arguments; for commutative symbols, particular argument positions are of no significance, so another condition is added which looks for arguments which unify with previously erased arguments, and flags these with *bdef* as candidates for erasure. Flagging extra arguments with *bdef* merely increases the generality of the analogue produced by the ACR, so the particular conditions under which *bdef* is used are not critical. The true significance of *bdef* (and the other special syntax introduced by the ACR) will only be clarified when the procedures which make use of the analogue steps are described in the next chapter.

- The ACR as defined above produces a structural correspondence between a term, T, and its analogue T^α, as a side effect (each symbol is associated with the symbol to which it is mapped). It is important for the following operations in plan application to maintain a *structural* correspondence between the terms in the base proof and their analogues in the target. Specifically, the structural correspondence is used in mapping inference positions (see below).

- The exotic cases which make the definition complicated, such as what to do if there is more than one prior pairing, and if arguments have been unmapped previously, are necessary for the definition to be complete; however, they do not, in practice, arise very often.

5.4   Analogous operator identification

As explained above, the purpose of analogous operator identification (AOI) is to find plausible analogues (from the axiom/theorem base) for axioms which were used in the base proof, given a mapping derived from the problem statements. In addition, as we shall see below, the AOI can produce an extension to the initial mapping between problems. As noted above, the analogue of an axiom, A, with respect to the existing mapping α, A^α, will not in general be in the knowledge base. This is why a separate procedure is required for the AOI. Kling's analogy system, ZORBA, forms unstructured plans for the solution of the target problem which consist entirely of potential analogues for the axioms used in the base — ZORBA makes no use of intermediate steps.

We first analyse Kling's procedure EXTENDER, for finding the analogues of axioms. The analysis involves a reconstruction of EXTENDER and assessment of its performance on some examples. In the following sections we propose an AOI which is an improvement on Kling's, and discuss its performance.

5.4.1 Kling's EXTENDER

Description

Given a mapping, α, and a set of axioms whose analogues are sought, first find the subset, $SOME_\alpha$, which consists of those axioms *some* (not all) of whose symbols are mapped by α. For each $A \in SOME_\alpha$, form a **description** of A, *descr(A)*. *descr(A)* is a list of the predicates[5] that occur in A, flagged by the polarities of the positions in which they occur — *pos* if all occurrences are positive, *neg* if they are all negative, and *impcond* if there are some of each. Thus if A is

$$\neg subgroup(h, g, *) \vee group(g, *)$$

then *descr(A)* is

$$[pos(group), neg(subgroup)]$$

Then map *descr(A)* to get $descr(A)^\alpha$ (this type of mapping is obviously much simpler than that described in the previous section). Express $descr(A)^\alpha$ as

$$\overline{descr(A)^\alpha} \cup Defs$$

where Defs consists of that part of $descr(A)^\alpha$ which was mapped by default, and $\overline{descr(A)^\alpha}$ is that part which was positively mapped. Then return as possible analogues for A those axioms B such that

$$descr(B) \supseteq \overline{descr(A)^\alpha} \qquad (a)$$

and such that

$$|descr(B) \cap Defs| \qquad (b)$$

is maximal over all axioms satisfying (a). We can think of (a) as a filter, and (b) as a metric which is applied to axioms which pass through the filter. The filter (a) is an application of the **consistent translation** heuristic — we look for axioms which contain symbols which are associated with ones in the base axiom. The metric (b) is a direct application of the **identical symbols** heuristic — analogous axioms are chosen which will lead to identical associations being added to the analogy.

Given such a B, the existing mapping is extended in the following way: Form the sets

$$descr(B) \backslash \overline{descr(A)^\alpha} \quad \text{and} \quad Defs = descr(A)^\alpha \backslash \overline{descr(A)^\alpha}$$

---

[5] Recall that Kling's clauses contain no functions or constants — in a less restricted syntax, the descriptions would obviously include the other symbols (see below).

For any pair of identical features (including the polarity signs) between these two sets, add the corresponding predicate association to the mapping, and delete the features from the sets. Out of the remainder, for any pair of features of the same polarity, whose predicates are of the same (unique) semantic type, add the predicate association to the existing mapping.

The procedure is repeated for each extended mapping, until the set $SOME_\alpha$ is empty.

Assessment of EXTENDER

The current author reconstructed EXTENDER in Prolog and analysed its performance on numerous examples. The following limitations of the routine became apparent:

1. It is likely that EXTENDER will fail to find analogues for certain of the axioms used in the base proof. Any axiom that has all its predicates mapped by the initial mapping will never be considered by the procedure. This is presumably an oversight on Kling's part; the situation perhaps never arose in the examples which he was considering. It is straightforward to change the procedure so that it takes account of such axioms, and this was done for the reconstruction.

2. Axioms whose descriptions contain only one feature, will tend to give rise to many possible analogues, most of them obviously unsuitable. For example, 12 analogues were found for the axiom $x = x$, out of a base of just 19 axioms, including such unlikely candidates as $x \cap (y \cup z) = (x \cap y) \cup (x \cap z)$. There is clearly something wrong with the metric for this to happen. As the axiom base expanded, this problem would become increasingly severe.

3. When an association is added to the mapping, no argument pairing information is included because all such information is lost in forming the descriptions. For example, if the axioms in question were $x \leq x \cup y$ and $x \cap y \leq x$, the extended match *ought* to include the association $(\leq, \leq, [(1, 2), (2, 1)])$, but Kling's procedure would produce $(\leq, \leq, id)$ by default. This could be important at later stages of the Basic APS process.[6]

4. The extension procedure is heavily geared towards adding identical associations, both in the metric for choosing possible analogues, and in

---

[6]This point does not apply to Kling's own system since it only uses the identity of analogous axioms, and not their structure; but it will apply to the application systems described in Chapter 6.

the procedure for extending the mapping based on them. For example, if A is

$$\neg rat(x) \vee \neg rat(y) \vee rat(x - y)$$

and '$-$' is not in the initial map, then the axiom B,

$$\neg rat(x) \vee \neg rat(y) \vee y = 0 \vee rat(x/y)$$

would not be considered as a possible analogue, since A itself has a higher default match than B. But if the initial mapping contained the association $(+, \cdot, id)$, then B would actually turn out to be the correct analogue for A. It is interesting that EXTENDER relies heavily on the identical symbols heuristic, while INITIAL_MAP (see Chapter 3) made no use of it at all, relying on the semantic type heuristic instead. The overall problem with both procedures is too much reliance on weak heuristics.

5. If A is

$$x \cap (y \cup z) = (x \cap y) \cup (x \cap z)$$

α contains

$$(\cap, \cup, id), (\cup, \cap, id)$$

and B is

$$x \cup (y \cap z) = (x \cup y) \cap (x \cup z)$$

then $descr(A) = descr(B) = descr(A)^\alpha = [pos(=), pos(\cap), pos(\cup)]$; so Kling's procedure, based on the abstracted descriptions, has no way of distinguishing between A and B as analogues for A. Yet, given the initial mapping, it is clear that B is the analogue of A (in fact $B = A^\alpha$, according to the ACR defined in the last section).

Some of the problems listed above are caused by the particular filter and metric which Kling uses: 1 and 2 are clearly of this type; 4 is also partly, since the filter could be changed so as not to bias towards identical associations. However, some of the problems indicate limitations of the reliance on abstracted descriptions, which take no account of the *structure* of the axioms: it is the structure which indicates argument pairings (3), which causes non-identical associations to be added to the mapping (4), and which enables us to distinguish between axioms which contain the same symbols (5).

Conclusions   EXTENDER is deficient in two respects. Firstly, its metric for choosing possible analogous axioms is unsatisfactory because it can cause many obviously unsuitable analogues to be found, particularly for small axioms, and leans too heavily on the identical symbols heuristic, causing the correct analogue often to be missed. Secondly EXTENDER is based on abstracted descriptions of the clauses, and thus cannot take account of the structure of the clauses, which is important for analogy.

5.4.2   An improved AOI

Value of structural match

EXTENDER seems to be based on the expectation that finding analogues for axioms should be easier than the initial analogy matching; i.e. that the knowledge of part of the analogy should make it easier to extend it further, and that the extension can be done solely on the basis of the abstracted descriptions of the axioms. However, we have seen that structural correspondence is relevant in deciding analogues for axioms. We summarise the reasons for this:

- The notion of structural similarity (the partial homomorphism heuristic) is crucial to the use of analogy in automated problem solving, as discussed in Chapter 3. In order to make effective use of this strong heuristic, we need a structural match between base axioms and their potential analogues. It is possible to get an idea of whether two axioms might possibly match well together structurally by analysing their abstracted descriptions (see below), but this is only a weak use of the heuristic.

- A structural match enables the existing mapping to be extended in a principled way, with non-identical argument pairings if indicated. The use of the strong partial homomorphism heuristic would remove the need to rely on the weak identical symbols heuristic to propose extensions to the mapping.

- If we have a structural match between a pair of axioms, we can map over the inference position, at which the base axiom was used in the base proof, to the target axiom. For example, if we have the following match between axioms from Boolean algebra

$$x = x \cup 0$$

$$1 \cap x = x$$

and we know that the upper axiom was applied by paramodulation from left to right in the base, we can predict that the lower one will be applied by paramodulation from right to left in the target.

Value of flexible filter

Kling's use of a filter based on abstracted descriptions has been seen to be both faulty in itself and limited in its discriminatory ability, being based on abstracted descriptions; while the latter point is true for any matching based on abstracted descriptions, a more flexible and less biased filter would nevertheless be a valuable part of an AOI: since some of the symbols in a base axiom will probably already have been mapped, we can use their analogues to 'get a handle' on potential analogous axioms; this will enable us to cut down considerably the number of candidates from the potentially very large knowledge base. Structural matching, as called for above, is bound to be more expensive than feature matching; without some way of pruning possible analogues, we would find that the AOI was extremely expensive.

However, we need a more flexible filter than Kling's, which does not, for example, allow inconsistencies to be introduced into the mapping; we would also want to remove the heavy reliance on the identical symbols heuristic.

Two-stage AOI

We are therefore led to a two-stage AOI:

1. A flexible filter, based on abstracted descriptions, is first called between a base axiom, and all clauses from the knowledge base; it returns a (short) ordered list of candidate analogues for the base axiom.

2. The candidate list is used to form the initial state of the match-ing and-agenda as described in Section 4.4; each partial match is started off with the existing mapping in its mapping slot, instead of the empty mapping. The analogy matching algorithm (described in Chapter 4.4) is then called to produce an ordered list of completed matches. The candidate analogues involved in the matches, together with the matches themselves and their assessments, are returned as the result of the AOI. Each candidate has an associated extension to the mapping — those associations added in the course of matching, which were not in the initial mapping.

Of the two stages, the second is much more complex; however, the com-plexity involved is that which has already been discussed in the design of the matching system FHM. Note that the facility FHM to be provided with guidance in the form of expected associations is being made use of here; the existing mapping is put in the initial mapping slot; this makes the matching faster and more accurate than it would be if the matching were done from scratch. It also has the virtue of guiding the AOI towards axioms which involve mappings which are consistent with the existing mapping; this is important, since we are looking for (relatively) consistent mappings throughout the analogy process. But we also do not rule out the introduction of inconsistencies into the mapping, if this is suggested by other analogy heuristics. The AOI inherits the flexibility of FHM with respect to the heuristics.

The filter stage is important, for the reasons given above, and we next consider its design.

A flexible filter   We first change the definition of the description function so that repeated occurrences of symbols are repeated in the descriptions (thus $x \cup x = x$ no longer has the same description as $x \cup (y \cup z) = (x \cup y) \cup z$). We then define a similarity function between descriptions which takes account of the symbols which do not match as well as the ones which do.

Since we are dealing with an unrestricted syntax, the descriptions are defined to be three lists, one each for predicates, functions and constants. So if A is $x \cup 0 = x$ then

$$descr(A) = (\ [=],\ [\cup],\ [0]\ )$$

(Unlike Kling, we do not include polarities in the description, although it would be simple to add them if it proved useful.) The similarity function $d(D_1, D_2)$ between two descriptions of this form is defined to be the sum of a similarity function f between individual components across the three components. The function f is defined below.

Suppose we have descriptions D_1 and D_2, and that D_1 is a mapped description; D_1 may thus contain default symbols, flagged by def, and optional symbols, flagged by $bdef$. Let these be $Defs$ and $Bdefs$ respectively, and let

$$Maps = D_1 \backslash (Defs \cup Bdefs)$$

be those symbols in D_1 which were positively mapped. Then

1. $f(D_1, D_2)$ should depend positively on $d_1(D_1, D_2) = |D_1 \cap D_2|$; i.e. the number of positively mapped symbols; note that default and optional symbols are excluded from this, since there are no defaults in D_2; this is an application of the **consistent translation heuristic** — we prefer axioms which may enable repeated associations.

2. $f(D_1, D_2)$ should depend negatively on the number of symbols in the descriptions which do not match. There are two qualifications to this. Firstly, default symbols should be excluded from the unmatched symbols, since they may match, without inconsistency, with symbols in D_2; furthermore, for each default symbol, two should be subtracted from the unmatched total, since the symbol with which a default might match should not be penalised either. Secondly, optional arguments should not count as unmatched, since they are optional; furthermore, for each optional symbol in $Bdefs$ which matches with a symbol in D_2, two should be subtracted from the unmatched total, since we can then consider the optional symbol to be included and to match with the other. These qualifications are designed to view the match as optimistically as possible. When all this is included, the expression obtained is

$$d_2(D_1, D_2) = |D_1 \cup D_2| - |D_1 \cap D_2| - 2 \cdot |Defs| - |Bdefs| - |Bdefs' \cap D_2|$$

where $Bdefs'$ is $Bdefs$ with the $bdef$ tags stripped off. This is also an application of the **consistent translation heuristic**, from the negative point of view — d_2 represents an estimate of the number of inconsistencies which would be introduced by matching with a particular axiom.

3. $f(D_1, D_2)$ should depend negatively on the difference in size between the descriptions. As above there is a qualification arising from $Bdefs$; since symbols in $Bdefs$ are optional, and we should be optimistic, we should retain just as many optional symbols in order to minimise the difference in sizes. Thus we define $d_3(D_1, D_2)$ as follows:

$$
\begin{array}{ll}
|D_2| - |D_1| & \text{if } |D_1| \le |D_2| \\
|D_1| - |Bdefs| - |D_2| & \text{if } |D_2| \le |D_1| - |Bdefs| \\
0 & \text{otherwise}
\end{array}
$$

This number represents a minimum on the number of unmapped symbols in an analogy match between the clauses giving rise to the descriptions. This is an application of the **partial homomorphism heuristic**: d_3 gives a lower bound on the number of unmatched symbols which would result from matching with a particular axiom.

4. $f(D_1, D_2)$ also depends positively on

$$|Defs' \cap D_2|$$

where *Defs'* is *Defs* with the *def* tags stripped out. That is, we reward default symbols which match symbols in D_2. This is an application of the **identical symbols** heuristic — we marginally prefer matches which promise identical associations.

All of the applications of analogy heuristics above are weak ones, even though some of the heuristics are strong; this is because the quantities can only estimate indirectly the prospects for a given heuristic being well satisfied by a match with the axiom. The filter which has been implemented has

$$f(D_1, D_2) = 3 \cdot d_1(D_1, D_2) - d_2(D_1, D_2) - 3 \cdot d_3(D_1, D_2) + d_4(D_1, D_2)$$

The weights attached to the four constituents reflect their relative importance.

The filter uses the similarity function just described together with a preset threshold — it finds the maximal similarity between the mapped description and the axioms in the knowledge base, and returns all axioms whose similarity with the mapped description differs from the maximum by less than the threshold. A small threshold will result in fewer axioms being returned, and thus in less work for stage 2, but risks missing plausible analogues. A large threshold has the reverse characteristics. A threshold of 5 has proved suitable for the filter, and is used in the examples that follow.

Examples

We now illustrate the behaviour of the new AOI routine on some examples. For both of the example problems considered below, the same knowledge base was used, consisting of 59 axioms and theorems from real number theory and Boolean algebra. The axioms/theorems for the two domains were mixed in order to simulate a large knowledge base, where many different sorts of axiom and theorem could be applied.

Example 1   Given the following initial match between problems

$$\neg rat(x) \lor rat(y) \lor \neg rat(x + y)$$

$$\neg rat(x) \lor rat(y) \lor x = 0 \lor \neg rat(x \cdot y)$$

we use the new AOI to find plausible analogues for the axioms used in the proof of the upper clause:

$$A_1: \quad \neg rat(x) \lor \neg rat(y) \lor rat(x - y)$$
$$A_2: \quad (x + y) - x = y$$

For A_1, the filter returns the following candidates, with associated scores:

$$A_1: \quad \neg rat(x) \vee \neg rat(y) \vee rat(x-y) \qquad (10)$$
$$A_3: \quad \neg rat(x) \vee \neg rat(y) \vee y = 0 \vee rat(x/y) \quad (9)$$
$$A_4: \quad \neg rat(x) \vee rat(y) \vee \neg rat(x+y) \qquad (9)$$

The matching stage produces three matches:

Axioms	Strength	Map extension
$A_1 \leftrightarrow A_1$	0.929	$\{- \leftrightarrow -\}$
$A_1 \leftrightarrow A_3$	0.811	$\{- \leftrightarrow /\}$
$A_1 \leftrightarrow A_3$	0.811	$\{- \leftrightarrow /\}$

The difference between the two matches with A_3 is that the association $- \leftrightarrow$ / has arguments preserved in one and swapped in the other. In the context of the solution of the target, A_3 will turn out to be the correct analogue (see Chapter 6); the match with A_1 has greater strength than that with A_3 because it is a better structural match, and it has more identical symbols. However, the match with A_3 is still returned as a plausible analogue; Kling's EXTENDER returns A_1 as the only analogue for itself, and would thus be led into trouble on this example.

For A_2, the filter returns the following 9 candidates:

$$A_5: \quad x \cdot y = y \cdot x \qquad (5)$$
$$A_6: \quad x \cdot y = x \cdot y \qquad (5)$$
$$A_7: \quad \neg x \mid y \vee y = x \cdot h(x,y) \quad (4)$$
$$A_8: \quad x^2 = x \cdot x \qquad (4)$$
$$A_9: \quad x = 0 \vee (x \cdot y)/x = y \quad (4)$$
$$A_{10}: \quad x \cdot 1 = x \qquad (2)$$
$$A_{11}: \quad x \cap \bar{x} = 0 \qquad (1)$$
$$A_2: \quad (x + y) - x = y \qquad (1)$$

Given these candidates, the matching stage produces 3 matches:

Axioms	Strength	Map extension
$A_2 \leftrightarrow A_2$	0.867	$\{+ \leftrightarrow +, - \leftrightarrow -\}$
$A_2 \leftrightarrow A_9$	0.833	$\{- \leftrightarrow /\}$
$A_2 \leftrightarrow A_{10}$	0.751	$\{(x + y) - x \leftrightarrow x \cdot 1\}$

The first of the matches is marginally preferred because the inconsistency which it entails ($+ \leftrightarrow \cdot$ previously, and $+ \leftrightarrow -$ now) is outweighed by the unmapped symbols in the other match. In the context of the target problem, the second match will turn out to be correct (see Chapter 6). Kling's EXTENDER returns 11 possible analogues from the knowledge base, including the correct one.

Example 2   Given the following initial match between problems:

$$x \cup x = x$$
$$\mid\mid\mid\mid\mid$$
$$x \cap x = x$$

we use the new AOI to find plausible analogues for the following axioms from the proof of the upper clause (see Chapter 6 for the full base proof):

$$B_1: \quad x \cup 0 = x$$
$$B_2: \quad x \cap \overline{x} = 0$$
$$B_3: \quad x = x$$

For B_1, the filter returns the following candidates, with associated scores:

$$B_4: \quad x \cap 1 = x \quad (6)$$
$$B_2: \quad x \cap \overline{x} = 0 \quad (3)$$
$$B_5: \quad x \cap 0 = 0 \quad (3)$$
$$B_6: \quad x + 0 = x \quad (2)$$
$$B_1: \quad x \cup 0 = x \quad (2)$$

The matching stage produces three matches:

Axioms	Strength	Map extension
$B_1 \leftrightarrow B_5$	0.980	$\{0 \leftrightarrow x,\ x \leftrightarrow 0\}$
$B_1 \leftrightarrow B_4$	0.960	$\{0 \leftrightarrow 1\}$
$B_1 \leftrightarrow B_1$	0.867	$\{0 \leftrightarrow 0, \cup \leftrightarrow \cup\}$

The second of these turns out to be correct in the context of the target proof. The second is a unification modulo commutativity and a single function mismatch. Kling's EXTENDER returns B_2 and B_5 as the possible analogues; it is unable to find B_4, the correct analogue, because of its heavy reliance on the identical symbols heuristic — the association with B_4 introduces a new non-identical association $0 \leftrightarrow 1$ into the mapping.

For B_2, the filter returns the following 8 candidates, with associated scores:

$$B_2: \quad x \cap \overline{x} = 0 \qquad (6)$$
$$B_7: \quad x \cup \overline{x} = 1 \qquad (4)$$
$$B_8: \quad x^2 = x \cdot x \qquad (3)$$
$$B_6: \quad x + 0 = x \qquad (2)$$
$$B_9: \quad (x + y) - x = y \quad (2)$$
$$B_{10}: \quad x \cap y = y \cap x \qquad (2)$$
$$B_1: \quad x \cup 0 = x \qquad (2)$$
$$B_4: \quad x \cap 1 = x \qquad (2)$$

The matching stage produces two matches:

Axioms	Strength	Map extension
$B_2 \leftrightarrow B_7$	0.967	$\{\cap \leftrightarrow \cup, \, - \leftrightarrow -, \, 0 \leftrightarrow 1\}$
$B_2 \leftrightarrow B_2$	0.880	$\{\cap \leftrightarrow \cap, \, - \leftrightarrow -, \, 0 \leftrightarrow 0\}$

The first of these will turn out to be correct; the second involves an inconsistency as to the analogue of $\cap$ from right to left. Kling's EXTENDER returns B_2 as the only analogue for itself, and thus would, once again, be led into trouble. The cause of the problem is again the reliance on the identical symbols heuristic.

For B_3, the filter returns just one candidate, B_3 itself, which leads to a single match. Note that this was the example which led Kling's EXTENDER to propose 17 different analogues.

Conclusions The examples given above show how the two stages of the AOI combine to find analogues which match well according to the analogy heuristics and the initial mapping between the problems. The flexibility of both the filter and the matcher enable good analogues to be found, even if this involves extending the mapping with non-identical associations. The map extension is based on the same general principles as the initial map formation between problems, rather than special purpose procedures, as with Kling's EXTENDER. The examples given above are typical, and were not carefully chosen so that Kling's procedures failed on them.

It would be quite possible to use each stage of the AOI without the other. We could try matching against all clauses in the knowledge base without first filtering; or we could just use the filter, and return the candidate list as the plausible analogues without using the matcher to distinguish between them. The problem with the first of these strategies would be that the AOI would be very expensive, and would become even more so as the knowledge base expanded. The problem with the second is that the AOI will not be so discriminating, and will not return structural correspondences; however, the latter problem will be mitigated by the fact that the candidates will be discriminated anyway when an attempt is made to apply them in plan application; the question is whether the extra cost of attempting and failing to apply bad analogues is greater than the cost of matching to find the promising ones beforehand. We cannot settle this question here, but will return to it again in Chapter 6.

5.5 Mapping inference positions

The ACR and AOI procedures described above are used to map the intermediate steps and axioms respectively of the base proof. However, important constituents of the base proof which are not covered by these procedures are the **inference positions**, i.e. the positions of the unified literals in their clauses in the case of binary resolution, and, in addition, the position of the rewritten subterm and the direction of application of the equality in the case of paramodulation. We can use an analogy to predict the positions of the corresponding inferences in the target proof – the analogous positions. For example, suppose we are considering the following base inference, an application of paramodulation:

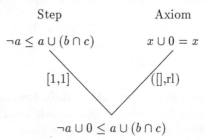

Step   Axiom

$$\neg a \leq a \cup (b \cap c) \qquad x \cup 0 = x$$

$$[1,1] \qquad\qquad ([],\text{rl})$$

$$\neg a \cup 0 \leq a \cup (b \cap c)$$

This means that the subterm at position $[1,1]$ in the step, a, is rewritten by the equation $x \cup 0 = x$ used from right to left. Suppose also that we have mapped the step and the axiom, using the ACR and AOI, in the following way:

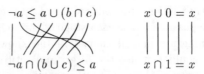

$$\neg a \leq a \cup (b \cap c) \qquad x \cup 0 = x$$

$$\neg a \cap (b \cup c) \leq a \qquad x \cap 1 = x$$

Then, using the structural correspondences shown,[7] obtained from the mapping procedures, we can map the entire step, including inference positions

---

[7]Recall that the ACR, described in Section 5.3, produces a structural correspondence between a term and its analogue as a side effect

to:

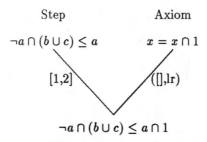

The inference positions, [1,1] and ([],rl), are mapped via the structural correspondences shown; without the correspondences, the positions could not be mapped. The value of the mapped positions is well illustrated by the current example. There are six ways of applying the axiom $x = x \cap 1$ to the clause $\neg a \cap (b \cup c) \leq a$: we can use the mapped positions to try the indicated way first; in the context of a developing analogy, we have good grounds for expecting the indicated inference to be the one most likely to lead to success; if it does not, we can return and try other ways. If the positions were not mapped, we would not have grounds for choosing between the six possible inferences; over several successive steps, this could lead to an unmanageable search space, even assuming that the analogous axioms were the correct ones.

Chapter 6

Plan application

In this chapter we consider the final stage of Basic APS, namely the application of the analogical plan. The analogical plan is constructed from the base proof by the procedures described in the previous chapter and is used to guide the search of the underlying problem solving system on the target problem.

It is possible to take a straightforward approach to the application of analogical plans. The advice given by the plan is interpreted strictly, with little or no deviation from the plan allowed. Such application systems are relatively easy to design and program, but tend only to work on simple analogies. Nevertheless, the ways in which simple systems fail is instructive for the design of more sophisticated application systems. In Section 6.1, we describe the design of some simple systems, and give examples of their performance. We also use these systems to consider some important issues in plan application, specifically:

- What information from the base proof should be used in the construction and application of the analogical plan.

- Should the construction and application stages be separated (i.e. we construct the entire plan before applying any of it) or interleaved (we construct the plan step by step as application proceeds).

In Section 6.2, we go on to describe research done on more sophisticated, flexible application systems. We will be particularly concerned with the **control architectures** of such systems, and with the **patching operators** which the systems use in order to overcome flaws in the plan. We motivate the discussion with numerous examples of apparently simple analogies which cannot be applied by the simple systems.

6.1   Simple plan application

In this section we describe some simple systems for applying analogical plans.
We demonstrate their effectiveness on some example analogies, and compare their performance with an unguided breadth-first theorem prover. Our
purpose is three-fold. Firstly to demonstrate that the matching and plan
construction procedures described in previous chapters can be co-ordinated
in a straightforward way to complete the Basic APS framework. Secondly to
address the issue of what information should be represented in the analogical plan — we present some comparative results and draw some conclusions.
Thirdly to motivate the following section — we will have a reference system
from which to discuss the **patching** of analogical plans, i.e. what to do
when they break down.

The systems we describe in this section are all based on *depth-first* exploration of the various choices in a plan, and are not able to patch plans, except
by appending inference steps onto the end. While the analogies which can be
successfully applied by these systems are close ones, the problems themselves
can be hard, in terms of having very large search spaces for an unguided theorem prover. Thus we demonstrate that the use of the analogy dramatically
reduces the amount of search and time spent on the problems.

We use a resolution theorem prover ([10]) as the underlying inference
mechanism in this section. Before developing the analogy application systems, we briefly describe the theorem prover.

6.1.1   A resolution/paramodulation system

Our underlying theorem proving system has two inference rules: **binary
resolution** and **paramodulation** (essentially the replacing of equals by
equals). The proofs which the analogy system accepts as base proofs and
those which it produces as target proofs are thus resolution/paramodulation
proofs.

The basic procedures of the system are those which apply the inference
rules to a pair of clauses: the **binary resolution procedure** takes as input
two clauses (skolemised disjunctions of literals; literals being either atoms or
negated atoms) with a pair of literal positions; resolution of the clauses on
the specified pair of literals is attempted. If successful the derived clause is
returned as output. If the literal positions are unspecified, all possible ways
of resolving the clauses are attempted, and the set of possible resolvents is
returned as output.

The **paramodulation procedure** also takes a pair of clauses as input,
with a pair of literal positions, a direction (left-to-right or right-to-left) for
the first position, and a subterm position for the second; paramodulation of

the second clause by the equality in the specified literal position of the first clause, in the specified direction at the specified literal and subterm position, is attempted. If successful the derived clause is returned as output. As with binary resolution, if the inference positions are not specified, paramodulation is attempted in all possible ways between the clauses, the set of derived clauses being returned as output.

The ability to specify the inference positions to the inference rules is important for the analogy systems since they try, if possible, to make inferences in the target at positions analogous to those which occurred in the base. As explained at the end of the previous chapter, this ability can reduce considerably the branching rate.

In addition to the basic inference rules, we refer to an unguided breadth-first search theorem prover which makes use of the inference rules. We use this simple theorem prover for two purposes. Firstly, as part of the analogy application systems — to take over from plan application when the latter has worked through the plan without completing the solution to the target problem. Secondly as an alternative problem solver with which we can compare the analogy systems. The theorem prover is based on the **set of support** strategy ([4]); the set of support consists of all clauses which are either goal clauses or which have goal clauses as ancestors in their derivations; inferences (by binary resolution or paramodulation) are made between a clause from the set of support and some other clause (whether on the set of support or not); i.e. axioms are never resolved or paramodulated with each other directly.

The breadth-first strategy works as follows. Initially the depth of the search is zero and the goal clauses are assigned depth zero; at a particular depth, each clause from the set of support at that depth is resolved and paramodulated with all other clauses from the search space; any inferred clause which is subsumed by a previously inferred clause is deleted; similarly, any previously inferred clause which is subsumed by a newly inferred clause is removed from the search space; each inferred clause which is retained is assigned depth one greater than the current depth. This procedure is repeated for successively increasing depths until either the empty clause is derived, the machine runs out of space or the program is stopped by the user.

6.1.2 A framework for analogy application

The application systems which are described in this section are all based on the same framework for the application of analogical plans: the steps in the plan are verified successively, starting from the negated goals and continuing to the derivation of the empty clause in the base proof. Where there is more than one possibility at a position in the plan, for example if a base axiom has several candidate analogues, each possibility is tried in turn; if a possibility fails — either the axiom cannot be applied successfully, or, if it can, the plan fails at a later stage — another candidate is tried. Thus the strategy for plan execution is depth-first search through the various choice points in the plan. Note that the choices will, in general, have been ordered according to an estimate of their plausibility (by the strength of analogy matches, for example). The most plausible will be tried first. The ordering may be fixed when the plan is constructed, or derived dynamically as application proceeds. Thus, the strategy is something between depth-first and best-first search.

6.1.3   Issues in plan construction and application

What information should the plan contain?

The tools so far described make the following information available for the plan for the solution to the target problem:

- *Goal analogues.* Analogues for the goal clauses used in the base proof.

- *Intermediate steps.* Analogues for steps in the base proof, produced by the ACR.

- *Candidate axioms.* Sets of candidate analogues for axioms used in the base proof, produced by the AOI.

- *The tree structure of the plan,* including the inference rules applied (binary resolution or paramodulation) and the inference positions, as described above.

Published analogy systems use plans involving different constituents: Kling's system ZORBA ([29]) only makes use of the axioms which were applied in the base proof; no attention is paid to the intermediate steps from the base proof, or to the structure of the base proof. The program synthesis system PRL ([11]) contains a small analogy component which also pays no attention to intermediate steps from the base — it uses axiom plans, like ZORBA, but also takes account of the structure of the base proof. Munyer ([33]) describes two analogy application systems neither of which pays any attention to the axioms from the base proof; the analogical plans in these systems consist principally of intermediate steps together with the structure of the base solution (apparently, no inference positions from the base are used though).

So, previous authors have differed in their opinions about the nature of analogical plans, just as they have in the heuristics which their systems use. Furthermore, as in the case of the matching algorithms (see Chapter 3), there has been little discussion of the relative usefulness of the various possible constituents of analogical plans. We consider the following possibilities for the composition of the plan:

- *Axiom plan.* The plan contains a candidate set of analogues for each axiom which was used in the base proof, produced by a call to the AOI routine. Intermediate steps are not used at all. This means that only the inference positions in the axioms can be used since those in the intermediate steps depend on the structural correspondence given by the ACR. In terms of the framework described above, local failure of the plan and backtracking is caused by the failure to apply any of the possible axioms at a step. That is, there are no intermediate steps which could be used to prune the search. However, the checking with intermediate steps (the special unification procedure described below) turns out to be an expensive process. So, while the search space may be larger with an axiom plan, it may nevertheless be searched more quickly. The (one-sided) inference positions can be used to order the possible inferences between an axiom and a step — that is, inferences (if any) at the specified axiom position can be tried first, others being tried on backtracking if these fail.

  As explained above, Kling's system ZORBA, and the analogy facility of PRL, both use axiom plans. Easy analogies tend to suggest axiom plans — solving the target problem merely requires applying the same, or similar, axioms to those used in the base, in the same order; checking with intermediate steps does not seem to be necessary. This view is criticised in the conclusion to this section.

- *Step plan.* The plan contains an analogue for each of the intermediate steps which were passed through in the base proof, constructed by the ACR. No attention is paid to the axioms which were used. This means that only the inference positions in the intermediate steps can be mapped since those in the axioms depend on the AOI. A step is verified by trying to make an inference with any axiom from the axiom base, and then checking that the inferred clause matches with the next mapped step. Since the mapped step may contain some of the special symbols produced by the ACR, which have special meanings, the matching process needs to be an extension of ordinary unification, and is explained below. Thus, the intermediate steps are used to prune the search. Again, the (one-sided) inference positions are used to order the possible inferences between an axiom and an intermediate step, those at the specified position being tried first.

As explained above, Munyer's application systems make use of step plans.

- *Full plan.* Both candidate axioms and intermediate steps are used, calling both the AOI and the ACR as appropriate. We can use either (a) the two-stage AOI or (b) just the filter stage, as suggested in the previous chapter. In the case of (a), all of the inference positions in the base proof can be mapped and included in the plan. In the case of (b), just the positions at the intermediate steps can be mapped since the filter stage of the AOI alone does not produce structural correspondences between a base axiom and its potential analogues. A step is verified by attempting an inference with a candidate analogue, and, if successful, checking that the inferred clause matches with the next mapped step, using the special unification described below. Any inference positions which are available are used to order the inferences, as before.

Should the plan forming and validating procedures be separate or interleaved?

- *Separation.* The entire plan is constructed before any validation is attempted. This type of system was assumed, for the sake of discussion, in the previous chapter. It is conceptually easier to grasp a plan which is entirely formed before it is validated. However, a great deal of time may be spent mapping the base proof only to find that the validation procedure fails on the first few steps. Kling's system ZORBA separates the construction and validation stages.

- *Interleaving.* Steps of the base proof are only mapped as they are needed for making target inferences. This type of system would have the benefit of failing relatively quickly on a bad analogy. Munyer's application systems interleave plan construction and validation.

If a step plan, or a full plan of type (b), is chosen, it seems advisable to interleave formation and verification of the plan rather than to have them separate; this is because the plan formation process, in this case, is essentially just the ACR and possibly the axiom filter, both of which are relatively cheap; thus it is no great cost to have to remap the steps after backtracking. This enables the special unification to be called with as few special symbols in the mapped step as possible. If the whole plan is formed in advance, with

	Separate	Interleaved
Axiom plan	A	B
Full plan (a)	C	D
Full plan (b)	-	E
Step plan	-	F

Figure 6.1: Implemented systems

the initial mapping, there will be many defaults throughout the plan, which will repeatedly slow down the special unification procedure, which is much more expensive when many special symbols are present.

6.1.4   Summary of possibilities

Figure 6.1 shows the various possible systems within the framework being discussed, with those which have been eliminated marked with dashes. The six systems which have been implemented are given letters so that they can be referred to in the discussion which follows. The various systems are compared with each other and with an unguided breadth-first search resolution procedure.

6.1.5   Special unification

As mentioned above, there is a special unification procedure to check whether an inferred clause matches with an intermediate step mapped by the ACR. We need a special unification procedure because the plan steps (constructed by the ACR) may contain the following special symbols:

- The function symbol def; $def(T)$ in a mapped step means that the head function symbol of T, f say, is not in the current match, i.e. f is a default symbol in the clause. When matching against an inferred clause, f should be allowed to match with any function symbol. If f matches with g, the association (f,g) can be added to the existing mapping. In this way the default is overwritten; in future calls to the ACR, occurrences of f will be replaced by g without the use of def.

- The function symbol $bdef$; $bdef(T)$ in a mapped step means that T is an 'optional' argument. The step should be allowed to match with an inferred clause whether or not T is matched. For example, the clause

$$[(a * b)/b = a, bdef(a = 0)]$$

should match both

$$[(a * b)/b = a]$$

and

$$[(a * b)/b = a, a = 0]$$

A *bdef* term is allowed to match with any number of terms on the other side (i.e. more than just one); furthermore, if the term contains variables, these are not shared between different bindings. Such terms are produced by the ACR if symbols have had unmatched arguments in the past.

- The function symbols *poss* and *list*; these represent multiple possibilities arising from inconsistencies in the match (see the previous chapter for more details). They should be allowed to match if any of the possibilities would succeed. Thus

$$list([f(a,b), f(a,a), g(6)])$$

would match

$$f(x, x)$$

by virtue of the second possibility. Similarly

$$poss([f, g], [a, b])$$

should match

$$g(a, b)$$

It is straightforward to implement a special unification procedure which takes account of these possibilities. The structure of the procedure is the same as that of ordinary unification; the main difference is that, in addition to a list of variable bindings, a list containing information about the special syntax, if any, in the terms is maintained; this list records whether a default symbol has been overwritten yet, and, if so, what it is matched to; whether an optional argument has been included or omitted; whether a list of possibilities, either in the form *list* or *poss* has been restricted by the matching so far. In ordinary unification, whenever a variable is encountered, the variable binding list is consulted to see whether it has been bound; in the special unification, whenever a special syntax symbol is encountered, the special syntax list is consulted to see whether it has been overwritten, modified or omitted, as the case may be.

In addition to the above features, the procedure we use unifies modulo commutativity, for all known commutative functions and predicates; this enables minor patches to be made to the plan as a side effect of the unification.

The procedure produces a list of unifiers; each unifier consists of the usual variable substitution together with any extension made to the analogy by overwriting defaults. Whether or not the latter is made use of depends on choices made elsewhere in the particular application system.

6.1.6 Performance

We will test and compare the performance of the six systems on seven examples, two from Boolean algebra, one from rational number theory and four from arithmetic.

Examples

Boolean algebra The two examples we consider are:

- Problem 1. Prove $x \cup x = x$ by analogy to a given (non-standard) proof of $x \cap x = x$.

- Problem 2. Prove $x \cap x = x$ by analogy to a given (standard) proof of $x \cup x = x$.

We use the following axioms from Boolean algebra:

$$
\begin{aligned}
&1. && x \cap 0 = 0 \\
&2. && x \cap 1 = x \\
&3. && x \cup 0 = x \\
&4. && x \cup 1 = 1 \\
&5. && x \cap (y \cap z) = (x \cap y) \cap z \\
&6. && x \cup (y \cup z) = (x \cup y) \cup z \\
&7. && x \cap (y \cup z) = (x \cap y) \cup (x \cap z) \\
&8. && x \cup (y \cap z) = (x \cup y) \cap (x \cup z) \\
&9. && x \cap y = y \cap x \\
&10. && x \cup y = y \cup x \\
&11. && x \cap \bar{x} = 0 \\
&12. && x \cup \bar{x} = 1 \\
&13. && \neg x \leq y \vee \neg y \leq x \vee x = y \\
&14. && x \leq x \cup y \\
&15. && x \cap y \leq x \\
&16. && x \leq y \cap z \vee \neg x \leq y \vee \neg x \leq z \\
&17. && \neg y \leq x \vee \neg z \leq x \vee y \cup z \leq x \\
&18. && x \leq x
\end{aligned}
$$

together with the reflexivity of equality. Axioms 1–12 are standard Boolean algebra axioms; 13–17 relate the partial order in the algebra, $\leq$, to the lattice operations.

The standard proof uses the standard Boolean algebra axioms; the non-standard proof uses the extra axioms 13–17. While the goals are essentially the same, the given proofs are different.

Rational number theory   We use the single example:

- Problem 3. Prove

$$\neg rational(x) \vee rational(y) \vee x = 0 \vee \neg rational(x \cdot y)$$

  by analogy to a given proof of

$$\neg rational(x) \vee rational(y) \vee \neg rational(x + y)$$

We use a large axiom base, consisting of 45 axioms, some relevant to the theory, others not. We do this in order to test the systems on a large base, where the branching rate for a resolution system would be very high.

Arithmetic   The problems set are:

- Problem 4. Prove $x/x = 1 \vee x = 0$ by analogy to a given proof of $x - x = 0$.

- Problem 5. Prove $(x \cdot y)/x = y \vee x = 0$ by analogy to a given proof of $(x + y) - x = y$.

- Problem 6. Prove $\neg inv(x) = inv(y) \vee x = y \vee x = 0 \vee y = 0$ by analogy to a given proof of $\neg min(x) = min(y) \vee x = y$.

- Problem 7. Prove $\neg inv(x) = inv(y) \vee x = y \vee x = 0 \vee y = 0$ by analogy to another proof of $\neg min(x) = min(y) \vee x = y$.

We use the following axioms from arithmetic:

$$
\begin{array}{rl}
1. & x + y = y + x \\
2. & x \cdot y = y \cdot x \\
3. & x + y + z = x + (y + z) \\
4. & (x \cdot y) \cdot z = x \cdot (y \cdot z) \\
5. & x + 0 = x \\
6. & x \cdot 1 = x \\
7. & x + min(x) = 0 \\
8. & x \cdot inv(x) = 1 \vee x = 0 \\
9. & x - y = x + min(y) \\
10. & x/y = x \cdot inv(y) \vee y = 0 \\
11. & x \cdot y = x \cdot y \\
12. & x + y = x + y
\end{array}
$$

together with reflexivity for equality; min/1 represents unary minus, to distinguish it from binary subtraction; similarly inv/1 represents inversion.

Results   The following table gives times for the solution of the various problems by the various systems. 'Fail' means that the program either runs out of space, or is interrupted having got irreparably bogged down. The times refer to compiled Quintus Prolog on a Sun 3 workstation.

Problem	A	B	C	D	E	F
1	42s	26s	48s	27s	11s	14s
2	1m29s	1m50s	1m1s	47s	17s	2m11s
3	1m11s	2m5s	1m19s	2m7s	42s	1m37s
4	23s	17s	25s	20s	9s	25s
5	fail	fail	45s	27s	23s	57s
6	fail	fail	1m55s	1m3s	57s	30m
7	fail	fail	3m45s	2m16s	2m33s	fail

- Problem 1. All the programs find the same proof for the target, without any backtracking, i.e. the plan suggests the right inference in every case. Figure 6.3 shows the base and target proofs[1] (Figure 6.2 explains the notation used in all of the application diagrams which follow). This example, and problem 2, are examples of 'perfect' analogies, where the target and base proofs are isomorphic, differing only in the identity of the symbols in the goals, axioms and steps. It is important for analogy systems to be able to solve easy analogies like this one; if they cannot, their claims on harder analogies become suspect; we argue below that previous analogy systems would not be able to solve problems such as 1 and 2.

The axiom plan systems (A and B) find the proof faster than the corresponding full plan systems (C and D); the latter are slowed up by the checking with mapped steps, which is not necessary in this case since the right inferences are always suggested anyway. The full plan (b) (E) system is the quickest of all; this is because the axiom filter which it uses is successful in reducing possibilities, and the extra work which other systems do to match axioms fully is not necessary. The step plan system (F) is also quick; the cost of trying to apply axioms and matching the results with the intermediate steps turns out to be less than the cost of the full matching within AOI.

Also, the interleaving systems (B and D) are quicker than the corresponding separate systems (A and C); their use of the extended match pays off, and there is no backtracking which would force them to re-match axioms.

---

[1]The labels on the steps in the proof show the number of the axiom which was used, and the inference rule which was used ('binres' for binary resolution and 'paramod' for paramodulation). The plan steps are not shown in the figures.

- Problem 2. Again, all programs succeed and find the same proof for the target. The full plan systems do so without backtracking, but the axiom plan systems (A and B) and the step plan system (F) do have to backtrack. The extra search made by A, B and F is shown with dotted lines in Figure 6.4; dead ends in the search are represented by triangles; for F, the extra search is caused by the application of axiom 4 at the second step, which matches with the corresponding plan step (not shown in the figure) but leads to a dead end; for A and B, the search arises because there are four ways to apply axiom 11, in the specified position, at the fourth step, the third of which leads to the solution; the first two inferences lead to dead ends after one more step. This extra search is responsible for the slower times for A and B; the interleaving system, B, is slowed down more by the extra search than the separate system A, since it involves rematching axiom 2 for each branch.

  For the same reasons as before the full plan (b) system (E) is quickest of all, while the step plan system (F) is slowest — in this case much time is spent trying to apply the wrong axioms.

- Problem 3. Again, all programs succeed and find the same proof (see Figure 6.5). However, all require some backtracking to do so; in all cases, axiom 1 is tried first at the first step, and leads to failure; the full plan and step plan systems fail after two steps, since the inferred clauses do not match with the plan; the axiom plan systems do some extra search since they do not have the intermediate steps to prune it; this leads to dead ends in each case after one more step. System A, which does not extend the mapping as application proceeds, makes a similar mistake again at the third step (preferring the association $- \leftrightarrow -$ to $- \leftrightarrow /$), and does some extra search, applying axiom 2 in seven ways before backtracking onto the solution path.

  The backtracking causes the interleaving systems to be slower than the corresponding separate systems on this example, the cost of rematching axiom 2 outweighing the advantage of using the extended match.

  Again the full plan (b) system is quickest of all; the lack of inference positions in the axioms does not lead to any extra search.

  This example is somewhat more difficult than the previous ones, in that the target and base proofs are not isomorphic — some clauses in the target have extra conditions, and the target proof contains extra steps; the last two steps in the target are made by breadth-first search after the plan has been exhausted without the empty clause being derived.

- Problem 4. This problem turns out to be very easy for all the systems, which find the proof (not shown) with no backtracking. The relative speeds are similar, with similar reasons, to those for Problem 1.

- Problem 5. The axiom plan systems both fail on this example, becoming bogged down in fruitless inferences. The other systems succeed, finding the proof shown with unbroken lines in Figure 6.6; the axiom plan systems make the wrong inference (shown with dotted lines) at the second step, get bogged down in the resulting search and so do not manage to backtrack to the second step and correct the inference. The wrong inference is made because of the lack of the inference position in the step, which is what enables the other systems to avoid the problem.

  For the full plan (a) systems, the interleaving one (D) is quicker than the separate one (C), since there is no backtracking to offset the advantage of using the extended match. Again, the full plan (b) system is quickest of all, for the same reasons as before.

  This example, and the two which follow, are similar to problem 3, in that the proofs are not isomorphic, the plan being patched by search at the end; they turn out to be more difficult because the choice of the wrong axiom can have more severe consequences in a long proof containing many applications of paramodulation (particularly for the axiom plan systems).

- Problem 6. The axiom plan systems again fail on this example, being unable to recover from the application of the wrong axiom at the first step. The other systems make the same mistake, but are able to prune the fruitless search by the special unification with plan steps. Systems C and F both do some more extra search later on in the solution, shown with dotted lines in Figure 6.7; the use of the extended match in the AOI enables systems D and E to avoid the extra search.

  Again, the interleaving systems prove to be much quicker on this more difficult example. The step plan system (F) is extremely slow; it is slowed down particularly on steps which contain variables, as many clauses paramodulate with these.

- Problem 7. The full plan systems are the only ones able to solve this problem. The axiom plan systems cannot recover from applying the wrong axiom at the first step (as all the systems do), getting bogged down again in fruitless search, and unable to prune it with the plan steps. The step plan system (F) does not recover from making the wrong inference at the fourth step. Figure 6.8 indicates the search spaces.

1. Steps in complete proofs are indicated by clauses joined with unbroken lines:

$$\neg a \cup a = a$$

13,binres

$$\neg a \cup a \leq a \vee \neg a \leq a \cup a$$

The label indicates that axiom 13 was applied using binary resolution.

2. Search steps not part of a completed proof are indicated with dashed lines:

$$\neg(a \cdot b) \cdot inv(a) = b \vee a = 0$$

A,B:2,paramod

o

In addition to the axiom and inference rule, the label on a search step indicates which of the implemented systems made the step (in this case, A and B). Where the systems are not indicated, they are the same as on the previous step. For search steps, the axiom number and/or inference rule may be omitted from the label.

3. Dead ends in the search are indicated by the symbol $\triangle$.

4. Failed searches are indicated by the symbol $\bowtie$.

Figure 6.2: Key to following figures

Of the successful full plan (a) systems, the interleaving one, D, is much quicker. This is because, having backtracked to the first step and corrected the inference, no further backtracking is required — the use of the extended mapping means that the next application of axiom 12 in the base proof is mapped correctly first time; whereas the separate system, C, makes the same mistake again with the next application of axiom 12, and a similar mistake with axiom 1, each of which leads to some extra search. This example illustrates the advantage of extending the mapping during application – the current step benefits from experience gained at previous steps.

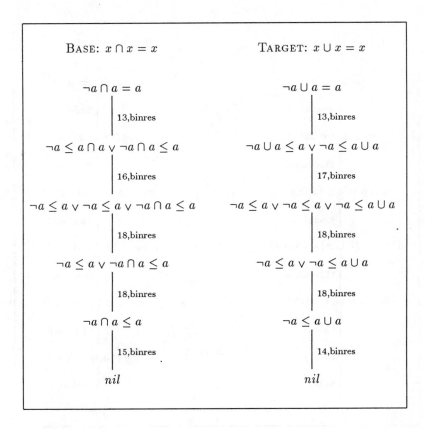

Figure 6.3: Problem 1

Discussion

Generally speaking, the analogy systems handled these simple analogy problems quite well. We contrast their performance with that of the unguided
breadth-first search theorem prover in the next section. We firstly consider
the relative performance of the various systems.

Full vs step vs axiom plans   The most clear answer to any of the issues
raised earlier is that the full plan systems are superior to the axiom plan
systems and step plan systems.

Their superiority over the step plan system is simply accounted for by
the pruning of search enabled by the AOI. Although the special unification

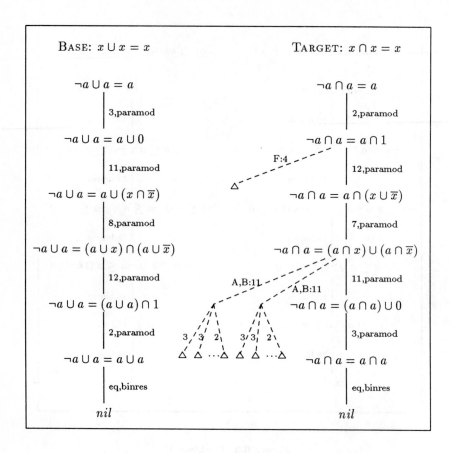

Figure 6.4: Problem 2

with intermediate steps enables the step plan system F to prune the search, the preceding diagrams do not show the many attempts which F makes to apply all possible axioms, which are blocked by the special unification; this accounts for the relative slowness of F, even when little extra search is shown on the diagrams.

The axiom plan systems work well for the easy examples, but their performance deteriorates rapidly on the more difficult examples. The full plan (a) systems are more expensive on the simple examples, but prove much more powerful on the more difficult examples. There seem to be two main factors in the shortcomings of the axiom plan systems:

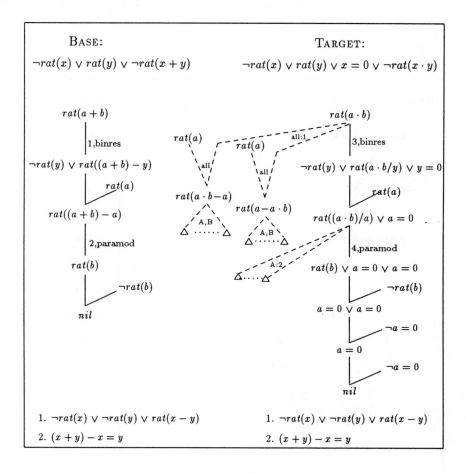

Figure 6.5: Problem 3

- The lack of inference positions in the steps leads to a higher branching rate for the axiom plan systems than for the others; the full plan systems benefit from being able to map inference positions in both axioms and intermediate steps; the lack of axiom positions in the step plan system turns out to be less important than the lack of step positions in the axiom plan system. This is because paramodulation, which is mainly responsible for the high branching rate, is usually applied with the equality as axiom and the intermediate step as the rewritten clause. The branching rate usually arises from being able to apply the equality

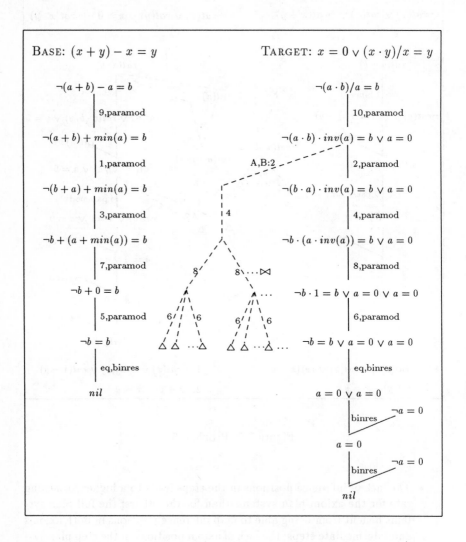

Figure 6.6: Problem 5

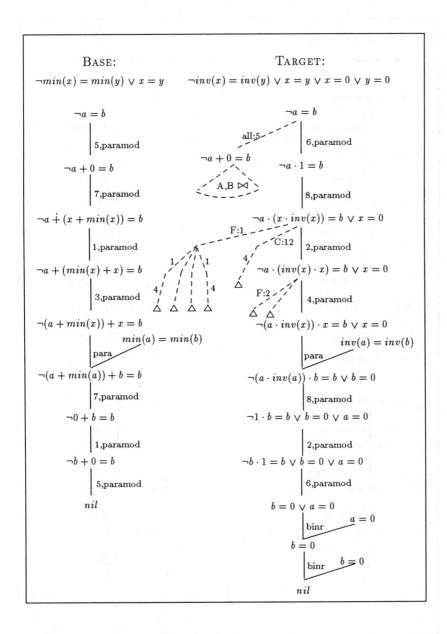

Figure 6.7: Problem 6

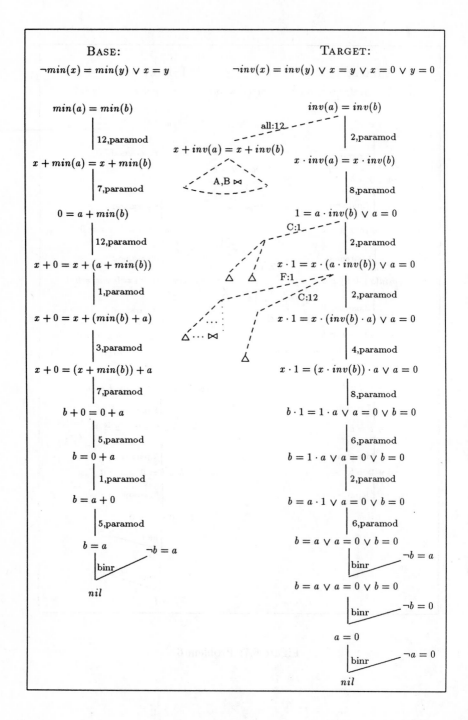

Figure 6.8: Problem 7

at various different subterms of the rewritten clause; thus is it particularly useful to be able to map the intermediate step inference positions in order to specify a preferred rewriting.

- The axiom plan systems cannot use intermediate plan steps to reject certain inferences and so reduce the branching rate, as the other systems can. This inability to prune the search is what leads to the failure of the axiom plan systems on some of the examples. In the full plan and step plan systems, the cost of matching inferred clauses with plan steps, using the special unification procedure, turns out to be easily outweighed by the benefit of pruning the search which it brings.

Separation vs interleaving   The results indicate that the extra matching involved in interleaving pays off, in terms of avoiding extra search, and quicker axiom matching and special unification. Of full plan (a) systems, the interleaving one, D, performs better, on the whole, than the separate one, C. The extra cost of rematching axioms after backtracking is outweighed by the advantages of using the extended match; the extended match not only makes matching with plan steps more efficient, but can avoid the need to backtrack by dynamically ordering the candidate analogues according to their consistency with the **current** match. The separate system, which computes analogues for all the axioms before any inference, can perform extra backtracking. This is most evident in problem 6, in which, as Figure 6.7 shows, system C makes two further incorrect inferences which system D is able to avoid by learning from its earlier mistake.

On most of the problems, the full plan (b) system (E) is the most efficient; the extra time spent in matching candidate inferences with mapped steps, using the special unification, is outweighed by the time spent by the full plan (a) system in calling the full analogy matching algorithm to distinguish further among the candidate analogues for axioms. On the more difficult examples (5, 6 and 7), there is not much difference between D and E. We cannot conclude from these results whether or not the two-stage AOI is preferable to the one-stage version; with the full plan (b) system, the special unification is effectively providing the second stage of the AOI; on more difficult examples, which require patching, (see the next section), it may be useful to have strong information about analogues for the axioms independently of our *immediate* ability to apply them successfully — the next plan step may be misleading, for example. In situations such as this, the two-stage AOI may well be superior to the one-stage version.

6.1.7   Comparison with unguided search and early analogy systems

The same problems were also given to the unguided breadth-first search the-orem prover described earlier; it was unable to solve any of them within 30 minutes. Furthermore, on only one of the problems (problem 1) had the prover managed to search beyond depth 2; since the proofs for the seven problems lie at depth at least 5, there was no point in letting the prover run longer. The average branching rate (including ancestor resolution and paramodulation) for problem 1 was around 30 (817 mutually non-subsuming clauses were derived at depth 2); assuming that this branching rate is main-tained at lower levels, the search space at level 5 would have size approxi-mately $2 \cdot 10^7$.

For problem 3, with a large axiom base, the branching rate was about 50 for the first level, and over 500 for the next level (the increase in branching rate is caused by the introduction of variables into inferred clauses, which causes them to paramodulate with many other clauses).

For the arithmetic problems, the average branching rate turned out to be around 50, which gives an estimated size for the search space to depth 10 (as in problem 6) of 10^{17}.

So it is clear that the analogy application systems are effective in guiding search in otherwise explosive spaces. The explosive nature of the search is indicated by the fact that the axiom plan systems are sometimes unable to recover from a single incorrect inference. While the analogies involved are intuitively close, the base and target proofs are significantly different, involving application of different axioms, and sometimes different numbers of steps.

6.1.8   Summary

In this section, we have seen how the techniques developed in earlier chapters can be used to guide search effectively within a resolution theorem proving system. We have seen the explosive nature of unguided breadth-first search within the domains we have considered, and have illustrated the dramatically reduced search spaces involved in the application of analogies.

We have also compared the effectiveness of different approaches to the formation and validation of analogical plans; we have concluded that the full plan systems, which make use of both the axioms and intermediate steps from the base proof, are more effective than either the axiom plan or the step plan systems. Furthermore, the extra work involved in interleaving the construction and validation of plans has proved to be worthwhile. We have not considered, in this section, any examples which, while intuitively close analogies, cannot be solved within the simple framework we have considered; we consider some such examples in the next section, and discuss how the application framework will have to be extended to cope with them. The conclusions we have drawn will also apply to the extended framework, i.e. the superiority of the full plan and interleaving systems does not depend on the simplicity of the examples which we have considered so far.

6.2 Flexible application

In this section, we discuss research done towards developing more advanced analogy application systems than the simple depth-first ones we looked at in the previous section. We first consider the limitations of the simple system.

Flawed plans We can define an analogical plan to be **correct** if there is a choice of axioms from the axiom nodes which allows each of the inferences suggested by the plan to go through, with the inferred clause matching the plan formula for the result, in the sense of the special unification procedure described in the last section, and the empty clause being derived at the last step. A plan is **flawed** if it is not correct.

To put it another way, we can think of the analogical plan as representing a large number of possible attempted proofs of the target problem: a plan is correct if one of these attempts is a valid proof of the target, and it is flawed otherwise.

The plan application strategy of the systems described in the previous section is to verify the plan steps successively, choosing axioms from the axiom sets, making inferences, and checking that the inferred clauses correspond to the plan according to the special unification procedure. Thus it seems that these simple strategies will never be able to apply flawed plans successfully. In fact, a certain type of flawed plan can be applied by the simple systems: when all of the plan steps go through successfully, except that the final clause derived is not the empty clause, the system attempts to finish the target proof by refuting the remaining clause in a breadth-first search. Problems 3, 4, 5 and 6 from the previous section involve flawed plans of this type which were applied successfully.

A more serious type of flaw is when a step in the plan will not go through for any choice of axioms at previous nodes, either because none of the candidate axioms will apply, or, if some do, the inferred clauses do not match with the next intermediate plan step. This type of flaw will cause failure in all the application systems of the previous section.

Of course, the plan might not be appropriate for the target problem at all, in which case it is right that it should fail; but many intuitively close analogies lead to plans which are flawed, in the strong sense (examples of these are given in the next section). As humans, we feel that these analogies provide useful guidance towards the solution of the target problem. Only close analogies lead to plans which are correct, in the sense defined above. Thus an analogy system which can handle more interesting and difficult analogies will have to be able to cope with flawed plans. The matcher FHM is able to construct many intuitively valid analogies which lead to plans which are at least slightly flawed. Several of the example analogies presented in Chapter 1 are of this form. This provides motivation for the development of more powerful application procedures able to apply flawed plans.

Often, the underlying cause of a flaw in a plan is that a 'short-cut' has been taken in the corresponding part of the base proof: in cases where the base problem is easier to solve than is the target, there is sometimes a direct way of completing a stage of the base proof which does not work in the target; a more roundabout sequence of steps in the base would achieve the same effect and have close analogue in the target. We will see examples of this phenomenon below. This phenomenon is similar to the **superficial difference problem** in matching which we described in Chapter 4: plan application must iron out superficial differences between the proofs (by patching) just as matching must do the same between problem statements. Overcoming these kinds of superficial difference facilitates post-generalisation: if, in order to match up the problems and then apply the analogical plan, we managed to remove the superficial differences, it is likely that some form of valid post-generalisation can be made.

For a flawed plan to be validated, it must be corrected or **patched**. That is, inferences other than those suggested by the plan must be made at some stage during application. As the examples given in the next section will show, flaws in analogical plans are often *local* problems — that is, extra inferences can be made which will allow the plan to be picked up again after one or a few steps. If the flaw can be successfully patched, the straightforward application can take over again.

6.2.1   Example flawed plans and patches

The question facing the designer of an improved application system is 'what to do when the next step will not go through?'. This happens if (a) the next indicated axiom will not apply to the step, or, if it does, (b) the inferred clause does not match with the next plan step. There are many possibilities that come to mind — try a different candidate axiom, backtrack to a previous step, try to add steps to make the axiom apply (if (a)), try to add steps to match with the plan step (if (b)), try to miss out plan steps, try a different plan altogether, try to develop some other part of the plan, and others. The plan need not necessarily be flawed for this situation to arise — it may be that a wrong choice of axiom has been made somewhere in the application. The first two possible actions mentioned above, choosing a different axiom and backtracking to a previous step, attempt to follow up this possibility. But these are the only actions which the simple systems can try. An improved application system will not immediately know whether a local failure arises because the plan is flawed or because a wrong choice has been made. It will not be feasible, in general, to search exhaustively the space indicated by the plan before deciding on what patching action to take. Therefore, the application system will have to consider the patching options along with the first two backtracking options.

The problem is which action to try first, and how to co-ordinate the investigation of the different possibilities. Before we consider the issues of control, we examine the possible causes of the local failure of a plan, assigning blame to particular parts of the plan, or choices made during its application. Each type of cause suggests a way of overcoming the local failure. We give examples of the different types.

- *Wrong axiom.* Perhaps the wrong axiom has been chosen out of the candidate set produced by the AOI, either at the present step or at a previous step. The analogy search spaces illustrated in the previous section (Figures 6.3–6.8) show cases where the axiom chosen first leads to a dead end, and it is another axiom from the candidate set, less favoured initially, which, when applied, leads to the solution.

  The cure for this problem is to try a different candidate axiom, either at the current step, or at a previous step.

- *Wrong plan.* Perhaps the entire plan which is being followed is inappropriate for the target problem, and should be abandoned in favour of another. In a realistic analogy system, this is bound to happen often because of the empirical nature of analogy.

  The cure for this is to stop developing the current plan and start on (or pick up again) another plan.

The above are the only situations which the simple analogy systems can deal with. The system is exploring the wrong branch of the analogy search space, and should backtrack to another branch. For the rest of the reasons for failure, we assume that the plan application is basically on the right track, in terms of the inferences that have been made so far. The failures are classified according to whether the step and the axiom suggested by the

plan are 'right' or 'wrong'— that is, whether they turn out to form part
of a solution to the target problem. These distinctions are not clear cut;
for example, an axiom suggested by the plan may turn out to be useful in
achieving the next step, but only along with the application of other axioms;
this would somewhat dilute its rightness. Here is the classification:

- *Step right, axiom right.* The hypothesised axiom and plan step for
  the next inference are right (in the sense that they both occur in the
  intended patch), but extra steps need to be inserted before and/or after
  the axiom is applied in order to allow the step to go through. Figure 6.9
  shows an example of a plan step which occurs in the attempt to prove
  the additive closure of the binary rationals by analogy to that of the
  ordinary rationals, i.e.

$$binrat(x) \wedge binrat(y) \longrightarrow binrat(x + y)$$

  by analogy to

$$rat(x) \wedge rat(y) \longrightarrow rat(x + y)$$

  The suggested analogue, A_1', for the base axiom A_1, does not apply at
  the expected step because the unification of the literals fails (symptom
  (a)). The problem is not that either the axiom A_1' or the next plan
  step is wrong, but that an extra step (boxed in Figure 6.9) needs to
  be added before A_1' is applied. When this step is made, A_1' applies,
  the inferred clause is found to match with the plan step, and the plan
  application proceeds, the problem having been overcome.

  A similar thing can happen with symptom (b), where the axiom applies, but extra steps need to be added **after** the axiom in order to
  match the inferred clause with the plan step. It may also be necessary
  to insert steps both before and after the axiom in order to allow the
  step to go through.

  So the cure here is to make extra inferences before and/or after the
  suggested axiom is applied (depending on which of (a) and (b) has
  happened), in order to infer a clause which matches with the next
  plan step.

- *Step right, axiom wrong.* It could be that, while the next plan step
  turns out to be right, none of the candidate axioms is right. This would
  happen if the analogue of the base axiom is not in the axiom base, and
  needs to be derived from the axioms which are in the base as a lemma.
  Similarly, the base axiom may itself have been a lemma, and thus it
  would not be surprising that the analogue would have to be proved as

a lemma. Figure 6.10 shows an example of this from Boolean algebra where, in the base $x \cap x = x$ is proved by using the lemma $x \cap (x \cup y) = x$. Supposing that the analogous lemma $x \cup (x \cap y) = x$ has not yet been derived, it is conjectured, being the analogue to the base lemma, and an attempt made to prove it by analogy to the proof of the base lemma.

The cure for this problem is to construct the analogue of the base axiom, conjecture it to be a theorem, attempt to derive it from the given target axioms, and then use it to make the next plan step. If a lemma was applied in the base, it would be reasonable to attempt the proof of the conjecture by analogy to the proof of the lemma in the base. The conjecture proving stage could be omitted, with the conjecture being recorded as a hypothesis for the target problem.

Alternatively, a number of steps (which would represent the proof of the lemma) could be inserted directly into the plan, without explicitly proving the lemma.

- *Step wrong, axiom right.* Perhaps the fault is not with the axiom, but with the plan step, which is misleading. Figure 6.11[2] shows an example of this which occurs in the attempt to prove

$$odd(x) \wedge odd(y) \longrightarrow odd(x \cdot y)$$

by analogy to

$$even(x) \wedge even(y) \longrightarrow even(x \cdot y)$$

The boxed plan step proves to be misleading,[3] while the analogous axiom proves to be (weakly) useful, along with other additional axioms. The step needs to be ignored, and the plan is picked up again at the next step after extra inferences are made.

So the cure here is to make inferences, with the candidate analogous axioms and perhaps others, and attempt to match the inferred clauses with steps later in the plan.

- *Step wrong, axiom wrong.* Perhaps the next inference in the base proof is not needed in the target, and both the axiom and the plan step should be missed out. Figure 6.9 with base and target swapped provides an example of this; there is an extra step in the (new) base which is not needed in the target.

---

[2] We have omitted some of the axioms used in this proof.

[3] Note the use of the list notation in the boxed plan step; recall, from Chapter 5, that the list represents multiple possibilities.

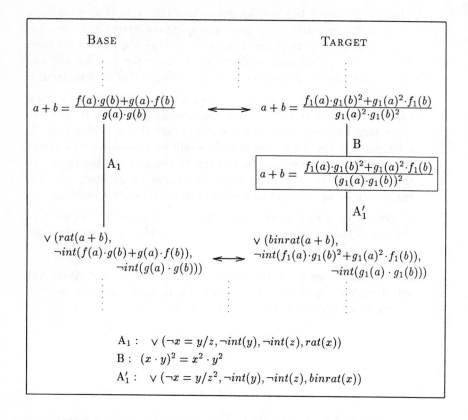

Figure 6.9: Extra step inserted

In order to patch in this situation, the following base axiom should be applied, and the result matched with the following base step. More generally, inferences may be made from the current step, and the plan picked up again at a later stage.

6.2.2   Structured versus unstructured application

One way of tackling the problem of flawed plans is to argue that the problem only arises because we are trying to follow the plan too closely. That is, the example flaws we have been discussing are only problematical because the application system *expects* a certain axiom to apply at a particular step and to produce a certain result. One way of avoiding the problem would therefore

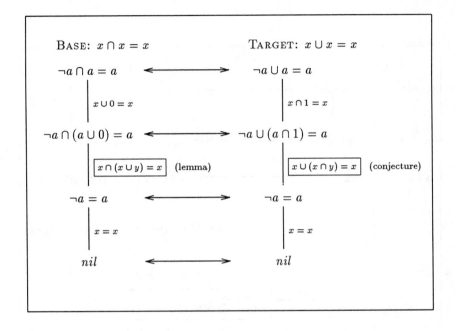

Figure 6.10: Conjecture made

be to use a looser notion of plan in the first place, which would not regard the above examples as flaws at all.

A good, if extreme, example of this approach to application is provided by Kling's system ZORBA ([29]). ZORBA constructs analogues for all of the axioms which were used in the base proof, as described in Chapter 5, and then simply restricts the underlying resolution theorem prover to these axioms in its search for a proof of the target problem. This does restrict the search to be a small fraction of what it would have been without the analogy (i.e. if the entire axiom base was used). However, no attempt is made further to direct the target search by attempting to follow the order and intermediate structure of the base proof. It is clear how this approach avoids some of the flaws which we have been discussing; for example, if a step which was made in the base needs to be omitted from the target proof, it will make little difference to ZORBA's application — perhaps only a subset of the analogous axioms will actually be needed in the proof of the target.

However, most of the flaws we have discussed would still result in flaws in ZORBA's application. For ZORBA, a plan is flawed simply when the theorem

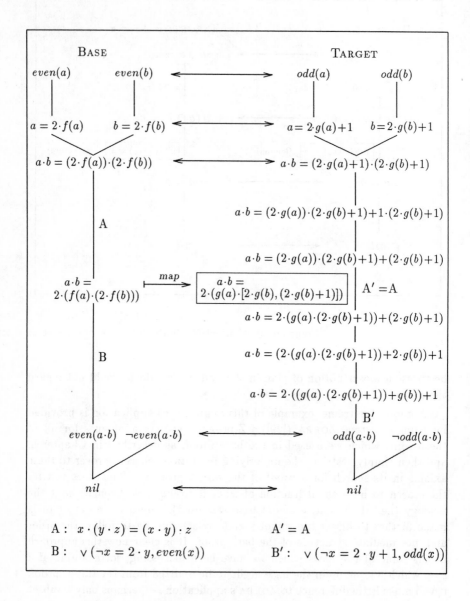

Figure 6.11: Plan step ignored

prover is unable to prove the target from the set of analogous axioms. Flaws which require the application of extra axioms in the target will tend to lead to flaws in ZORBA too. ZORBA has one patching operator — to extend the set of analogous axioms and then to try again. Thus it would be able, in theory at least, to recover from these types of plan breakdown.

So ZORBA is able to avoid some plan breakdowns by using a looser notion of plan. But this comes at considerable cost, since it loses the ability to use the structure of the base proof to guide the target proof. The examples of analogy application which we discussed in detail in Section 6.1 indicate how serious this loss of direction can be: the axiom plan systems, if they strayed from the correct track, frequently got irreparably bogged down in the search space of applications of the axioms in the plan. ZORBA uses considerably less direction than these, as it ignores the order in the base proof. Hence, we would expect that ZORBA would find the easy analogies of Section 6.1 very difficult to apply.

So, in comparison with ZORBA anyway, the structured application approach taken by [33, 1, 35] is more promising. The general goal of structured application systems is to exploit as much as possible of the base proof to guide the target proof, while being flexible enough to overcome differences between the base and target.

Munyer's **implicit planning method** ([33]) is some way between ZORBA and fully structured plan application. This method modifies a breadth-first search for a solution to the target problem by favouring the application of operators which are analogous to ones used in the base solution. Some of the structure of the base solution is used in application: operators from the base solution are chosen to be mapped on the basis of an assessment of similarity between *sequences* of operators in the base and the steps made so far in the target. As with ZORBA, this approach avoids certain flaws in a plan. Munyer reports some successes for the implicit planning method, but goes on to discard it in favour of his **explicit planning method**, which is a more structured application method. Munyer observes ([33]) that the implicit planning method is unable to exploit a base solution to the extent that seems possible intuitively. His argument is essentially the same one put forward in the previous paragraph.

6.2.3 The need for agenda-based control

The examples given above show that a competent analogy system will have to be able to perform a variety of patching operations. We now consider the important issue of the control mechanism which will direct the application of the various operations available in the analogy application system, both normal plan development operations and patching operations (in some cases there will not be a clear distinction between the two types).

The procedure for co-ordinating the various patching strategies described above should take account of the following points:

- In a given situation, we will not normally know which operation will lead to success, indeed if any of them will. We may well be able to heuristically order the possibilities according to some measure of likelihood, but the heuristics used will be weak; hence we should not follow the ordering slavishly.

- If the chosen operation does not lead to success (or indication of future success) after having been investigated for a while, we should devote some resources to one of the other possible operations. This will involve suspending the development of the first operation rather than aborting it, in order to give us the option of returning to the suspended operation if the others do not work out well.

- How far we develop a given operation will depend on how promising are the other operations which have previously been suspended or which have not been tried yet at all, as well as how successful the current operation is turning out to be.

These points rule out the depth-first application systems of the previous section — they will exhaustively pursue a given axiom, say, at the current node in the plan before they would consider the next possible axiom at the current node or previous nodes. This makes the ordering of the analogous axioms at a node critical to the success of the application; but there is often little reason to prefer one possibility over another initially. These simple systems are fine as long as they stay on the track of the analogy, but are poor at finding the track again if they ever stray off it.

We argue, along with [1, 2], that an **agenda-based** application system is needed to support the kind of flexibility called for above. The idea is that the current state of application is represented by a list of currently active development paths ordered by a heuristic measure of their promise. The most promising of these is developed further. As in matching, development will usually lead to a number of offspring nodes which are assessed as to their promise and merged with the rest of the agenda in order. An active node on the agenda will represent a partial application of the analogical plan from the base problem. That is, target inferences corresponding to some of the base steps will have been made leading to the derivation of an intermediate step, but there are more steps to make before the application is completed.

In the successful application of simple analogies, such as the examples given in the previous section, normal plan development operations (i.e. the application of one of the axioms returned by the AOI) are repeatedly applied to the most promising node; since each operation would be successful, the assessment of the offspring node will be at least as high as the parent node (in fact higher); hence the offspring will be installed at the head of the agenda and will be developed next. In simple cases, therefore, only normal development operations need be called on and no unnecessary search need be performed. Thus the agenda allows the application of simple analogies to be simple, and is therefore able to easily reproduce the results of the depth-first systems on the easy analogies of the previous section.

Of course the agenda is really designed to be able to handle less close analogies. Such analogies are characterised by breakdowns in normal plan development in ways that we have described and exemplified above. Given failure of the normal development operators on the current node, it will be reassessed by giving a numerical assessment of promise to the applicable patching operators — the new assessment of the node will be related to that of the most promising of the patching operators. The overall assessment of the node will probably drop somewhat. This may mean that another node is now top of the agenda, in which case control transfers to it. If the original node is still top, the most promising patching operator is pursued next.

In this way the application system can coroutine between different branches in the application space while directing most of its effort to the most promising possibilities.

There is some evidence to be had initially for the relative promise of the strategies, which can be used to set their initial assessments:

- If there are no good untried analogues at the present step, patching by conjecture is suggested.

- If the local failure occurs with symptom (b), i.e. the candidate axiom applied but the inferred clause did not match with the plan step, patching by search is suggested, rather than patching by conjecture.

The above evidence is not very strong however, and certainly not strong enough to fix a permanent ordering on the strategies. The evidence is used to put an initial ordering on the strategies, which may be altered later.

Note that the agenda may include nodes from previous steps, as well as those from the latest step; the present step could be the result of a patch made at a previous step; so, if the present step proves fruitless, other strategies at the previous step may need to be investigated. It seems wise to reward a node for the number of plan steps which have been made to reach it; that is, we should be prepared to put more effort into patching (by conjecture or search) after many plan steps have gone through successfully.

The agenda offers another flexibility not possible with the depth-first framework. The agenda can represent the partial application of more than one initial analogy match with a single base problem, and also matches with more than one base problem. Thus if initial matching does not distinguish clearly between candidate base problems, which is likely often to be the case in a realistic analogy system, the application system can be allowed to make the choice according to which base problem leads to a successful plan.

6.2.4   Patching operators

Having described a control regime capable of supporting a number of patching operators, we now describe some patching operators which have been proposed and/or used. We also give examples of their use in applying analogies outside the scope of the depth-first systems.

MEA rules for small patches

Various patching operators have been proposed in order to overcome particular occurrences of symptoms (a) and (b) above. With (a) for example an axiom suggested by the AOI has been applied but the result does not match with the plan step according to the special unification procedure. An appropriate patching operator would make a resource-limited attempt to bridge the gap between the inferred clause and the plan step by inserting one or more extra steps. With (b), a strongly suggested axiom does not apply at all. In this case, we attempt to bridge the gap between the current step and the axiom to enable it to be applied. We call these operators MEA (means-ends analysis) operators, as they choose steps to apply based on where they are and where they wish to end up.

The following patching operator is designed to make bridges of this sort:

> *MEA patching operator*
> Find pairs of subterms where unification (or special unification)
> fails. Attempt to rewrite the subterms from the current step
> to be unifiable (or specially unifiable) with the corresponding
> subterms from the axiom or plan step (depending on whether it
> is case (a) or (b)).
>
>   Use analysis of the head symbols in the subterms to choose
> which axioms to apply in order to accomplish the rewriting —
> i.e. if the pair of subterms have hfs's f and g, look for axioms

which can replace an f-headed term by a g-headed term, such as ones of the form

$$f(\ldots) = g(\ldots)$$

If the rewriting attempt fails, try again with the containing subterms at the next highest syntactic level.

This patching operator is very similar to the **double entry fetching** operator described in [1, 2], which attempts to enable the application of the next inference rule in the plan by finding a lemma which matches with both the current clause and the rule to be applied.

The technique of **gazing** ([37]) would provide a way of extending this operator to a more powerful but expensive one. In gazing, a more complete analysis of the symbols contained in formulae is used to produce a plan for the expansion of definitions. In our case, we would want a mini-plan for the application of rewrites to make the pair of terms unifiable.

For an example of the patching operator in action, we return to the example of Figure 6.9. In this case, the candidate axiom will not apply because the unification of

$$\frac{f_1(a) \cdot g_1(b)^2 + g_1(a)^2 \cdot f_1(b)}{g_1(a)^2 \cdot g_1(b)^2} \quad \text{and} \quad \frac{x}{y^2}$$

fails. From the unification algorithm it could be seen that the failure is caused by the two subterms

$$g_1(a)^2 \cdot g_1(b)^2 \quad \text{and} \quad y^2$$

The MEA procedure looks for axioms which can produce a rewrite of the form

$$x \cdot y \rightarrow z^2$$

The axiom

$$(x \cdot y)^2 = x^2 \cdot y^2,$$

assuming it was in the axiom base, would be selected and applied left to right, obtaining

$$\frac{f_1(a) \cdot g_1(b)^2 + g_1(a)^2 \cdot f_1(b)}{(g_1(a) \cdot g_1(b))^2}$$

The candidate axiom now applies and the inferred clause matches with the plan step, thus completing the patch described in Figure 6.9.

Another patching operator in this category is also described by [1, 2]: the **variable elimination operator**. This operator attempts to insert extra steps in order to allow the *variable elimination inference rule* to be applied. This is a special purpose inference rule used in the underlying natural deduction theorem prover on top of which the analogy system is built. An example of variable elimination is the inference of the goal

$$0 < a \wedge c \leq f(a)$$

from the goal

$$X < a \wedge 0 \leq X \wedge c \leq f(a) \tag{6.1}$$

The variable X is eliminated from the goal, using properties of the inequality predicates. To illustrate the patching operator, suppose that the step above had been made in the base proof, the following analogous step to 6.1 had been reached in the target

$$X < a \wedge 0 \leq X \wedge c \leq f(X) \tag{6.2}$$

and the application system next tries to apply variable elimination to X in 6.2. The inference rule does not apply directly, as there is another occurrence of X in the goal, within the literal $c \leq f(X)$. The term $f(X)$ is said to be a *shielding term* for X. The variable elimination patching operator would now be invoked, and would attempt to make inferences to 6.2 — specifically to the literal $c \leq f(X)$ — which remove the occurrence of X. For example, if the clause

$$g(a) \leq f(Y)$$

is an hypothesis in the current proof, it can be chained with 6.2 to produce

$$X < a \wedge 0 \leq X \wedge c \leq f(a)$$

This extra inference enables variable elimination to be applied, producing the new goal

$$0 < a \wedge c \leq g(a)$$

The search for hypotheses to apply in order to remove a shielding term is guided in a similar way to the double entry fetching operator described above: hypotheses containing terms which share constant and function symbols with the shielding term are given high priority.

The relax operator

Suppose that the inferred clause does not match with the plan step according to special unification, but would do so if the current mapping were extended.

We may decide to extend the mapping accordingly and hence accept the step.
For example, suppose the inferred clause were

$$q^3 = 4.r^3$$

and the plan step were

$$q^{[2,3]} = [2,3] \cdot r^{[2,3]}$$

which had been constructed from the base step

$$q^2 = 2 \cdot r^2$$

according to a current mapping

$$
\begin{array}{ccc}
q & \longleftrightarrow & q \\
r & \longleftrightarrow & r \\
2 & \longleftrightarrow & 2 \\
2 & \longleftrightarrow & 3
\end{array}
$$

This situation occurs in an example discussed below. The plan step does not
match with the inferred clause. However, allowing the match to go through
would add just one more association

$$2 \longleftrightarrow 4$$

to the current mapping. This would lower the assessment of the mapping,
but not by much. Hence this is a plausible action in this case. The plausibility is increased if the MEA operator is attempted first between the terms,
and fails to bridge the gap.

We term this patching operator the **relax operator**. The intuition
behind the name is that the application system should relax a little, and not
be so fussy over what it allows to match with what.

6.2.5 Operators for larger patches

Identifying the key step

The restricted patching operators described in the previous section handle
some flaws but not most. We now describe operators designed to make
larger patches than these. The idea behind these operators is that we can
often identify certain steps in the base as being the crucial ones, and we
can regard the other steps as being there only to enable the important ones.
If the analogy has broken down on one of the less important steps, we can
attempt to make a bridge to the (analogue of) the next important step. Such
a patch may involve several inferences.

Three ways of identifying the important steps in the base have been
proposed:

- *Motivation.* It is assumed that the base proof already contains the information as to what the next key step and hence the purpose of the current step is. In practice this information is provided by the user of the analogy system. This approach is described in [1, 2] where it is claimed to increase the power of the analogy system considerably. The term motivation is taken from [1, 2]. An example of how the base proof is annotated is:

$$... \text{(motive   ve   } X$$
$$\text{(chain (1) (2))}$$
$$\text{(chain (3) (5))}$$
$$\text{(ve } X))$$
$$...$$

The above covers three basic steps in the base proof: two applications of the 'chaining' inference rule (the numbers in brackets specify the clauses earlier in the proof which are being chained) followed by an application of the variable elimination inference rule (ve) on the variable X. In addition, the above specifies that the purpose of the chaining steps is to enable the variable elimination step to be made — this is the motivation for the chaining steps.

In [2] the key step is attempted *before* the less important step, which is only attempted if the key step cannot be applied immediately.

With the use of motivation, and the MEA rules discussed above, the MCC researchers report the ability to apply a number of impressive analogies, such as the following one from real analysis:

BASE: for sequences S_n and T_n, if S_n converges to s and T_n converges to t then $S_n \cdot T_n$ converges to $s \cdot t$.

TARGET: for sequences S_n and T_n, if S_n converges to s and T_n converges to t then $S_n + T_n$ converges to $s + t$.

- *Bottle-neck axioms.* In the absence of user-supplied motivation, we can sometimes guess the next important step in the base. The application of certain axioms, such as definitions, normally represents important stages of the base proof. The definition of a predicate or function is sometimes the only axiom which can make the necessary connection between symbols in the base proof. The analogue of the definition will be likely to play an equally important part in the target proof.

- *Symbol removal heuristic.* When proving something about certain objects (represented by symbols) it is common to introduce temporary symbols into the proof which are manipulated for a number of steps and then discarded to produce a statement about the original symbols. A step where such symbols are removed therefore represents the completion of a section of the proof. We can thus regard the step immediately following the removal as being an important one.

The use of these operators normally involves a search procedure which attempts to bridge the gap between the current clause and the step or axiom which has been identified as being important. Since we expect the patches to be small, breadth-first search is appropriate for this. Analogues of intervening base axioms can be given higher priority than others by not incrementing the depth counter for applications of them.

We illustrate these operators on one of the examples given in Chapter 1, and mentioned again earlier in this chapter:

$$even(x) \wedge even(y) \rightarrow even(x \cdot y)$$

$$\backslash \; | \; | \; | \; | \; | \; | \; /// $$

$$odd(x) \wedge odd(y) \rightarrow odd(x \cdot y)$$

Figure 6.11 shows the base and target proofs, and illustrates how the application breaks down. The first three steps go through analogously in the base and target, giving analogous steps

$$a \cdot b = (2 \cdot f(a)) \cdot (2 \cdot f(b))$$

and

$$a \cdot b = (2 \cdot g(a) + 1) \cdot (2 \cdot g(b) + 1)$$

The next step in the base rewrites the term into the form

$$a \cdot b = 2 \cdot (f(a) \cdot (2 \cdot f(b))$$

so that the definition of *even*

$$\neg x = 2 \cdot y \vee even(x)$$

can be applied again to complete the proof. This step cannot be mapped directly to the target, as illustrated in Figure 6.11. Both the bottle-neck axiom rule and the symbol removal rule would indicate that the next important step in the base is the application of the definition of *even* (B) — the symbols 2 and f are removed from the base proof by this step. The search procedure has therefore to make a bridge between the current step in the target

$$a \cdot b = (2 \cdot g(a) + 1) \cdot (2 \cdot g(b) + 1)$$

and the analogous definition of *odd*:

$$\neg x = 2 \cdot y + 1 \vee odd(x)$$

An MEA procedure like that described above would suggest the subgoal

$$(2 \cdot g(a) + 1) \cdot (2 \cdot g(b) + 1) = 2 \cdot y + 1$$

in which the variable y can be matched with any term in solving the subgoal. This subgoal would be relatively straightforward for a system with moderate algebraic manipulation capabilities — we assume that the analogy application system has such capabilities to hand and can solve the subgoal, rewriting the current target step as

$$a \cdot b = 2 \cdot (g(a) \cdot (2 \cdot g(b) + 1) + g(b)) + 1$$

This completes the patch; the next step goes through to complete the application of the plan and the solution of the target problem.

We now describe another example of analogy application which is enabled by the patching operators we have introduced. The analogy problem is as follows:

> Prove the irrationality of the cube root of two by analogy to a given proof of the irrationality of the square root of two.

The problems are formalised and matched as follows:[4]

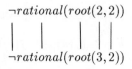

The base theorem is one of the most famous in the history of mathematics. Its proof eluded the Greeks for many years. In fact, the discovery of the proof undermined Greek mathematics which had been based on the belief that all numbers were rational. We now sketch the base proof and then consider how the analogy can be applied to prove the target theorem.

---

[4]We represent the root function by a binary function symbol *root* rather than the normal form $\sqrt[y]{m}$ so that we can show the analogy match more clearly.

We prove the conjecture by contradiction; i.e. we assume that $root(2,2)$ is rational; i.e., by the definition of rationality, that there exist integers p and q such that

$$root(2,2) = p/q \qquad (6.3)$$

and p and q have no common factors, i.e. that

$$hcf(p,q) = 1$$

We then rearrange 6.3 to obtain

$$p^2 = 2 \cdot q^2 \qquad (6.4)$$

which implies that 2 divides p^2, hence that 2 divides p, since 2 is a prime number; hence there is an integer r such that $p = 2 \cdot r$. We can now substitute for p in 6.4, obtaining

$$(2 \cdot r)^2 = 2 \cdot q^2 \qquad (6.5)$$

and rearrange to obtain

$$q^2 = 2 \cdot r^2 \qquad (6.6)$$

$$2 \mid q^2 \qquad (6.7)$$

$$2 \mid q \qquad (6.8)$$

Since we now know that 2 divides both p and q, we can infer that

$$2 \mid hcf(p,q) \qquad (6.9)$$

Since $hcf(p,q) = 1$

$$2 \mid 1 \qquad (6.10)$$

which gives us a contradiction, thus completing the proof of the theorem. A full proof of the theorem, with all of the steps expanded to applications of basic axioms takes 63 steps.

With the initial match between the problems as shown above, application proceeds in a straightforward way, with no patching required, up to the analogue of step 6.5 above:

$$root(3,2) = p/q \qquad (6.3')$$

$$p^3 = 2 \cdot q^3 \qquad (6.4')$$

$$(2 \cdot r)^3 = 2 \cdot q^3 \qquad (6.5')$$

However, the next step in the base, which is to reduce 6.5 to obtain 6.6, does not go through directly in the target. If we apply the reduction

procedure to 6.5′ (in an attempt to apply an analogous operator), we obtain
the equation

$$q^3 = 4.r^3 \qquad (6.6')$$

which does not match with the plan step computed from 6.6:

$$q^{[2,3]} = [2,3] \cdot r^{[2,3]}$$

There are various ways in which patching operators can be applied to
recover the track of the analogy. The agenda-based architecture allows them
all to be tried out. Which one actually succeeds will depend on the numerical
scheme which is used to assess promise. We just describe one of the possibilities. The relax operator described above is promising for this situation,
as allowing the step to go through just adds one new association

$$2 \leftrightarrow 4$$

to the current mapping. We assume that the relax operator is applied. The
next step in the base is the application of the axiom

$$x = y \cdot z \wedge int(z) \longrightarrow y \mid x$$

The same axiom is applied to 6.6′ to obtain

$$4 \mid q^3 \qquad (6.7')$$

The next step in the base is the application of the axiom

$$p \mid x^y \to p \mid x \quad [prime(p)] \qquad (6.11)$$

The $prime(p)$ condition in square brackets is checked as a pre-condition
for the rule's application. This avoids having to apply the basic definition of
primeness, which would be complicated. The attempt to apply this axiom
in the target fails, since 4 is not prime. Since this axiom is the only plausible
analogue for itself, another patching operator must be applied. The MEA
procedure between the current step

$$4 \mid q^3 \qquad (6.7')$$

and the antecedent of the axiom 6.11

$$p \mid x^y \quad [prime(p)] \qquad (extra)$$

would be a plausible candidate for a patching operator.

Again, we assume that this patching operator would be tried. It is straightforward for the MEA procedure to apply the extra axiom

$$x \mid y \wedge y \mid z \longrightarrow x \mid z$$

to infer $2 \mid q^3$ from 6.7′, which matches with (*extra*), allowing the axiom to be applied in the target, producing

$$2 \mid q \tag{6.8′}$$

which matches with the plan step computed from 6.8. Thus, the patch is made, and the analogy application is back on track. The rest of the steps in the target go through without further patching, completing the proof of the target theorem:

$$2 \mid hcf(p, q) \tag{6.9′}$$

$$2 \mid 1 \tag{6.10′}$$

Munyer's explicit planning method Munyer ([33]) describes an application system, the explicit planning method, which uses explicit plans constructed from the base solution to guide the target search. Munyer uses the term **skew** to describe a breakdown in plan application. To recover from such breakdowns, Munyer proposes the use of unguided breadth-first search. We can think of this patching operator as being a kind of MEA in that the goal is to bridge a specific gap in the plan; however, the unguided search operator uses no further guidance from the base proof, in contrast to those we have discussed above.

Comparison with Carbonnell's transformation operators In Chapter 1 we briefly discussed Carbonnell's proposals for application of analogies. Carbonnell proposes that the base proof be transformed into a valid proof of the target by successive application of certain operators, such as

'insert an operator application at a particular point in the plan'

and

'swap a consecutive pair of operator applications in the plan'

These transformation operators correspond to what we are calling patching operators. We could clearly define patching operators which perform operator insertion and swapping. It is noticeable that the patching operators we have described are more directed than the ones which Carbonnell proposes. For example, the result of the application an MEA patching operator, such as those described above, may be the insertion of an extra step into the target solution. However, the operator achieves this in a directed way, in order to apply some later operator, or reach some specified step in the plan. In Chapter 1, we observed that a Carbonnell-style application system would face a difficult problem of the control of the transformation operators. The patching operators we have described have been designed to alleviate the problem of control — they are designed to apply when and where normal plan application breaks down, and to achieve specific goals to enable the resumption of normal plan application. While the control of patching operators is still an important issue, it is made more tractable by their directed nature. This seems to be a more useful way of defining patching operators than by general-purpose perturbations to a plan.

Abstracting the base proof

The techniques for identifying important steps in the base can be thought of as ways of **abstracting** the base proof; that is, viewing the base proof at a level slightly higher than the sequence of axioms that was applied. This slightly higher level expresses the *purpose* of steps and indicates a strategic view of the proof. We have seen how this kind of abstraction can be exploited by an analogy application system. We now look at other ways in which the base proof can be abstracted which are useful to analogy; these methods involve direct re-expression of the base proof.

Abstracting subexpressions   In Chapter 4 we described how it is useful for the analogy matcher to be able to abstract subexpressions such as the following

$$2 \cdot f(x)$$

$$2 \cdot g(x) + 1$$

re-expressing them as

$$exp_1[x]$$
$$exp_2[x]$$

to enable the associations shown to be made, where

$$exp_1[<v>] = 2 \cdot f(<v>)$$

$$exp_2[<v>] = 2 \cdot g(<v>) + 1$$

That is, we produce an abstracted description of the subterms which just records the variables contained in the subterms. We now describe how this kind of abstraction can also facilitate the application of such analogies.

The example we discuss is the analogy between the following two theorems from analysis:[5]

> The sum of two uniformly continuous functions is itself uniformly continuous.

> The sum of two convergent sequences is itself convergent.

$$unif\_cts(F_1) \wedge unif\_cts(F_2) \rightarrow unif\_cts(F_1 + F_2)$$

$$cgt(F_1) \wedge cgt(F_2) \rightarrow cgt(F_1 + F_2)$$

We first describe the base proof to a level of detail sufficient to discuss the application of the analogy. The base proof we use proceeds by refutation: i.e. we begin by assuming that we have functions f_1 and f_2 (skolem constants) which are both uniformly continuous but whose sum, $f_1 + f_2$ is not uniformly continuous:

$$unif\_cts(f_1) \tag{6.12}$$

$$unif\_cts(f_2) \tag{6.13}$$

$$\neg unif\_cts(f_1 + f_2) \tag{6.14}$$

Expanding 6.14 with the definition of uniform continuity gives the following statement: there is an $e_0 > 0$ such that, for any D, there are $x_0(D)$ and $y_0(D)$ such that[6]

$$\neg |(f_1 + f_2) * (x_0(D)) - (f_1 + f_2) * (y_0(D))| < e_0 \tag{6.15}$$

$$|x_0(D) - y_0(D)| < D \tag{6.16}$$

In the following few steps, 6.15 is rearranged, using the definition of $+$ for functions, some simple rewrite rules and the property $|X + Y| \leq |X| + |Y|$, to derive

$$\neg |f_1 * (x_0(D)) - f_1 * (y_0(D))| + |f_2 * (x_0(D)) - f_2 * (y_0(D))| < e_0 \tag{6.17}$$

---

[5]In discussing this example and its application, we will use upper case letters to denote variables and lower case letters to denote constants, predicates and functions. This will enable the quantification of the formulae presented to be understood more readily.

[6]We use the infix function symbol $*$ to denote the function application operator, i.e. $f * x$ denotes the result of applying the function f to the value x.

We next expand 6.12 and 6.13 with the definition of uniform continuity:

$$\neg |X - Y| < d(E) \vee |f_1 * X - f_1 * Y| < E \qquad (6.18)$$

$$\neg |X - Y| < d(E) \vee |f_2 * X - f_2 * Y| < E \qquad (6.19)$$

Expressions 6.18 and 6.19 are then combined with 6.17, using a rule for reasoning with inequalities, to derive

$$\neg |x_0(D) - y_0(D)| < d(E_1) \vee \neg |x_0(D) - y_0(D)| < d(E_2) \vee \neg |E_1 + E_2| < e_0 \qquad (6.20)$$

We now apply the following rule

$$X < Y_1 \wedge X < Y_2 \rightarrow X < min(Y_1, Y_2) \qquad (6.21)$$

to 6.20 producing

$$\neg |x_0(D) - y_0(D)| < min(d(E_1), d(E_2)) \vee \neg |E_1 + E_2| < e_0 \qquad (6.22)$$

We now resolve 6.22 with 6.16 to derive

$$\neg |E_1 + E_2| < e_0 \qquad (6.23)$$

To refute this statement, it now only remains to show that we can choose values for the variables E_1 and E_2 so that $|E_1 + E_2| < e_0$. This is done by choosing $E_1 = e_0/3$ and $E_2 = e_0/3$ and using the fact that $e_0 > 0$. This completes the base proof.

We now describe the progress of the application of the analogy shown above in an attempt to prove the result for sequences. The first steps apply directly:

$$cgt(s_1) \qquad (6.12')$$

$$cgt(s_2) \qquad (6.13')$$

$$\neg cgt(s_1 + s_2) \qquad (6.14')$$

To make the next few steps, the definitions of uniform continuity and convergence are matched up by the AOI; for example, the definitional clauses

$$\neg unif\_cts(F) \vee \neg |X - Y| < d(E) \vee |F * X - F * Y| < E$$

$$\neg cgt(S) \vee \neg X > n(E) \vee \neg Y > n(E) \vee |S * X - S * Y| < E$$

Matching these two (and the other parts of the definition) involves abstracting subexpressions in the way discussed above. Given the current mapping, some parts of the above two clauses match easily, as shown above, leaving the residual matching subproblem:

$$(\neg|X - Y| < d(E), \quad \neg X > n(E) \vee \neg Y > n(E))$$

Variable analysis indicates that the two sides of the subproblem are compatible (i.e. each contains three variables). Hence simple abstraction is invoked, replacing the subproblem with

$$(\neg exp_1[X, Y, d(E)], \quad \neg exp_2[X, Y, n(E)])$$

where

$$exp_1[V_1, V_2, V_3] = |V_1 - V_2| < V_3$$

and

$$exp_2[V_1, V_2, V_3] = V_1 > V_3 \wedge V_2 > V_3.$$

Thus the original clauses are rewritten and matching completed as follows:

$$\neg unif\_cts(F) \vee \neg exp_1[X, Y, d(E)] \vee |F * X - F * Y| < E$$

$$\neg cgt(S) \vee \neg exp_2[X, Y, n(E)] \vee |S * X - S * Y| < E$$

This abstraction enables step 6.16 to be rewritten as

$$exp_1[x_0(D), y_0(D), D]$$

and for the analogous steps to 6.15 and 6.16

$$\neg|(s_1 + s_2) * (x_0(N)) - (s_1 + s_2) * (y_0(N))| < e_0 \qquad (6.15')$$

$$exp_2[x_0(N), y_0(N), N] \qquad (6.16')$$

to be made in the target. The rearrangement of 6.15' proceeds isomorphically in the target, producing

$$\neg|s_1 * (x_0(N)) - s_1 * (y_0(N))| + |s_2 * (x_0(N)) - s_2 * (y_0(N))| < e_0 \qquad (6.17')$$

Expanding 6.12' and 6.13', as indicated by the base proof involves re-expressing 6.18 and 6.19 in terms of exp_1 and matching with the corresponding steps in the target

$$\neg exp_2[X, Y, n(E)] \vee |s_1 * X - s_1 * Y| < e \qquad (6.18')$$

$$\neg exp_2[X, Y, n(E)] \vee |s_2 * X - s_2 * Y| < e \qquad (6.19')$$

The base proof then recommends combining 6.17′, 6.18′ and 6.19′ using the same equality rule as was used in the base proof; this goes through to derive

$$\neg exp_2[x_0, y_0, n(E_1)] \vee \neg exp_2[x_0, y_0, n(E_2)] \vee E_1 + E_2 < e_0 \qquad (6.20')$$

matching with the abstracted base step

$$\neg exp_1[x_0, y_0, d(E_1)] \vee \neg exp_1[x_0, y_0, d(E_2)] \vee \dot{E}_1 + E_2 < e_0$$

Notice that we are having to abstract all the intermediate steps in the base proof in order to make analogous steps in the target. The next step in the base proof causes a problem for our abstraction because it uses the internal structure of exp_1 to infer

$$exp_1[x_0, y_0, min(d(E_1), d(E_2))]$$

from

$$exp_1[x_0, y_0, d(E_1)] \quad \text{and} \quad exp_1[x_0, y_0, d(E_2)]$$

With the current match, which simply pairs exp_1 with exp_2 as wholes without further elaboration we cannot predict *how* the corresponding step will be achieved in the target. However, we can set up an abstracted plan step, analogous to the abstracted version of 6.22:

$$\neg exp_2[x_0(N), y_0(N), def(min(n(E_1), n(E_2)))] \vee \neg |E_1 + E_2| < e_0$$
$$(6.22' : plan)$$

Notice the presence of the $def/1$ function symbol in this plan step; this records the fact that we do not yet know what the analogue of min should be. It would be straightforward for an MEA procedure such as those described above to bridge the gap between 6.20′ and 6.22′ : *plan* once the occurrences of exp_2 had been expanded; the rule

$$X > Y_1 \wedge X > Y_2 \rightarrow X > max(Y_1, Y_2) \qquad (6.21')$$

would be applied twice to the expanded version of 6.20 to produce

$$\neg exp_2[x_0(N), y_0(N), max(n(E_1), n(E_2))] \vee \neg |E_1 + E_2| < e_0 \qquad (6.22')$$

in which the abstraction has been reintroduced. Notice that the abstraction has been used to recommend the correct goal in the target, even though achieving it is somewhat different from the corresponding step in the base. Thus the abstraction has enabled a patch to be made.

The analogy next recommends resolution between 6.22′ and 6.16′. Unlike the previous step, this step does not involve the internal structure of exp_2 and so can be made directly at the abstracted level.

The remaining steps in the base proof map over to the target isomorphically, completing the proof of the target theorem. This example shows how a
facility to abstract the base proof allows the application system to overcome
superficial syntactic differences between the base and target. Steps where
the differences do not play a part can be applied without patching; steps
where the differences do play a part indicate where a patch is likely to be
necessary. In this case, the patching operator was called *before* normal plan
development had broken down.

For another example which illustrates the importance of abstracting the
base proof in applying an analogy, we consider the application of the geometrical analogy which has already been introduced (see Chapters 1 and
4):

> The three lines joining the vertices of a triangle to the midpoints
> of the opposite sides meet at a point (the orthocentre).

> The four lines joining the vertices of a tetrahedron to the ortho-
> centres of the opposite faces meet at a point.

Figure 6.12 gives formal statements of these two theorems. In Chapter 4,
we described how a matcher can use symmetry analysis to re-express the
formal statements as follows and hence find the strong match between them
shown:

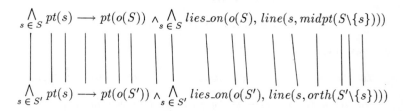

$$\bigwedge_{s \in S} pt(s) \longrightarrow pt(o(S)) \wedge \bigwedge_{s \in S} lies\_on(o(S), line(s, midpt(S\backslash\{s\})))$$

$$\bigwedge_{s \in S'} pt(s) \longrightarrow pt(o(S')) \wedge \bigwedge_{s \in S'} lies\_on(o(S'), line(s, orth(S'\backslash\{s\})))$$

If the base theorem is proved in the form in Figure 6.12, it will have to
be rewritten in order for the analogy between the abstracted problems to be
applied to it. This is because the base proof will not involve the same symbols
as the new form of the problem. Given such a major problem abstraction,
it is clear that the base proof will have to be re-expressed *before* application
begins. The re-expression of the base proof essentially amounts to extending
the symmetry, found within the problem statement during matching, to the
proof. How easy this is depends on how symmetrically the base proof is given.
To make things easy for ourselves, we assume a symmetric presentation. We

---

HYPOTHESES	HYPOTHESES
point(x) $\wedge$	*point*(x) $\wedge$
point(y) $\wedge$	*point*(y) $\wedge$
point(z)	*point*(z) $\wedge$
	point(w)
CONCLUSIONS	CONCLUSIONS
point($o(x,y,z)$) $\wedge$	*point*($p(x,y,z,w)$) $\wedge$
lies_on($o(x,y,z)$,	*lies_on*($p(x,y,x,w)$,
$line(z, midpt(x,y))$)) $\wedge$	$line(w, orth(x,y,z))$)) $\wedge$
lies_on($o(x,y,z)$,	*lies_on*($p(x,y,z,w)$,
$line(x, midpt(y,z))$)) $\wedge$	$line(x, orth(y,z,w))$)) $\wedge$
lies_on($o(x,y,z)$,	*lies_on*($p(x,y,z,w)$,
$line(y, midpt(z,x))$))	$line(y, orth(w,z,x))$)) $\wedge$
	lies_on($p(x,y,z,w)$,
	$line(z, orth(w,x,y))$))

Figure 6.12: Formal statements of analogous geometry theorems

assume that the base proof is structured as follows: each of the three *lies_on* conjuncts in the conclusion in Figure 6.12 is proved in a separate chunk of the base proof. For example, the chunk which proves the second of these,

$$lies\_on(o(x,y,z), line(x, midpt(y,z)))$$

would be as follows:

$$\forall a\ lies\_on(a \cdot x + (1-a) \cdot midpt(y,z)\ ,\ line(x, midpt(y,z)))$$

$$\forall a\ lies\_on(a \cdot x + (1-a) \cdot (y+z)/2\ ,\ line(x, midpt(y,z)))$$

$$lies\_on(1/3(x+y+z)\ ,\ line(x, midpt(y,z)))$$

This proves the second conjunct with

$$o(x,y,z) = 1/3(x+y+z)$$

The first step is an instance of the axiom

$$\forall \lambda, x, y\ lies\_on(\lambda \cdot x + (1-\lambda) \cdot y\ ,\ line(x,y))$$

The second and third steps are derived by expansion of the definition of *midpt* and simple rearrangement respectively. In the third step, the variable

a is instantiated to 1/3. The other conjuncts are proved symmetrically, the chunks being obtainable from the one given above by cycle permutations of (x, y, z). The essence of abstracting the base proof is noticing this symmetry, which is the same symmetry that exists within the problem statement. The abstraction of the base proof then proceeds in a similar way to that of the base problem statement did, giving the following abstracted proof:

$$\bigwedge_{s \in S} \forall a \; lies\_on(a \cdot s + (1 - a) \cdot midpt(S \backslash \{s\}) \;, \; line(s, midpt(S \backslash \{s\})))$$

$$\bigwedge_{s \in S} \forall a \; lies\_on(a \cdot s + (1 - a) \cdot 1/2 \cdot \sum (S \backslash \{s\}) \;, \; line(s, midpt(S \backslash \{s\})))$$

$$\bigwedge_{s \in S} lies\_on(1/3 \cdot \sum S \;, \; line(s, midpt(S \backslash \{s\})))$$

which gives

$$o(S) = 1/3 \cdot \sum S$$

where $\sum S$ refers to the vector sum of all the elements of the set S.

Given this abstracted form and the analogy match shown above, construction and application of the analogical plan is straightforward. The abstracted target proof is:

$$\bigwedge_{s \in S'} \forall a \; lies\_on(a \cdot s + (1 - a) \cdot orth(S' \backslash \{s\}) \;, \; line(s, orth(S' \backslash \{s\})))$$

$$\bigwedge_{s \in S'} \forall a \; lies\_on(a \cdot s + (1 - a) \cdot 1/3 \cdot \sum (S' \backslash \{s\}) \;, \; line(s, orth(S' \backslash \{s\})))$$

$$\bigwedge_{s \in S'} lies\_on(1/4 \cdot \sum S' \;, \; line(s, orth(S' \backslash \{s\})))$$

giving

$$o(S') = 1/4 \cdot \sum S'$$

Hence, at the abstract level, the two proofs are isomorphic. If an analogical plan was attempted at the given level of description, the application would involve major patches.

Both intuitively and computationally, abstraction seems to be necessary for this analogy to be found and exploited. The abstraction used, and our method for obtaining it, correspond closely with our intuitions about this problem. Notice how the abstraction needed for the proofs is a straightforward extension of that for the problems.

Chapter 7

Learning global analogies

In this chapter we consider how an analogical reasoning system of the type described in this book could improve its ability to reason by analogy in a domain, by learning global analogies within the domain or between domains. The motivation for this is that the analogical reasoning systems so far described exhibit a similar kind of dumbness as ordinary theorem provers, one level up: that is, APS systems are called for so that theorem provers will be able to learn from their experience, and not repeat exactly the same behaviour when faced with a problem similar to one which they have solved before. However, the analogical reasoning systems, as described so far, in searching for and then applying an analogy which was essentially the same as one which had been encountered before, would go through the same steps of matching, plan construction and application as they would have done had they never encountered the previous analogy. Just as superficially different problems can sometimes be solved in analogous ways, superficially different examples of analogical reasoning, where the respective base problems and target problems may be very different, can involve essentially the same analogy.

We claim that, by abstracting out important aspects of successful attempts to solve problems by analogy, we can re-use them beneficially in new attempts at APS. The aspects which will be abstracted will amount to a description of the analogy which was found and used, without details which are specific to the problems that were involved. Since the description is not tied to particular problems, but could potentially apply to any from the domain in question, we can think of it as describing a *global analogy* within or between domains. Thus, our technique for transferring experience over different instances of APS is to learn global analogies, which we hope will be relevant to many different situations.

In Chapter 3, we criticised Kling's analogy matching algorithm because of its use of **semantic types**. Recall how analogy matchers, such as Kling's, can make use of semantic types:

> Associations between symbols of the same (or similar) semantic type are preferred over those of disparate types.

How strong the preference is and how a given matcher implements it are separate matters. In Kling's case, the preference is very strong (in fact mandatory) and is built into the structure of his algorithm. We argued (Chapter 3) that the types which Kling provided for the matcher encoded a global analogy between group theory and ring theory; the matcher merely reconstructed parts of this global analogy between individual problems from group theory and ring theory respectively. However, we also argued that the use of semantic types would be valid as long as the types could be learnt automatically in some way. In this chapter, we consider the construction or refinement of type hierarchies corresponding to the global analogies that are learnt over the course of APS experience.

We then consider how the global analogies, or semantic types, can be used within the Basic APS framework as described in the previous chapters; that is, how they can improve the performance of the analogical reasoning system. This includes their use in matching, as discussed earlier, but also extends to other parts of analogical problem solving.

We also discuss how the knowledge of global analogies, independent of particular pairs of problems, would enable a broader and more varied approach to the construction and use of analogies; we discuss how this more varied approach reflects better the use of analogies by humans than does Basic APS alone. However, we argue that the Basic APS process, which has been the main concern of this book, is a necessary part of the other uses of analogy.

7.1 Semantic types and dualities

Before we describe the techniques for learning global analogies and semantic types, we define more closely the structures which we intend to learn.

7.1.1 Semantic types

The simplest definition of a **type hierarchy** is as a **tree**, the leaves[1] of which are labelled with symbols (function symbols, for instance) from the object language, and each non-terminal node is labelled with a set of symbols

---

[1]The **leaves** of a tree are nodes which have no daughter nodes.

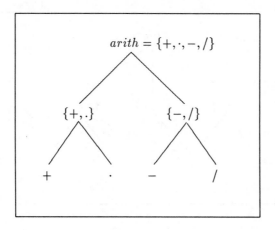

Figure 7.1: An example of a hierarchy

— the set containing just those symbols which label leaves below it in the tree. Figure 7.1 shows an example of a hierarchy.

(This example is intended to illustrate the definition — no significance should be attached to the particular choices of node made here.) However, it is sometimes useful to consider more general structures than these, such as is shown in Figure 7.2. So some researchers [36] have defined a type hierarchy as an **upper semi-lattice**. This definition is motivated by the desire to make the version spaces/focusing algorithm [32] work (i.e. for there to be unique least upper bounds in the hierarchy), rather than by any direct reasons why concepts should be clustered in this way. For example, the dotted line in Figure 7.2 would not be allowed, but there seems to be no good reason why the resulting concept structure should not occur.

7.1.2 Dualities

We have argued that we should learn *global* analogies within or between domains; that is, analogies that are not tied to particular pairs of problems, as those which we have considered so far are. We will use the term **duality** to refer to such a global analogy, in order to distinguish it from the local analogies between pairs of problems. We give the following somewhat vague definition of a duality within a domain:

A duality is (a) an association between some of the symbols in the domain together with (b) an association between

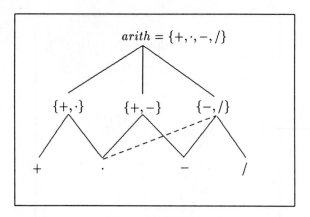

Figure 7.2: An alternative hierarchy

axioms/theorems of the domain such that associated axioms or theorems are approximately mapped to each other by the symbol association.

Remarks

- The definition is phrased for dualities *within* a domain. Dualities *between* domains are defined in the same way, except that, of course, corresponding symbols or clauses must belong to corresponding domains. All of what follows applies equally well to this kind of duality.

- The definition is vague because we have not said what 'approximately mapped' means. However, the notion is the same as that encountered in analogies between individual problems. We could define a measure of the closeness of a duality, reflecting the degree of correspondence between the associated axioms, based on the assessment procedure for analogy matches described in Section 4.4.

Examples

A: Real number theory.

$$(a) \quad \left\{ \begin{array}{ccc} + & \longleftrightarrow & \cdot \\ - & \longleftrightarrow & / \\ 0 & \longleftrightarrow & 1 \end{array} \right.$$

$$
\text{(b)} \left\{
\begin{array}{ccc}
x + 0 = x & \longleftrightarrow & x \cdot 1 = x \\
x + y = y + x & \longleftrightarrow & x \cdot y = y \cdot x \\
x - x = 0 & \longleftrightarrow & x = 0 \ \lor \ x/x = 1 \\
& \text{etc.} &
\end{array}
\right.
$$

B: Boolean algebra.

$$
\text{(a)} \left\{
\begin{array}{ccc}
\cup & \longleftrightarrow & \cap \\
\cap & \longleftrightarrow & \cup \\
0 & \longleftrightarrow & 1 \\
1 & \longleftrightarrow & 0
\end{array}
\right.
$$

$$
\text{(b)} \left\{
\begin{array}{ccc}
x \cup y = y \cup x & \longleftrightarrow & x \cap y = y \cap x \\
x \cap 1 = 1 & \longleftrightarrow & x \cup 0 = 0 \\
x \cup 0 = x & \longleftrightarrow & x \cap 1 = x \\
& \text{etc.} &
\end{array}
\right.
$$

C: Trigonometry.

$$
\text{(a)} \left\{
\begin{array}{ccc}
sin & \longleftrightarrow & cos \\
cos & \longleftrightarrow & sin
\end{array}
\right.
$$

$$
\text{(b)} \left\{
\begin{array}{ccc}
sin^2(x) = 1 - cos^2(x) & \longleftrightarrow & cos^2(x) = 1 - sin^2(x) \\
d/dx(sin(x)) = cos(x) & \longleftrightarrow & d/dx(cos(x)) = -sin(x)
\end{array}
\right.
$$

D: Abstract algebra.

$$
\text{(a)} \left\{
\begin{array}{ccc}
group & \longleftrightarrow & ring \\
subgroup & \longleftrightarrow & subring \\
normal & & \\
subgroup & \longleftrightarrow & ideal \\
& \text{etc.} &
\end{array}
\right.
$$

$$
\text{(b)} \left\{
\begin{array}{c}
\neg subgroup(h, g) \lor group(g) \\
\longleftrightarrow \quad \neg subring(h, g) \lor ring(g) \\
\text{etc.}
\end{array}
\right.
$$

Remarks on examples

- Example A shows the need for the word 'approximate' in the definition — one of a pair of associated sentences has a condition which the other does not have.

- There is no need for a duality to apply to all axioms/theorems on each side; we fully expect that some properties of one side will not have close analogues (or analogues at all) on the other. For example, the equation

$$
sin(2 \cdot x) = 2 \cdot sin(x) \cdot cos(x)
$$

does not have a syntactically close analogue in C.

- Example B is an example of a **formal duality**, where the symbol
  mapping represents a perfect symmetry in the axiomatisation of the
  domain, which ensures that, for any theorem in Boolean algebra, its
  dual under the mapping is also a theorem. Other dualities may be
  regarded as partial symmetries.

The idea behind the definition of dualities given is to be able to represent,
and hence exploit, situations where a part of a theory has similar structure
to another part (or a part of a different theory). Formal dualities, such as
B, are a limiting case of dualities, and do not seem to arise nearly so often
as partial dualities do. Thus we claim it is worthwhile to study the more
general kind, involving approximate mappings.

We discuss the exploitation of dualities in Section 7.6; to give a brief idea
here, they can be used in matching (in a similar, although potentially more
powerful, way to semantic types), in plan construction (by implicitly extending the mapping between problems, thus making the plan more accurate)
and in making and proving conjectures.

For partial dualities, successful exploitation will involve taking advantage
of the duality where it applies, while not wasting too much time trying to
use it where it does not.

7.2   Justification for use

In Chapter 3. we argued that the semantic type heuristic would be effective
in analogy matching if the types encode global analogies (what we are now
calling dualities). The means of encoding provides the basic connection
between types and dualities (which we will explore further in Section 7.3):

> Symbols which are associated by a duality should have the
> same or similar semantic type (i.e. are sibling leaves, or close to
> being sibling leaves, in the hierarchy).

Recasting the effectiveness argument in terms of dualities (i.e. using the
connection just given), we get a similar argument in justification of the use
of dualities in matching:

> *Analytical justification.* Pairs of symbols associated by a du-
> ality are plausible as analogues because they have structurally
> similar axioms/theorems associated with them: thus, given that
> the dual symbols occur in structurally similar formulae, and re-
> garding a solution as a sequence of structural rearrangements
> leading from a start to a finish, each arising from an axiom or
> theorem, it is likely that the two formulae will have similar solu-
> tions.

We could also take a more pragmatic approach to the justification for dualities, as in the following argument:

> *Empirical justification.* Analogies between individual problems often contain part of a global analogy (a duality) as well as more problem-specific elements: the associations
>
> $$+ \longleftrightarrow \cdot \; , - \longleftrightarrow / \quad \text{and} \quad 0 \longleftrightarrow 1$$
>
> often form part of specific analogies between problems, together with associations which do not belong to the global analogy. For this reason, symbols which are associated by a known duality are plausible as analogues within specific problems.

Just as it is possible to take both an empirical and an analytical approach to the justification of the use of dualities, we will see below that we can take both an empirical and an analytical approach to learning them.

Comparison with version spaces

As a brief digression, let us look at the success criterion for the use of the semantic type hierarchy in the inductive generalisation system LEX [32], discussed in Chapter 2: the hierarchy is used, by the **version spaces** technique, to **bias** the program towards making some generalisations, those that involve types from the hierarchy, rather than others. Once made, a generalisation will be applied to new problems containing symbols of the appropriate types in the appropriate places, i.e. if corresponding function symbols between the new and old problems are of similar types. The technique will be successful if the new problems, which match the generalisation, can be solved in suitably similar ways. This will be true if the types encode global analogies within the domain; i.e. the success criterion for the use of types in version spaces is the same as that in analogy matching.

This point is significant as it indicates that hierarchies may be shared between the different techniques. A refinement or addition to the hierarchy made by one of the techniques would be available for use by the other. Both uses for type hierarchies have associated methods for learning and refining them: [45] and [46] describe learning methods for generalisation; Section 7.5 describes learning methods for analogy.

7.3 Connection between types and dualities

In Chapter 3 we introduced the basic connection between semantic types and dualities:

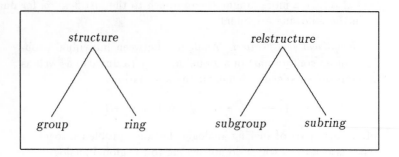

Figure 7.3: Algebraic hierarchies

Symbols which are associated by a duality are given the same or similar semantic type in the hierarchy.

Now that we have been more specific about the nature of the types and dualities, we can look at the connection in more detail. Notice, first of all, that some of the information in a duality is lost when it is represented as types. For example, the duality

$$
\begin{array}{ccc}
group & \longleftrightarrow & ring \\
subgroup & \longleftrightarrow & subring
\end{array}
$$

might be represented as in Figure 7.3.

Analogous symbols are given the same type, but the dependency between the associations in the duality (i.e. *if* groups are seen as rings *then* subgroups are seen as subrings) is lost in the type structure. In Section 7.5, we will see that this information could be relevant for inductive generalisation.

On the other hand, dualities, as presented up to now, cannot *directly* model type situations such as shown in Figure 7.4, where a node has more than two descendants. We need to extend the definition to where the associations (of symbols, or axioms/theorems) could be ordered tuples. For example, a three-way symbol association is represented as (s_1, s_2, s_3); clearly the more expressive notation $x \leftrightarrow y$ available for binary associations cannot be used for ternary (or higher) associations.

Furthermore, dualities do not explicitly represent the hierarchical structure of types: suppose we had the fragment of type structure shown in Figure 7.5. The level 1 nodes correspond to the duality

$$
\begin{array}{ccc}
+ & \longleftrightarrow & \cdot \\
- & \longleftrightarrow & /
\end{array}
$$

or

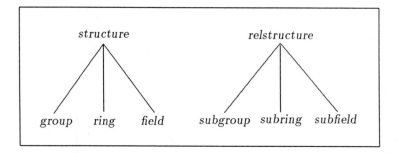

Figure 7.4: Extended algebraic hierarchies

$$(+,\cdot)$$
$$(-,/)$$

and the *arith* node corresponds to the duality

$$(+,-,\cdot,/)$$
$$(-,+,/,\cdot)$$

together with the four-way associations of axioms and theorems that justify this duality. But the dualities do not, as presented, explicitly represent the subset connection between the two. However, such connections could easily be derived in going from dualities to types.

7.4 Learning dualities

7.4.1 Outline of learning methods

In the last section, two arguments were given justifying the use of dualities in providing *a priori* plausibility judgements in analogy matching: one was *empirical*, claiming that dualities frequently recur as parts of matches between individual problems; the other was *analytical*, arguing that two symbols having structurally similar axioms/theorems associated with them suggests that they make good analogues.

These two lines of argument directly indicate two different ways that an analogy system can learn dualities within a domain (or between domains), over the course of its APS experience.

Empirical method The first method, the empirical one, would work by examining analogy matches which the system had constructed when solving

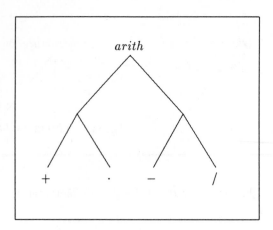

Figure 7.5: Arithmetic hierarchy

problems by analogy with other problems. The method would look for recurring submatches and for the operators (axioms or theorems) which had been found to be analogous by the application routine. The recurring submatches would form the (a) part of the dualities, and the associated operators would form the (b) part.

Analytical method   The second method, the analytical one, would work by examining the knowledge base (composed of axioms, theorems and possibly unproved conjectures) and constructing explicit analogy matches between the constituents. From the successful matches, the method would group together those that were consistent with each other. The union of the matches in a group would form the (a) part of a new duality, and the pairs of axioms/theorems which gave rise to the matches would form the (b) part.

7.4.2   Requirements for the learning methods

The above are rough outlines of how the two methods would work. Before considering them in more detail, we consider some aspects of dualities which the methods will have to cope with.

Dualities are statistical   Within $arith = \{+, \cdot, -, /\}$, we can find evidence for different dualities which are inconsistent with each other. Apart from duality A of Section 7.1.2, we could find evidence for

(a) $\left\{ \begin{array}{ccc} \cdot & \longleftrightarrow & \cdot \\ + & \longleftrightarrow & - \\ sin & \longleftrightarrow & sin \\ cos & \longleftrightarrow & cos \end{array} \right.$

(b) $\left\{ \begin{array}{l} sin(x+y) = sin(x) \cdot cos(y) + cos(x) \cdot sin(y) \\ \quad\quad \longleftrightarrow sin(x-y) = sin(x) \cdot cos(y) - cos(x) \cdot sin(y) \\ x \cdot (y+z) = x \cdot y + x \cdot z \\ \quad\quad \longleftrightarrow x \cdot (y-z) = x \cdot y - x \cdot z \end{array} \right.$

and for

(a) $\left\{ \begin{array}{ccc} + & \longleftrightarrow & + \\ \cdot & \longleftrightarrow & / \end{array} \right.$

(b) $\left\{ \begin{array}{l} (x+y) \cdot z = x \cdot z + y \cdot z \quad \longleftrightarrow \quad z = 0 \vee (x+y)/z = x/z + y/z \end{array} \right.$

If we tried hard enough, we could probably find evidence for almost any possible association within arith. We must be wary of this when looking for dualities. There is no reason why mutually inconsistent dualities should not be constructed and used, but there would be a danger of being swamped by too many. We would construct those which either (a) recur frequently (relative to others) or (b) are supported by at least several inter-related axiom/theorem matches such as duality A of Section 7.1.2. It may also be useful to weight certain sentences, perhaps on syntactic grounds, as being important (for example, a statement of the form $f(x,x) = const$ might be regarded as important) and to favour dualities involving important sentences.

Rewriting problem Even if a strong duality 'exists' in a domain, it is likely that the axioms will not be presented in a form which makes the duality clear, and thus amenable to the analytical method. In cases where the duality is clear, this is often because the provider of the axioms knows about the duality and deliberately presents the axioms in an elegant, symmetrical form. We would like the learning technique to work in unfamiliar domains which had not been tidied up in this way. (In fact, the technique, where successful, would have the effect of doing the tidying up itself.) What would happen would be that *axioms* on one side would correspond to *theorems* on the other which would have to be proved from the (non-dual) axioms. In simple cases, it might be feasible to perform the inference when looking for matches within the analytical method (that is, if the necessary theorems had not already been proved). But, in general, this would present a massive search problem, and a rather unmotivated one since the system would have little reason to believe that there was a duality there to be found until it had performed the inference.

In general, the establishment of the duality could involve an arbitrarily difficult re-expression of the axioms on one side, which would be beyond the scope of our techniques. However, if the difference between the forms of the axioms was relatively superficial, we might be able to combine the two learning techniques to overcome the difference. If a potential duality is masked by superficial differences between the axioms, we should still find that analogous *theorems* are provable. If these proofs are successfully achieved by analogy, we would find that the plan would have been patched: where a single axiom had been applied on one side, several axioms, or a single lemma (perhaps conjectured by analogy), would have been applied on the other side. Analysis of the trace of the successful APS by the empirical method would then suggest that the analytical method should attempt a corresponding rewriting in the axiom base in looking for its direct matches.

This suggests a control strategy for the two learning methods something like as follows:

1. Use the analytical method, without trying to do much, if any, inference. (This will pick up only obvious fragments of dualities.)

2. Use any dualities derived from 1 to help with solving problems by analogy.

3. After some successful attempts had been made, use the empirical method to suggest new dualities.

4. Attempt to justify and extend these new dualities by the analytical method. Where extra steps were needed on one side of an analogy, use this to suggest what inferences to make.

5. Go to 2.

A more sophisticated approach would be to perform an agenda-based best first search, making progress on any of 1 to 4, whichever seemed most promising.

Making conjectures and refutations An addition to the analytical method as described so far is its use in making conjectures. Suppose the empirical method suggests a duality with some axioms/theorems to back it up. At stage 4 above, the analytical method tries to extend the duality to other axioms/theorems associated with the symbols already involved in the duality: that is, it tries to find new axiom/theorem pairs which have analogy matches consistent with the existing duality. However, it may find, say, a theorem on one side with no apparent analogue on the other. If the duality is strong enough, the method could construct the analogue of the given theorem via the analogue construction rule (see Chapter 5), and conjecture it to be true. It would pass the problem to the application routine, which would try to prove the conjecture *by analogy* to the proof of the theorem from which it was constructed.

It would be necessary to use a falsification routine (search for counter-examples) to prune out obviously false conjectures before much effort was expended in trying to prove them. If the conjecture turned out to be false, this information would be passed back to the duality, where the fact would be recorded. An attempt could also be made to modify the conjecture so that the proof would go through. Negative information is important in dualities as well as positive information; negative information is usually provided by omission: when we give the duality $sin \longleftrightarrow cos$ it is implicit that it cannot be extended to, say, (sin, cos, tan) i.e. that the analogous conjectures for *tan* do not in general hold. However, in order to distinguish cases when conjectures had been falsified from those where they had not been made at all, we will need to add negative information explicitly as part of the dualities.

7.4.3   An example

We illustrate this technique on a database containing axioms for arithmetic. We consider three 'scenarios' arising from different possible axiomatisations of arithmetic.

Suppose that a four-way duality connecting the four arithmetic operators is known to the system; it could have been provided by the user or derived from the axioms/theorems shown (either at stage 1 or stage 3):

(a) $\left\{ \begin{array}{l} (+, -, \cdot, /) \\ (-, +, /, \cdot) \end{array} \right.$

(b) $\left\{ \begin{array}{l} (rat(x) \wedge rat(y) \rightarrow rat(x + y) \\ rat(x) \wedge rat(y) \rightarrow rat(x - y) \\ rat(x) \wedge rat(y) \rightarrow rat(x \cdot y) \\ \neg y = 0 \wedge rat(x) \wedge rat(y) \rightarrow rat(x/y) \ ) \end{array} \right.$

(possibly others)

(*rat* stands for *rational*)

(It should perhaps be possible for the user to specify a duality without a (b) part and force the system to consider it even if there is no apparent evidence for it; this would amount to specifying the type *arith* with no justification for why it is a type.)

Scenario 1   At stage 4 of the control strategy, the analytical method tries to extend the duality, by looking at axioms/theorems involving arithmetic operators and trying to find their analogues. Suppose for now that the axiom base has been set up symmetrically with respect to $+$ and $\cdot$; we would have among the axioms and theorems:

$$x \cdot y = y \cdot x \qquad\qquad x \cdot (y \cdot z) = (x \cdot y) \cdot z \qquad (*)$$

$$x + y = y + x \qquad\qquad x + (y + z) = (x + y) + z$$

$$1 \cdot x = x \qquad\qquad\qquad x = 0 \vee x/x = 1$$

$$0 + x = x \qquad\qquad\qquad x - x = 0$$

FHM would produce the matches shown above. No obvious analogues for $(*)$ involving $-$ and $/$ have been found, and similarly for the rest. So the following conjectures are made:

$$x - y = y - x \qquad\qquad\qquad x - (y - z) = (x - y) - z$$

$$bdef(y = 0) \vee x/y = y/x \qquad\qquad bdef(y = 0) \vee x/(y/z) = (x/y)/z$$

and so forth

The $bdef$ terms are produced by the ACR as a result of the extra condition in one of the original analogy matches; recall the interpretation of these terms, normally enforced by the special unification procedure: the $bdef$ term can stand for any number (usually 0 or 1) of occurrences of terms which match its argument, with the convention that variables are not shared between different occurrences, or with the rest of term; thus

$$bdef(y = 0) \vee x/y = y/x$$

would match with all of the following

$$x/y = y/x \; , \quad y = 0 \vee x/y = y/x \quad \text{and} \quad x = 0 \vee y = 0 \vee x/y = y/x$$

In the case of proving or refuting conjectures, corresponding interpretations would be made; for example, in this case, the refutation procedure would only succeed if all the variables in the counter-example failed the extra condition.

The falsification routine should be able to refute each of these conjectures easily. So these sentence forms are not true for the whole of *arith*; this indicates that there is a more specific duality within *arith*, which would then be constructed:

(a) $\left\{\begin{array}{ccc} + & \longleftrightarrow & \cdot \\ - & \longleftrightarrow & / \\ 0 & \longleftrightarrow & 1 \end{array}\right.$ (b) $\left\{\begin{array}{ccc} 0 + x = x & \longleftrightarrow & 1 \cdot x = x \\ x + y = y + x & \longleftrightarrow & x \cdot y = y \cdot x \\ & \text{etc.} & \end{array}\right.$

together with the information that this duality does not extend to the whole of arith. Even this duality is not perfect: the axiom $x \cdot (y + z) = x \cdot y + x \cdot z$ has no obvious analogue among the axioms. The best guess at an analogue, $x + (y \cdot z) = (x + y) \cdot (x + z)$, would be rejected by counter-example.

Scenario 2   Now let us retract the assumption that the axiom base had been set up symmetrically, and consider a slightly more difficult situation where the axiom base had not been set up quite symmetrically. Suppose we had:

$$\left\{\begin{array}{c} 1 \cdot x = x \\ \text{but} \quad x + 0 = x \end{array}\right. \quad \text{and} \quad \left\{\begin{array}{c} x \cdot (y \cdot z) = (x \cdot y) \cdot z \\ \text{but} \quad x + (y + z) = z + (x + y) \end{array}\right.$$

as axioms.

In fact, FHM, given access to the commutativity axioms for $+$ and $\cdot$, would be able to straighten the matches out itself. However, for the sake of illustration, let us assume that it could not. Furthermore, assume that the matches that were found by the analytical method at stage 4 were not strong enough to activate the conjecture-making process; whether or not this was so could depend, among other things, on whether the system had 'spare time' which it could use making and testing conjectures.

The system returns to stage 2, i.e. solving problems by analogy. Suppose the system has a proof of

$$(y + x) - x = y$$

in its knowledge base and, when asked to prove

$$x = 0 \vee (y \cdot x)/x = y$$

decides to do it by analogy to the stored result. Assuming that the application procedure was able to do this, we might have the analogous proofs for the two statements shown in Figure 7.6.

(Again, the existing application routines take into account any known commutativity of functions, and so would not need to make even this simple patch in this case; again, for the sake of illustration, we assume that the ability to deal with commutativity has been 'turned off'.) The third step in the base proof corresponds to two steps in the target. At stage 3 of the learning process, the duality

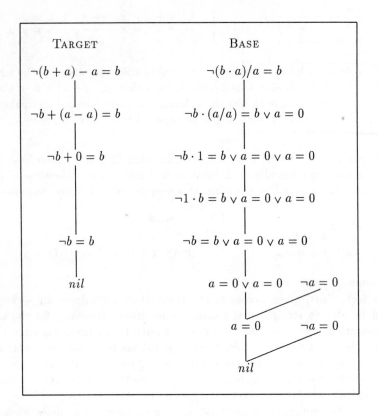

Figure 7.6: Analogous proofs

(a) $\left\{ \begin{array}{ccc} + & \longleftrightarrow & \cdot \\ - & \longleftrightarrow & / \\ 0 & \longleftrightarrow & 1 \end{array} \right.$

(b) $\left\{ \begin{array}{ccc} (y+x)-x = y+(x-x) & \longleftrightarrow & (y \cdot x)/x = y \cdot (x/x) \vee x = 0 \\ x-x = 0 & \longleftrightarrow & x/x = 1 \vee x = 0 \\ y+0 = y & \longleftrightarrow & y \cdot 1 = y \end{array} \right.$

would be suggested, where $y \cdot 1 = y$ is a theorem, proved during the course of the larger theorem, which is the analogue of the single axiom on the left-hand side.

At stage 4, the analytical method would extend the duality with

$$x \cdot y = y \cdot x \quad \longleftrightarrow \quad x + y = y + x$$
$$0 + y = y \quad \longleftrightarrow \quad 1 \cdot y = y$$
$$\text{etc.}$$

where $0 + y = y$ would be conjectured and proved, perhaps by analogy to the proof of $y \cdot 1 = y$.

Thus the asymmetry in the knowledge base would be removed, the duality would have been learnt and would be available for future use in the ways described in Section 7.6.

Scenario 3 Lastly, we consider a much more serious case of misleading asymmetry in the knowledge base. Suppose that the axiom base for arithmetic had been set up in a different way from that given and used in Section 6.1.6 of the previous chapter, where analogous axioms for addition and multiplication were used. Suppose that the additive axioms

> 7. $x + min(x) = 0$
> 9. $x - y = x + min(y)$

were retained, but the analogous multiplicative axioms

> 8. $x \cdot inv(x) = 1 \vee x = 0$
> 10. $x/y = x \cdot inv(y) \vee y = 0$

were replaced by the superficially non-analogous

> 8'. $x/x = 1 \vee x = 0$
> 10a'. $inv(x) = 1/x \vee x = 0$
> 10b'. $x \cdot (y/z) = (x \cdot y)/z \vee z = 0$

The equivalence between the two sets of multiplicative axioms (modulo the rest of the multiplicative axioms) is sufficiently obscure for it to be out of the question to make the necessary inferences during matching.

Suppose the system was asked to prove

$$\neg x \cdot y = 1 \vee x = inv(y) \vee y = 0$$

and decided to do it by analogy to a stored proof of

$$\neg x + y = 0 \vee x = min(y)$$

using the following match constructed by FHM

$$\neg x \cdot y = 1 \vee x = inv(y) \vee y = 0$$

$$\neg x + y = 0 \vee x = min(y)$$

Assuming that the application system was able to do this (a big assumption, since a major patch is required), we might have the corresponding proofs shown in Figure 7.7. The axioms applied have been left out at the easy steps, those that go through without patching. Corresponding to the two applications made in the base of the axiom

$$7. \quad x + min(x) = 0$$

there are applications of a *lemma* in the target,

$$x \cdot inv(x) = 1 \vee x = 0$$

which would have been conjectured by the existing analogy, and proved, as in Figure 7.8 (or perhaps left as an unproved assertion). Thus, we assume that 'patching by conjecture' has been used. Alternatively, 'patching by search' could have been used, with extra steps being put in the target proof (in effect, the proof of the lemma would need to be transcribed into the plan for the target, twice).

With the analogies between the two theorems, and between the axiom and the corresponding lemma having been established, there would be enough evidence for the empirical method to propose the duality

$$+ \longleftrightarrow \cdot$$
$$min \longleftrightarrow inv$$
$$0 \longleftrightarrow 1$$

In order to extend the duality, the analytical method would need to conjecture and prove analogues for axioms 9, 8′, 10a′ and 10b′. If this could be done, the equivalence of the alternative multiplicative axiomatisations would in effect have been proved.

The proofs of the conjectures made by analogy in this example are quite hard and would need a quite powerful theorem prover to be found automatically. This is simply because the equivalence between the two axiomatisations is not at all obvious.

The control strategy proposed for the co-ordination of the learning methods is just one way it might be done, and the details should not be taken too seriously; the important point is that the two methods should be able to help each other, especially when one gets stuck — the empirical method suggests symbol mappings, axiom associations and inferences to the analytical method, while the latter makes conjectures and extends the proposed dualities so that the empirical method becomes better at solving problems by analogy.

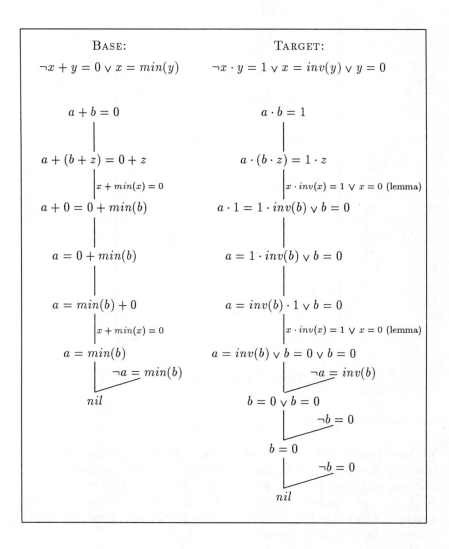

Figure 7.7: Analogous proofs with lemma

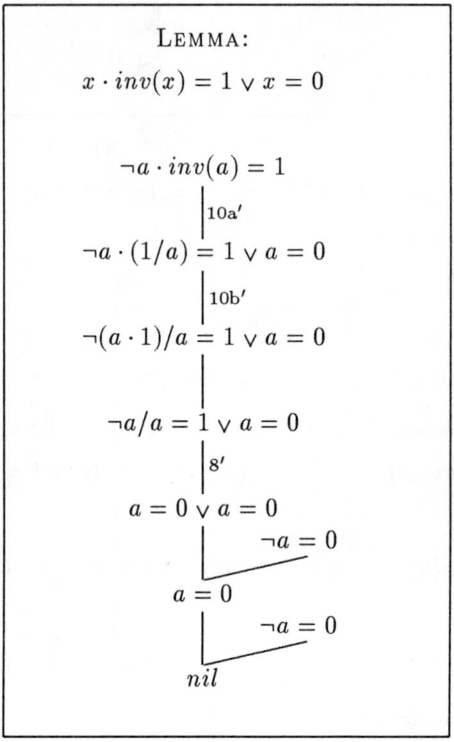

LEMMA:

$$x \cdot inv(x) = 1 \vee x = 0$$

$$\neg a \cdot inv(a) = 1$$

$$\Big| 10a'$$

$$\neg a \cdot (1/a) = 1 \vee a = 0$$

$$\Big| 10b'$$

$$\neg (a \cdot 1)/a = 1 \vee a = 0$$

$$\neg a/a = 1 \vee a = 0$$

$$\Big| 8'$$

$$a = 0 \vee a = 0$$

$$\neg a = 0$$

$$a = 0$$

$$\neg a = 0$$

$$nil$$

Figure 7.8: Proof of lemma

7.5   Learning types

We have argued that dualities provide a means for type formation, and that they provide the justification for the use of type hierarchies in analogy matching and inductive generalisation. In order for the creation of types to be of much use, the new types will have to be assimilated into the existing hierarchy, which may have been prespecified by the user, previously learnt, or derived by some other means.

We should also note that the remarks about the statistical nature of dualities, made in Section 7.4.2, apply equally to types — the types that we form should correspond to *strong* dualities. Consider the arithmetic example of the last section. Having done all the work to learn about the new duality, the corresponding refinement to the type structure is easy. Initially, we had the type structure:

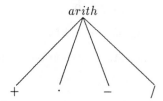

corresponding to the known duality (or this type could have been specified by the user). Following the principle that symbols associated in a duality should be given the same type, we obtain

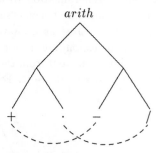

from the new duality. The dotted lines indicate that the connected symbols were on the same side of the duality; this is the dependency information that is traditionally excluded from the hierarchy. However, the following example of inductive generalisation indicates that it might be wise to retain the dependencies:

Type hierarchies

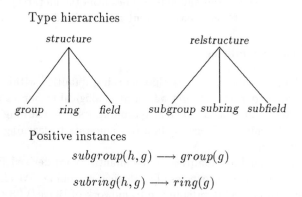

Positive instances

$$subgroup(h, g) \longrightarrow group(g)$$

$$subring(h, g) \longrightarrow ring(g)$$

The version space technique, briefly described in Section 7.2, would generalise them to

$$p_1(h, g) \longrightarrow p_2(g)$$

where $p_2 \in \{group, ring, field\}$

and $p_1 \in \{subgroup, subring, subfield\}$ independently.

This is a large over-generalisation. Attention to the dependencies indicates the generalisation

$$p_1(h, g) \longrightarrow p_2(g)$$

where
$$(p_2, p_1) \in \{(group, subgroup), (ring, subring), (field, subfield)\}$$

which is the intuitively reasonable generalisation to make. It may be that types which were once thought significant become superseded by stronger types for which evidence accumulates. Just as we have a notion of strength for dualities, we will map over a corresponding notion of strength for types. If a type is too weak, we may wish to remove it from the hierarchy altogether, linking any types below it directly to any above it. For example:

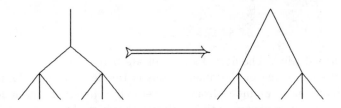

By being able to both add and delete types from the hierarchy, the system will be able to adjust its own bias without necessarily diluting it.

7.6   The use of dualities

The main claim of this chapter is that learning dualities within a domain will allow an analogy system to get better at analogical reasoning within the domain over time. Just as analogical reasoning itself is learning from past problems, the learning and use of dualities amounts to learning from past analogical reasoning.

We now consider how dualities, and semantic types derived from them, once learnt, can assist the processes of analogical reasoning. We also consider how dualities can be useful outside the framework of Basic APS with which we have been mainly concerned in this book: we briefly mention some other uses for analogy within an automated reasoning system, which, together with Basic APS, may begin to reflect the variety of uses made for analogy by humans.

7.6.1 Use within matching

One of the original motivations for the introduction of dualities was the desire to make the use of the **semantic type heuristic** within matching 'respectable'. The idea behind the semantic type heuristic was to favour associations between symbols of the same, or similar, semantic type over those of disparate types. Expressing this in terms of dualities, we should favour the association of pairs of symbols which are associated often in known dualities more than those which are not. Obviously the **strength** of the dualities (as discussed above, involving the consistency of the mapping, and the number of associated axioms) which involve a given symbol pair would contribute to the judgement of semantic closeness.

The FHM system, described in Section 4.4, makes the incorporation of extra heuristic criteria straightforward. Firstly, the match assessment procedure would be modified to reflect the degree of semantic closeness of symbols in the mapping, whether arising from types, dualities or both. Since all candidate matches are reassessed after each stage of match development, this would have the effect of moving matches consistent with the types and dualities towards the top of the agenda, and thus preferring them for development. Additionally, a heuristic development criterion could be added to the set which FHM already uses — that is, semantic closeness could be used as a criterion for proposing new associations for a developing match, rather than just assessing those which had been made. The criterion, being a default criterion, would presumably be put in at level 2, along with the identical symbols criterion which it generalises.

Furthermore, just as the dependency information within dualities is relevant to inductive generalisation, it is relevant to analogy matching as well. Rather than just making *a priori* plausibility judgements for isolated pairs of symbols, we could also regard associations as more plausible if they occur in a match with other associations from the *same* duality than if the dualities are separate. Thus the first of the following two matches would be judged to be more plausible than the second:

$$(x + y) - y = x \qquad\qquad (x + y) - y = x$$
$$\backslash\backslash\backslash\;////\;\qquad\qquad \backslash\backslash\backslash\;||||||$$
$$(x \cdot y)/y = x \qquad\qquad (x \cdot y) - y = x$$

A refinement to this would be to increase the plausibility attached to the first match if the solution to the base problem involved the use of axioms or lemmas which were known to be associated in the duality, and to decrease it if not.

7.6.2   Use within application

Dualities contain information about analogous axioms or theorems. So, if a duality is involved in a particular match between problems, and the solution to the base problem involved application of some of the axioms or theorems (as lemmas) from the duality, then the duality can be used to suggest the probable analogues for these in the solution to the target. This would avoid having to search for these analogues during the application phase, and so would speed up the process.

In a similar way, if a symbol occurs in the solution to the base problem which does not occur in the problem statement (and thus is not in the problem match) but does occur in a duality involved in the match, then its analogue can be predicted from the duality. Where applicable, this replaces the default clause in the analogue construction rule, and is likely to save time in application by making the right prediction straight away. This use for dualities would find application in problem 3 of the previous chapter: as the right-hand side of Figure 6.5, of that chapter, shows, all of the application systems make the wrong inference at the first step, and only recover after varying amounts of fruitless search. The problem is caused by a marginal preference for the association

$$- \longleftrightarrow -$$

over

$$- \longleftrightarrow /$$

given an initial mapping containing the associations

$$rat \longleftrightarrow rat$$
$$+ \longleftrightarrow \cdot$$

This preference would be reversed given knowledge of the duality

$$+ \longleftrightarrow \cdot$$
$$- \longleftrightarrow /$$
$$0 \longleftrightarrow 1$$

since the dependency implicit in the duality would suggest $/$ as analogue for $-$.

7.7   'Conjectures and refutations' – alternative uses of analogy

We have already seen that the ability to make and test conjectures is a necessary part of duality formation, as well as being interesting and useful in its own right. It is possible to use the same mechanism in the problem solving phase. Given a problem to solve which has no close analogue among previously solved problems, but which involves symbols from a duality, we could apply the mapping from the duality to the given problem in order to construct a new problem; we would then attempt to solve the new problem and, if successful, try to map the solution back to a solution to the original problem. This is the paradigm for reasoning by analogy used by [3]. Similarly, if the dual problem were rejected by counter-example, we could try to construct a counter-example to the target problem by analogy.

It would be useful to have some measure of the relative difficulty of the two sides of a duality in order to make the technique successful — we would want to map problems from the harder side to problems on the easier side, and then to use the solutions to the easier problems as models for the solutions of the harder ones. For example, we might map a problem in three-dimensional geometry to its analogue in two-dimensional geometry rather than the other way around. One way of deriving such a measure would to be to consider the relative complexity of the solutions to pairs of dual problems which had previously been encountered; this would involve the number of steps in the solution, the number of applicable operators and other relevant factors.

A more radical departure from the Basic APS framework, but one which has been suggested as an important use for analogy by humans, is to use a hypothesised analogy to refine the axiomatisation of a domain. That is, rather than taking the axiomatisations and the problems as given, and constructing an analogy based on these, we would take a complete axiomatisation of the base domain, a partial/provisional axiomatisation of the target, (part of) an intended global analogy, or duality, between the domains, and some properties of the base domain which we wanted to hold in the target. The aim of the process would be to extend or refine the axiomatisation of the target domain and the analogy mapping, so that the specified properties of the base would have analogues in the target. We could approach this vaguely specified, but interesting, problem as follows. We take the proof of one of the specified properties in the base and attempt to transfer it to the target, using the analogy mapping provided to construct a plan for the target proof. As we attempt to validate the plan, we will probably be unable to find analogues for the axioms used in the base; we will use the patch by conjecture strategy to assert analogous axioms in the target, except that, rather

than conjecturing them as lemmas, we will propose them as axioms. In the
process, the duality between the domains will presumably be extended; its
extension may involve the introduction of new symbols into the target as
analogues for known symbols in the base. This can therefore be thought of
as a kind of definition by analogy.

Examples of this kind of use of analogy are, by definition, hard to find in
standard mathematical literature, since, by the time textbooks are written,
the domain axiomatisations have been fixed, and the exploratory processes
involved in arriving at a good axiomatisation are not discussed. However,
by looking at the historical development of certain branches of mathematics,
we can see how axiom systems have evolved by analogy to other areas. For
example, the theory of vector spaces developed from co-ordinate geometry
to basis-free axiomatisations by analogy with existing branches of abstract
algebra.

Notice that, while these more varied uses of analogy extend the Basic
APS framework, the process of solving a problem by analogy to another one
is still at their heart; the differences lie in where the problems and underlying
axiomatisations come from. We therefore suggest that a competent Basic
APS system is a prerequisite for the more exotic uses of analogy. This is
why we have been almost entirely concerned with Basic APS in this book.

7.7.1   Inductive generalisation

Inductive generalisation programs such as LEX are based on type hierarchies.
The learning techniques described in this chapter provide mechanisms for
the creation/refinement of type hierarchies. Moreover, by the discussion in
Section 7.2, the hierarchies produced in this way will be particularly suited
to inductive generalisation because the success conditions on the hierarchy
are the same between analogy and generalisation — we saw an example
in which types learned from analogy could improve the performance of an
inductive generalisation algorithm. Thus it seems like a good idea for the
analogy system to suggest new types to the generalisation system.

One problem might be that, since we have put no restrictions on the
type structure derived from dualities, it might turn out not to be an upper
semi-lattice, i.e. least upper bounds may not be unique. One way of getting
around this would be to pick out a maximal substructure which is an upper
semi-lattice. The choice could be made on the basis of the strengths of
the types. However, the problem really seems to lie with the generalisation
technique which requires an upper semi-lattice; the solution could be to
extend the version spaces technique to deal with more general structures.

7.8 Summary

We have argued for the learning of global analogies, or dualities, as a means of transferring experience from successful attempts at solving problems by analogy, to subsequent attempts. We have outlined two complementary learning techniques, one analytical and one empirical, for constructing dualities; we have also considered how the techniques can be co-ordinated, with each other and with normal analogical problem solving. Using the link between global analogies and semantic types, established in Chapter 3, we have discussed the creation and refinement of type hierarchies, based on dualities which have been learnt.

We then considered how dualities and semantic types, once learnt, can be used to improve performance within the Basic APS framework. We also discussed some other uses of analogy which are suggested by the use of global analogies, which persist over varying problem situations. We argued that Basic APS is a crucial component in the extended systems.

Bibliography

[1] B. Brock, S. Cooper and W. Pierce. Some experiments with analogy in proof discovery (preliminary report). MCC Technical Report AI-347-86, Microelectonics and Computer Technology Corporation, 1986.

[2] B. Brock, S. Cooper and W. Pierce. Some experiments with analogy in proof discovery: A natural deduction approach. MCC Technical Report ACA-AI-274-87, Microelectonics and Computer Technology Corporation, 1987.

[3] R.M. Brown. Use of analogy to acheive new expertise. Master's thesis, MIT, 1977.

[4] A. Bundy. *The Computer Modelling of Mathematical Reasoning.* Academic Press, 1983.

[5] A. Bundy. Discovery and reasoning in mathematics. In *Proceedings of the Ninth IJCAI*, 1985.

[6] A. Bundy. The use of explicit plans to guide inductive proofs. DAI Research Paper 349, University of Edinburgh, 1987.

[7] M.H. Burstein. Concept formation by incremental analogical reasoning and debugging. In R.S. Michalski, J.G. Carbonnel and T.M. Mitchell, editors, *Machine Learning.* Morgan Kaufmann, 1986.

[8] J. Carbonnell. Derivational analogy. In *AAAI-83*, 1983.

[9] J. Carbonnell. Learning by analogy: formulating and generalizing plans from past experience. In *Machine Learning.* Tioga, 1983.

[10] C. Chang and R.C. Lee. *Symbolic Logic and Mechanical Theorem Proving.* Academic Press, 1973.

[11] R.L. Constable, S.F. Allen, H.M. Bromley et al. *Implementing Mathematics with the Nuprl Proof Development System.* Prentice Hall, 1986.

[12] T.R. Davies and S.J. Russell. A logical approach to reasoning by analogy. In *Proceedings of the Tenth IJCAI*, 1987.

[13] K. Duncker. *On Problem Solving*. Psychological Monographs, 58 (Vol 270), 1945.

[14] T.G. Evans. A program for the solution of geometric analogy intelligence test questions. In M. Minsky, editor, *Semantic Information Processing*. 1968.

[15] B. Falkenheimer, K. Forbus and D. Gentner. The structure-mapping engine: algorithm and examples. *Artificial Intelligence*, in press.

[16] R.E. Fikes and N.J. Nilsson. Strips: a new approach to the application of theorem proving to problem solving. *Artificial Intelligence*, 2:189–208, 1971.

[17] D. Gentner. Are scientific analogies metaphors? In D. Miall, editor, *Metaphor: Problems and Perspectives*. Harvester Press, 1982.

[18] D. Gentner. Structure-mapping: a theoretical framework for analogy. *Cognitive Science*, 7, 1983.

[19] D. Gentner. Mechanisms of analogical learning. Technical Report UIUCDCS-R-87-1381, Department of Computer Science, University of Illinois at Urbana-Champaign, 1987.

[20] D. Gentner. Mechanisms of analogical learning. In A. Ortony and S. Vosniadou, editors, *Similarity and Analogical learning*. Cambridge University Press, 1990.

[21] D. Gentner and D.R. Gentner. Flowing waters or teeming crowds: mental models of electricity. In D. Gentner and Stevens A.L., editors, *Mental Models*. Erlbaum Associates, 1983.

[22] D. Gentner and R. Landers. Analogical reminding: a good match is hard to find. In *Proceedings of the International Conference on Systems, Man and Cybernetics*, 1985.

[23] M. Gick and K.J. Holyoak. Analogical problem solving. *Cognitive Psychology*, 12, 1980.

[24] M.B. Hesse. *Models and Analogies in Science*. Notre-Dame, 1963.

[25] K.J. Holyoak and P.R. Thagard. Analogical mapping by constraint satisfaction. *Cognitive Science*, in press.

[26] K.J. Holyoak and P.R. Thagard. A computational model of analogical problem solving. In A. Ortony and S. Vosniadou, editors, *Similarity and Analogic learning*. Cambridge University Press, 1990.

[27] B Indurkhya. A computational theory of metaphor comprehension and analogical reasoning. PhD thesis, Boston University, 1985.

[28] S. Kedar-Cabelli. Purpose-directed analogy. In *Proceedings of the Seventh Annual Conference of the Cognitive Science Society*, 1985.

[29] R.E. Kling. A paradigm for reasoning by analogy. *Artificial Intelligence*, 2, 1971.

[30] D.B. Lenat. AM: an artificial intelligence approach to discovery in mathematics as heuristic search. In *Knowledge-based systems in artificial intelligence*. McGraw Hill, 1982.

[31] S. MacLane. *Categories for the Working Mathematician*. Springer-Verlag, 1972.

[32] T.M. Mitchell. Version spaces: an approach to concept learning. PhD thesis, Stanford University, 1978.

[33] J.C. Munyer. Analogy as a means of discovery in problem-solving and learning. PhD thesis, Univ. Calif. Santa Cruz, 1981.

[34] S.G. Owen. Heuristics for analogy matching. In *Proceedings of the Seventh ECAI*. ECAI, 1986.

[35] S.G. Owen. Finding and using analogies to guide mathematical proof. PhD thesis, Edinburgh University, 1988.

[36] G. Plotkin. Notes on focusing – university of edinburgh (unpublished). 1981.

[37] D. Plummer. Gazing: controlling the use of rewrite rules. PhD thesis, University of Edinburgh, 1977.

[38] G. Polya. *Induction and Analogy in Mathematics*. Princeton University Press, 1954.

[39] A. Robinson. *Logic Form and Function*. Edinburgh University Press, 1979.

[40] D.E. Rumelhart and A.A. Abrahamson. A model for analogical reasoning. *Cognitive Psychology*, 5, 1973.

[41] B. Silver. *Meta-level inference: Representing and Learning Control Information in Artificial Intelligence.* North-Holland, 1985.

[42] L. Sterling, A. Bundy, L. Byrd, R. O'Keefe and B. Silver. Solving symbolic equations with PRESS. Research Paper 171, Dept Artificial Intelligence, Edinburgh, 1982. In *Proceedings of* EUROCAM-82.

[43] R. Sternberg. Component processes in analogical reasoning. *Cognitive Psychology*, 9, 1977.

[44] P. Thagard, K. Holyoak, G. Nelson and D. Gochfield. Analog retrieval by constraint satisfaction. Technical report, Cognitive Science Laboratory, Princeton University Press, 1989.

[45] P.E. Utgoff. Adjusting bias in concept learning. In *Proceedings of the Eighth IJCAI.* International Joint Conference on Artificial Intelligence, 1983.

[46] J. Wielemaker and A. Bundy. Altering the description space for focusing. Research Paper 262, Dept Artificial Intelligence, University of Edinburgh, 1985.

[47] P.H. Winston. Learning and reasoning by analogy. *Communications of the ACM*, 23(12):689–703, 1980.

Index

Perspectives in Artificial Intelligence